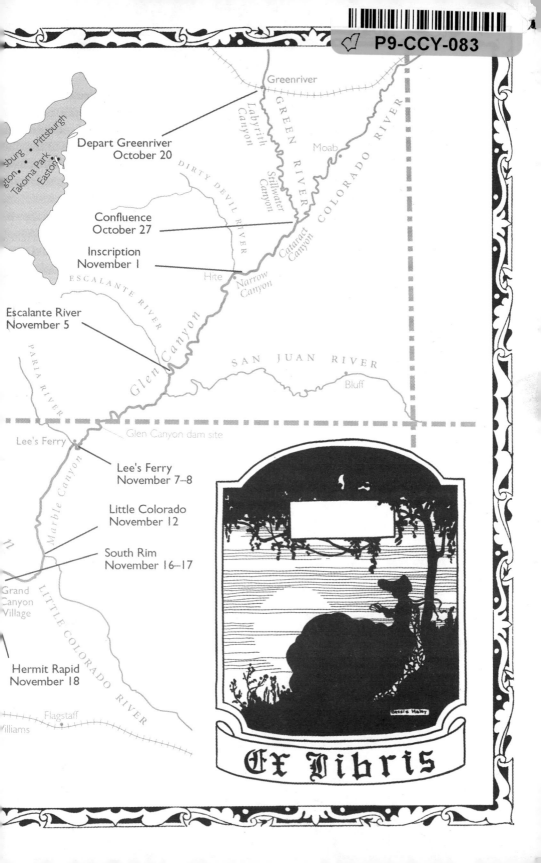

Greenriver

GREEN RIVER

Labyrith Canyon

DIRTY DEVIL RIVER

Depart Greenriver
October 20

sburg • Pittsburgh
gton • Takoma Park
Easton

Moab

COLORADO RIVER

Stillwater Canyon

Confluence
October 27

Cataract Canyon

Inscription
November 1

ESCALANTE RIVER

Hite

Narrow Canyon

Escalante River
November 5

Glen Canyon

SAN JUAN RIVER

PARIA RIVER

Bluff

Glen Canyon dam site

Lee's Ferry

Lee's Ferry
November 7–8

Marble Canyon

Little Colorado
November 12

South Rim
November 16–17

Grand Canyon Village

LITTLE COLORADO RIVER

Hermit Rapid
November 18

Flagstaff

illiams

Ex Libris

National Outdoor Book Award, 2001 • Finalist, Western PEN Award, 2001

OneBookAZ Book of the Year 2005 • Arizona Highways Nonfiction Book Award

With a gift for storytelling and the obsession of a sleuth, Brad Dimock captivates us with the kind of mystery only reality and a great river can invent.

—**Bruce Berger**
author, *There Was a River; The Telling Distance; Facing the Music*

This mystery takes us down a wild river into a hole in the ground and then flings us at the heart of a lost country. Glen and Bessie Hyde make us tremble as they face those jagged rocks and that last wave. And they fill us with envy for the freedom, guts, and joy of the funky and hardscrabble America they knew in their bones and we only know of as rumor. Brad Dimock deserves a medal for bringing them back alive to confront us all. And it's a helluva read, too.

— **Charles Bowden**
author, *Blue Desert; Blood Orchid; Desierto; Mescal*

It's a mezmerizing tale, skillfully told, and almost certain to be recognized as a classic in the field of outdoor adventure writing.

— **David Lavender**
author, *One Man's West; A Fist in the Wilderness; Let Me Be Free*

All the ingredients of a compelling mystery. Dimock has all the right credentials. A thorough history. Highly recommended.

— **Library Journal**

Brad Dimock cannot know the Hydes' story without knowing the river. He places us inside their adventure by placing us inside his own, a ride on the wild Colorado in a replica boat that resembles a sort-of-floatable wooden horse trough. His writing is clear, suspenseful, and keenly edged—prepare for delicious outbursts of dry wit—and his compassion for Glen and Bessie makes the story: how a dream, a boat, and a river of terrifying beauty could blind any one of us to our own fatal innocence.

—**Ellen Meloy**
author, *Eating Stone, Raven's Exile, The Anthropology of Turquoise*

Dimock wrote about two real people who gambled and lost. He writes with poignance about Glen's honor and Bessie's spunk. He draws a remarkable picture of Glen's father, tenaciously clinging at first to a thin hope, then left haunted by disaster. And Dimock does a beautiful job of depicting the Canyon in which this drama played out. He knows and loves this country and it shows. His story-telling runs as high and fast as the river.

— *Michael Collier in* **High Country News**

A damned good book. Hard to put down.

— **Tony Hillerman**

Sunk Without a Sound

Brad / Jeri - modern rafters
↓
Brian - their friend

Rollin + Mary
↓
Glen
Henry - Rollins BIL
Terry Nesbet - Glen's friend

Other river titles from Fretwater Press

The Very Hard Way
Bert Loper and the Colorado River

Brad Dimock

The Doing of the Thing
the Brief, Brilliant Whitewater Career of Buzz Holmstrom

Vince Welch, Cort Conley, and Brad Dimock

Every Rapid Speaks Plainly
the River Journals of Buzz Holmstrom

Brad Dimock, editor

The Brave Ones
the River Journals of Ellswoth and Emery Kolb

William Suran, editor

Glen Canyon Betrayed
a Sensuous Elegy

Katie Lee

Riverman
the Story of Bus Hatch

Roy Webb

Desert Riverman
the Free-Spirited Adventures of Murl Emery

Robert S. Wood

The Books of the Colorado River & the Grand Canyon
a Selective Bibliography, 1953

Francis P. Farquhar

The Books of the Grand Canyon, the Colorado River,
the Green River & the Colorado Plateau
a Selective Bibliography, 1953 — 2003

Mike S. Ford

Glen and Bessie Hyde leaving Phantom Ranch, November 18, 1928, Adolph Sutro photo

Bessie and Glen Hyde departing Lee's Ferry,
November 8, 1928

Sunk
Without
a Sound

The Tragic
Colorado River
Honeymoon of
Glen and Bessie Hyde

Brad Dimock

FRETWATER · PRESS ·
FLAGSTAFF · ARIZONA
· 2001 ·

FRETWATER PRESS
1000 Grand Canyon Avenue
Flagstaff, Arizona 86001
www.fretwater.com

09 10   8 7 6 5

ISBN
(cloth) 1-892327-28-7
(paper) 1-892327-98-8
(paper 13-digit) 978-1-892327-98-7

Library of Congress Card Number: 00-111578

This book was set in Adobe Minion and Gill Sans,
designed and typeset in Adobe InDesign, on a
Macintosh G3. Cover and interior design by Fretwater Press

Front cover photograph by Dugald Bremner, ©1996
Back cover photograph by Adolph G. Sutro,
courtesy Huntington Library

for Glen and Bessie

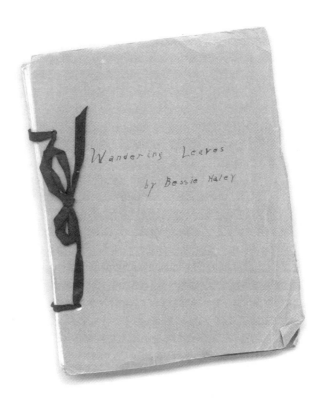

Wandering Leaves
by Bessie Haley

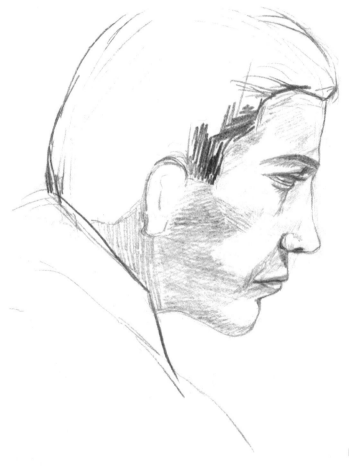

Glen Hyde
by Bessie Hyde

Preface

*I*T HAS BEEN SAID there is no such thing as nonfiction—that every version of the truth is merely what its author *believes* to be the truth. Each author chooses which details are significant, ignoring or down playing those that seem spurious or irrelevant. Yet another author may find those very discarded details to be the key to the *real* truth.

The very "facts" themselves are often questionable. Even today, witnesses at the scene of an accident often give contradictory accounts, each witness swearing their story is absolutely true. The farther into the past one delves, the more the "truth" is obscured by opinion, bias, and lack of complete records.

A history, then, depends on which ingredients its author selects, and in what proportions; how they are combined and how long they are cooked; whether the mix is oversalted or underspiced, too dry or sophomorically runny.

With that preface I offer this tale of Glen and Bessie Hyde. It is as complete and truthful as I could make it, yet is by definition a reflection of my own experience. Because so little is known of the Hydes and their disappearance more than seventy years ago, this story is, by necessity, a mosaic, a collage, a pastiche of bits and pieces. Newspapers, public records, and history books supplied some of the early information and context. Interviews with some of the few people who can remember back that far gave breadth and detail. Hyde family albums and collections did much to enrich the story of Glen's early years and the life of his father, R.C. Hyde. Research libraries throughout the country supplied letters, interviews, and memorabilia invaluable to the saga.

In places I have had to depend on the collection of the late Otis "Dock" Marston, a river running historian who, beginning in the late 1940s, spent three decades collecting everything he could find on the history of those who traveled the Green and Colorado Rivers. In some aspects of the Hyde story the Marston Collection overwhelms—in many other respects it is frustratingly spare. In still other facets, Marston's notes are biased, incomplete, or contradictory.

Much of the Hydes' story can only be inferred from tales of others who had similar experiences, yet left more complete records. I have explored many tangential stories in order to illuminate the Hydes.

The history of the Hydes has been overrun in the past thirty years by imaginative legend and sensational myth. After laying down what is known of the Hydes, their disappearance, and the search for the lost honeymooners, I have tried to guide the reader through the Hydes' evolving legacy, as the line between fact and fancy began to dissolve.

Historians, by and large, are supposed to stay out of their own books, yet I found that to be quite impossible. On the rivers where the Hydes spent just over forty days, I have spent much of the past thirty years. During my research on this story I have revisited places the Hydes went and tried to recreate similar circumstances, at times risking my fool neck and that of my patient and long-suffering wife, Jeri Ledbetter. Our retracing of the Hyde voyage, conceived on a whim, not only launched this book, but the experiences we had and perspectives we gained form a crucial part of understanding who the Hydes were, and what may or may not have happened to them. For this reason, you will find us ducking in and out of the narrative.

Lastly, one of the sparest and most incomplete facets of this story is the one many of us want to know the most about: who was Bessie Haley Hyde and what was she really like? Unfortunately, her family line is extinct, their records, letters, photo albums, and memories nonexistent. Bessie herself left precious few clues as to her persona and beliefs, her hopes and dreams. The most revealing single document is a handbound, typewritten manuscript of fifty poems she wrote around 1927, a year or two before her disappearance, entitled *Wandering Leaves*. I have included more than thirty of these poems as chapter openings in the hope that her poetry will infuse this tale with her elusive character.

BRAD DIMOCK
Flagstaff, Arizona

Table of contents

Glen on Devil, Bessie on Terry,
Murtaugh, Idaho, 1928

Glen and Bessie Hyde at the South Rim of Grand Canyon
Photo by Emery Kolb

Part One

Glen and Bessie

House Rock Rapid, 1996

We
Of the night,
Will know
Many things
Of which
You sleepers,
Have never
Dreamed.

— *Bessie Haley*

⌒ 1996 ⌒

*I*HEAVED ON THE TWENTY-FOOT SWEEP OAR again and again and again. The boat was still hurtling to the left side of the rapid—the wrong side. Jeri was giving everything she had on the rear sweep but things just weren't working. We were slipping broadside into the massive, crashing lateral wave in House Rock Rapid. The river had utterly overpowered us. As we slammed into the wave, Jeri and I both hurled ourselves instinctively onto the left gunwale of the boat—as if our combined 320 pounds could do anything to stop the Colorado River from rolling our two-ton sweep scow like a giant log. The wave pitched the boat on edge and inundated us.

Somehow we didn't capsize. I fought to regain control of the forward sweep as it windmilled in the waves, and wrestled it into submission. The rear sweep swung wildly, slammed the deck hard, barely missing Jeri's helmeted head, and kept swinging. But the lateral wave had stopped our leftward momentum, and we coasted past the huge drop-off on the bottom left, missing it by a good five feet. We lunged through the ten-foot tailwaves at the foot of the rapid. The boat was half-full and out of control, and I yelled to Jeri to kick open the self-bailing drain. "It *is* open!" she screamed back. "The water's pouring *in*!" That was the wrong answer. The water was supposed to be going out. We were sinking. "*Well...*" I shouted, nearing full panic. "Well *close* it then!"

3

By now we were in calm water. Jeri, of course, had already wedged the self-bailer shut without my advice. We bailed madly for several minutes, the bilge pump kicked on, and we calmed down enough to talk. But we had little to say. Our usual jubilation below a rapid was strikingly absent. We were scared witless. This was only day two of a two-week trip through Grand Canyon, and House Rock is not one of the really big rapids. It was becoming hideously apparent that our river trip just might not work out.

I STILL BLAME the whole misbegotten adventure on rum drinks. Two years earlier, my wife Jeri and I were relaxing in our boats after another big day in Grand Canyon. We were both commercial guides, running whitewater trips for adventurous tourists. The passengers were making camp, the cooks were preparing dinner, and the boatmen were having cocktails after a long day at the oars. We were discussing the merits of various river craft, in particular the ponderous wooden sweep scow used by Glen and Bessie Hyde in 1928. "I think it was a perfectly good boat," I said, pouring another drink.

"But didn't it kill the Hydes?" asked Ben, a trainee.

"Well, no one knows," I said. "The boat was found in good shape, fully loaded, and ready to go. It was the *Hydes* that vanished. Why blame it on the boat?"

Ben wasn't buying my argument, but I could see that Jeri was scheming. In another two years her name would rise to the top of the ten-year Park Service waiting list, and we would be able to run our own private trip through Grand Canyon. "Let's build a scow, Brad!" she said. "We can take it on our private trip—just you and me! Wouldn't it be romantic?" Jeri was on her third rum drink.

I was on my fourth. I grinned, shrugged, and said, "Okay. Let's do it." That was that. That's what we told people we were going to do. And that's what we did. For two years, the plan seemed little more than a dream. Now it was becoming a nightmare.

The idea was to re-create, to a large extent, the lost honeymooners' trip down the Colorado. In October of 1928, Glen and Bessie Hyde launched a crudely built sweep scow in Greenriver, Utah. They wound through Labyrinth and Stillwater Canyons, and navigated the rapids of Cataract Canyon. They drifted on through the calm waters of Glen Canyon, and eighty-six miles into the whitewater of Grand Canyon. They made record time. The Hydes climbed to the canyon rim at Grand Canyon Village, talked to the press, resupplied, and returned to their scow. They were seen the next day at Hermit Rapid, heading downstream into the gloom of early winter darkness. Their scow was found a month later, near the end of Grand Canyon, upright, intact, and with all gear aboard. Glen and Bessie were never seen again.

Or were they? In the seventy years since they vanished, at least two women thought to be Bessie Hyde appeared. As did two Glens. Each appearance carried hints of murder, mayhem, and mystery. But regardless of whether the Hydes drowned or survived, our reasoning, if it can be called that, was that the scow was not to blame. The boat was in fine shape. The Idaho sweep scow was getting an undeserved bad reputation. We figured the tragedy, if there was one, was more likely due to Glen and Bessie not having life jackets and not being familiar with Grand Canyon. Jeri and I had nearly two hundred trips through the Canyon between us, and wore the best life jackets money could buy. We had run the river in many different boats—it would just be a matter of learning the eccentricities of a scow. We were figuring on an educational and entertaining vacation.

I researched the construction of the Hyde scow as best as I could, collected pictures, and talked to a few old-timers up in Idaho who had built and run the last of the old wooden sweep scows for the Idaho Centennial. They were helpful but not encouraging. The construction of the boat was going to be simple—it was just a big box. But running the thing—that's where the trick lay. I asked Bob Smith, a laconic old-time sweepboatman what would happen if I accidentally hit a wall straight on with the tip of one of my sweeps. "Oh," he said. He paused. "You wouldn't want to do that."

I drove east to the White Mountains near the New Mexico border to pick up a load of rough-cut pine. Two weeks before the trip, we invited all our boatman friends to a scow-raising at our Flagstaff, Arizona, home. We gathered in our driveway at eight on a Saturday morning. First we hammered together a series of U-shaped frames out of old wooden posts, fastening them upside-down to two heavy eighteen-foot long planks. We screwed two layers of one-by-ten inch planking on the bottom, then turned the boat right side up and loaded it on our trailer before it became too heavy to move. We covered the sides and ends with more one-by-ten boards. Although Glen Hyde put his scow together with nails, we cheated, shooting in deck screws with power drills. I hoped to salvage much of the lumber, should the boat survive, to use as part of a garage.

In the midst of construction a friend pulled us aside and said, "Look, I'm going to feel really bad if you get killed in this thing." He wasn't smiling. We were. What could happen? In the past twenty-five years we had seen about every possible wreck in Grand Canyon. It always worked out somehow. We remained confident.

The following afternoon we floated the fully built replica in Lake Mary, five miles south of town. The scow had taken a scant fifteen hours to assemble, at a cost of less than five hundred dollars. It was twenty feet long, five feet wide, and three feet tall—a large wooden trough, little more. A very heavy, very solid, wooden trough. Protruding from each end was a sweep—a massive oar-like device. Each sweep was twenty feet long, with a two-by-ten inch blade eight feet long. The shafts were made of paired two-by-six inch fir planks. Each sweep had thirty pounds of lead shot built into the inboard end to counterbalance it enough that we could lift the massive blade from the river. Protruding from the inboard ends were wooden grips made from the sawed off handles of old broken oars. Fully assembled, each sweep weighed nearly 150 pounds. At the ends of the boat we mounted sections of one-inch black iron pipe as thole pins on which to pivot the sweeps.

In the center of the scow was a raised platform, five feet square, some

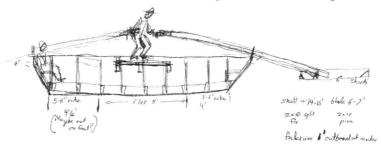

The extent of our blueprints

Scow skeleton

two-and-a-half feet above the floor of the boat. Sweepboatmen call this the dance floor. This is where the boatmen stand and heave on the sweeps. A scow of this size can be run by one or two boatmen, depending on the situation and desires of the crew. We planned to dance together.

The boat floated. The sweeps swept. We were giddy and optimistic.

SEVERAL DAYS LATER, with a group of friends, we took the scow on an overnight test cruise through the last few rapids of Grand Canyon and out onto Lake Mead. For months I had been talking to sweepboatmen from Idaho, trying to grasp the concept of maneuvering a craft in whitewater with no means of propulsion. We would have but one long lever protruding from the bow to point the beast, a second in the stern to help aim. Other than that we would be part of the river. Flotsam. But, said the Idahoans, there were ways to make the river put the boat where you wanted it; theories of becoming one with the proper currents. "Stay in the fastest current. Gather the river's momentum and use it to make maneuvers." I listened, squinted, and tried to visualize it. Once on the river, we tried those theories. They didn't work at all. Six rapids, six fiascoes. We were pummeled by the sweeps and knocked to the floor, spun crosswise to the current, and thoroughly spanked. Although I had a great deal of experience in kayaks, canoes, motorboats, and rowboats, each of those craft had the ability to move laterally across the current to avoid obstacles. The scow did not. Everything we knew about rowing a boat, every instinct we had, was working against us. We nicknamed the scow *Driftwood Struggling*. To make matters worse, the caulking had dried and contracted. Water gushed through every crack and the scow began to sink. We barely got it to shore.

Throughout the summer leading up to this, Jeri had asked me several times if I really thought this would work out. I blithely assured her it would. And as long as I remained confident, Jeri seemed willing to have faith in my judgment. I had been on the river fifteen years longer than she, and had run a wider variety of craft. But my confidence was waning. The scow sank again overnight.

We bailed it out, motored it across Lake Mead, and drove back toward Flagstaff. I had quit smiling. My infallible sense of humor was failing me. At a gas stop I inadvertently blockaded a pickup truck in an alley. The truck driver wanted out. I ran to our truck and jumped in to move it, slamming the door behind me. I was in the back seat. My brain had utterly seized.

Several days remained before our launch for the big trip, and we busied ourselves recaulking the scow with roofing tar and fine-tuning a few details. Jeri had the wits to go buy an electric bilge pump and a marine battery. We installed them and borrowed several inflatable tubes to put beneath the floorboards. We were cheating, of course, but we hoped to do something the Hydes had not: survive. And at this point I was having serious doubts. So was Jeri, as it turns out, but neither of us wanted to shake the other's confidence. Another close friend called, asking me very seriously if we were really going through with this. I mumbled something, hung up, and went down to our driveway to try and figure the best way out of the whole stupid idea.

At that time I was working on the biography of Buzz Holmstrom, the first man to run the Green and Colorado Rivers alone in 1937. Nine years after his feat, after many thousands of miles of rowing,

Holmstrom was asked to build and operate a sweep scow for a government survey trip on the Grande Ronde River in northeast Oregon. He knew nothing of how to operate a sweepboat, but was game. He hammered the scow together, then struggled with the ungainly craft for one day on the river. The following evening, the camp cook found his body slumped over a .22 rifle. "My God," I thought. "*Now* I know why he killed himself. It was the damned scow!*"

I tried to think of a way to disable the boat before it disabled me. That's when Brian Dierker drove up—one of my closest friends and one of the most experienced boatmen in Grand Canyon. I told him I was ready to abort, that I couldn't do this to myself or to Jeri. I had no clue how to control the craft, and it was probably going to sink or explode before I got the chance to learn. Brian pondered it for a moment and said, "What if I come along in my sportboat and run safety?"

Brian had a high-horsepower inflatable speedboat he had been using in Grand Canyon for several years for scientific expeditions. He had run a rescue boat in the midst of Kootenai Falls during the outlandish whitewater stunt photography for the movie *The River Wild*. He was well versed running flatwater and rapids, upstream or down, day or night. I lunged at his offer. "Will you? *Will you, Brian?* Oh *please?*" I think I was sobbing.

Whether he meant the offer or not, I was now clinging to him so desperately that he couldn't back out. He rearranged his schedule and enlisted his friend Cooper Carothers to ride along and pluck us out of the river. On August 13, 1996, we drove to Lee's Ferry, Arizona, the standard launching point for trips through Grand Canyon. We had four people and two boats—probably the fastest, most maneuverable boat ever to run the river, accompanying the most ponderous and lumbering. By mid-afternoon we were as ready as we were ever likely to be. With great trepidation, we pulled out from shore. We were committing ourselves to 225 miles of some of the heaviest whitewater in North America. We waved good-bye to the friends who had driven us to the river and drifted into the first minor turbulence, Paria Riffle. It knocked me flat.

Launching at
Lee's Ferry

WE MAY NOT have been the first to attempt a scow trip through Grand Canyon after the Hydes' disappearance. The wooden sweep scow fell from usage as soon as rubber pontoons appeared in the 1950s, and a few of the more modern inflatable sweepboats have since run Grand Canyon. These inflatables, as we understood it, carried a small motor for flatwater, and used the engine to build up speed for the rapids. Yet there is no written record of another attempt in a wooden scow— just this story: Early one spring in the late 1970s, Grand Canyon River Ranger Tom Workman walked down to the river at Lee's Ferry. The launch ramp was deserted save for a small group of people loading gear onto a large boxlike contraption. Recalls Workman:

"I was amazed to see this thing with these *huge* sweeps. I'd never seen a sweepboat. I said 'What *is* this thing?'" They invited him aboard and explained how the craft worked. "They were older than I, maybe forty-five. Farmers from Rupert, I think, in southern Idaho. They had on their old ball caps. They ran the Snake River with this thing—did it quite a bit, it sounds like. They loved to run rivers." Although he had never seen such a contraption, Workman was willing to believe the men knew what they were doing. He wished them the best of luck. As he was leaving, one of the men reached into the scow and handed him a gift: a fifty-pound sack of potatoes.

Boatman Mike Yard remembers seeing something scowlike around that time, pulling out of Redwall Cavern in Marble Canyon, thirty-three miles downstream from Lee's Ferry. He recalls seeing the men, dressed in flannel and denim, heaving on the sweeps, and thinking "Wow. That is so—so—romantic!"

No one seems to know who the men were, precisely what their craft really was, nor how they fared in Grand Canyon—whether they completed the trip without incident, or burned the beast and hiked out.

IN THE WEEKS preceding the trip we dug up everything we could find about Glen and Bessie Hyde. There wasn't much. Several books on river history carried a few pages on them, but told little about Glen's or Bessie's background. Glen was a tall, slender Idaho farm boy, rumored by some to be an uneducated brute. Bessie was short, demure, a poet, and not really that excited about the boat trip. Just how much river experience Glen Hyde had was not clear, but Bessie had none. Our trip, we hoped, would tell us more about them.

It did that and more. It piqued both our interests deeper into the story of Glen and Bessie Hyde. Frustrated with the utter lack of available or reliable information on the Hydes, I launched into an obsessive nationwide search for their story. After thousands of hours of digging through boxes of memorabilia, poring through archival collections, knocking on doors of timid old women, calling strangers from New Hampshire to Hawaii, driving to the four corners of the country, searching for buildings and streets that no longer exist, and surviving dozens upon dozens of dead ends, what I found was not what I expected. I found the story of Glen and Bessie Hyde—two brilliant young people on a daring adventure—and the phenomenal devotion of Glen's father, Rollin C. Hyde.

The Hyde family:
Edna, Rollin, Mary,
Glen, Jeanne

Some ships
Sail from port to port,
Following contentedly the same old way.

While others
Who through restlessness,
Watch new seas at the break of each day.

— Bessie Haley

2

Glen's
father ↑

~ 1859 – 1915 ~

ROLLIN CHARLES HYDE arrived in the rustic settlement of Spokane, Washington, in 1881 with his older brother Eugene, sisters Clara and Mattie, and their widowed mother, Susan Spencer Hyde. Their eldest brother Samuel had arrived two years earlier, when the population was less than one hundred, after living briefly in both Seattle and Tacoma. The potential of the small new forest town, situated beside spectacular Spokane Falls, had impressed Samuel. The seemingly endless virgin forest, the new silver mines near Cœur d'Alene, and the elbow room all showed great promise. The 230-foot drop of the falls could supply an estimated 300,000 horsepower to mills and industry. Spokane was an easy sell to the rest of the family, who had been farming near Oshkosh, Wisconsin.

The Hydes wasted little time in establishing themselves. Samuel became the prosecuting attorney and later a Justice of the Peace. When not serving in public office, he shared a law firm and acquired a reputation as one of the best lawyers in town. "Oh, go ahead and shoot the guy," went a local saying. "We'll get Sam Hyde to defend you." In 1894 he was elected to Congress. His booming voice in the House chamber was said to rival that of William Jennings Bryan.

Eugene became city marshal, chief of police, chief of the volunteer fire department, and served as a city councilman and state senator. He was not a man to back away from an uncomfortable situation and was known to be especially quick and effective with his .44-caliber double-action revolver. To his successor as marshal he passed on this advice: "Read the ordinances and never lose a fight."

Mattie Hyde taught school and soon married John Blalock, an up-and-coming shoe merchant. Clara, who was widowed by Dolphus Olmsted in Wisconsin before coming west with her three children, taught school as well.

Rollin, tall, slender, handsome, mustachioed, and the youngest of the family, got off to a slower start. Born April 29, 1859, in Elo, Wisconsin, Rollin had only a sixth-grade education, yet he taught school before coming west. In contrast to his gregarious and overtly public brothers, Rollin was a quiet, behind-the-scenes man. He filed for and proved up a homestead forty miles west in Davenport, Washington. Returning to Spokane, he entered into what became the family trade, real estate speculation. Between 1880 and 1890 Spokane's population grew from a few hundred to nearly twenty thousand residents. That would double in the next ten years. The Hyde sisters Clara and Mattie, and even their mother Susan, were actively buying and selling land, but Eugene, Rollin, and their brother-in-law John Blalock went into dealing with the greatest passion. In the years 1890–1892, the family recorded more than four hundred land transactions.

Rollin
Charles
Hyde

Mary
Thérèse
Rosslow
Hyde

On November 7, 1889, Rollin married beautiful Mary Thérèse Rosslow. Mary had been born into a small French-speaking community in Ohio, not learning English until grade school. Her parents, Suzanne Ameay, of France, and Augustus Rosselot, a master carpenter of French descent, moved to Spokane in 1887 with their six children. Once in Spokane, the family Americanized their name to Rosslow. Augustus built and sold one house after another, bringing in a steady income for the rest of his life. Although not as ambitious as the Hyde family, the Rosslow children did well. Henry and Louise opened the Lucerne portrait photography studio; Joseph became a lawyer. Augustus Jr. followed his father in the building trade.

At the time of Rollin and Mary's wedding, the Hyde brothers were engaged in their most ambitious real estate projects yet. Eugene built the three-story Hyde Building in 1889, only to have it burn in the great fire that swept the town on August 4. Undaunted, he erected the six-story brick Hyde Building in 1890 and founded the Citizen's Bank. Rollin followed suit with another six-story brick structure, the Fernwell Building. Brother-in-law John Blalock put up the Blalock Building. Meanwhile Rollin traveled back and forth to Davenport, where he worked another federal claim called a Timber Culture—"To encourage the Growth on the Western Prairie"—receiving title in 1892.

Fernwell Building

Edna Mae Hyde

But the Hyde clan's fortunes were fickle. Rollin and Mary's first son, Fernwell Albon Hyde, died at twelve weeks. In the spring of 1893, chaos hit Wall Street. In the East, banks and financial firms began to fail. The Panic of '93 spread west rapidly. During three days in May, Rollin Hyde, well on his way to becoming a millionaire, went flat broke. Overextended when the panic hit—he later said if he had not built those last two stories on the Fernwell building he would have survived—he lost everything. He took a night job as a janitor in the Fernwell, the building he had so recently built and owned. Within a month, Eugene Hyde's Citizen's Bank failed. He lost the Hyde Building as well. John and Mattie Blalock forfeited the Blalock Building. In 1896 Rollin and Mary's second son, Lynn, died at nineteen months. Sam Hyde, running for reelection to Congress that year, was tossed out on his ear along with every other Republican in the state. Mary's health was poor, and each winter she took ill, often having to have her tonsils lanced.

Rollin and Mary's bad luck finally abated. In October, 1896, Edna Mae Hyde was born. Rollin continued to work at the Fernwell Building, and purchased a home on Pacific Avenue. On December 9, 1898, Glen Rollin Hyde was born. Two years later, their last child, Jeanne Ethel Hyde, arrived. Life in the Hyde household was loving but austere,

Glen, Edna, and Mary Hyde

Glen Rollin Hyde

as Rollin's puritanical mother lived with them much of the time. In later life, Edna could not remember a single Hyde family gathering. Christmas was a holy day, not a holiday—no presents, no tree, no family dinner.

In the early years of the century Rollin began dabbling in real estate again, but his heart was no longer in it, nor did he have sufficient finances to get a foothold. In 1904, with his family, he left Spokane for his Timber Culture Patent in Davenport, the one piece of land he had been able to salvage from the Panic of '93. There, in the rolling scab-lands called the Palouse, forests were falling to the plow. Wheat prices had been holding high, and there were several large flour mills in Spokane. Hyde logged his timber, planted wheat, and began slowly to recover his financial and spiritual well-being.

Hyde worked hard. He was something of a Luddite, shunning new innovations in favor of horses and old iron machinery. Edna Hyde remembered harvest time, following the four-horse team as it hauled the header through the fields. A two-horse wagon followed alongside, catching the wheat heads as they dropped. Although Hyde experimented with a new twenty-horse combine, he found it wasteful. He went back to the old way.

Glen
Hyde

Schools were few in the rural Davenport area. By combining three children from a neighboring district with Glen and Edna, Hyde gathered the minimum number of pupils to open a small one-room school for five months of the year. The Hydes made their rare trips to town by buckboard, pulled by their draw horse, Old Dobbin. Edna recalled driving the cart with Glen one day and being astonished to see an actual motorcar coming the other way. Dobbin, said Edna, was unimpressed.

Outdoor living seemed a tonic; Mary's health improved on the Davenport farm. In the summers, when the wheat was taking care of itself, the family traveled north to Tiger, Washington, near Rollin's nephews, Arden and John Olmsted. There, on the shore of Leo Lake, they raised a second crop of grain.

Wheat prices continued to rise. In the fall of 1907 Hyde sold the Davenport farm for a record price. The family moved into the town of Davenport while Rollin made plans to return to Spokane and take up real estate again. He began collaborating with Mary's brother, Henry Rosslow, to buy a block of houses. But once off the farm, Mary became ill again, and the Spokane plans were scrapped. The family took the train south. In San Francisco, amid the ruins of the great earthquake and fire of a year earlier, they visited Mary's brother Augustus. They continued south to Santa Barbara.

Once away from the frozen-fog winters of inland Washington, Mary's health improved. The children loved California and spent much of their time at the beach. A year later they moved again, to Glendale, still a small town of two thousand. Edna recalled how odd the actors looked in the streets of neighboring Hollywood, as they silently gesticulated for the cameras. After a year the Hydes moved south again, to San Diego. The salubrious climate was helping Mary, but a brief return to Spokane proved detrimental. Returning south, they bought a citrus farm seven miles east of San Diego in Lemon Grove, and began to build a home. Mary's sister Louise moved in with them to help care for Mary. But for Mary, the southern climate was no longer enough. On December 20, 1911, she died of Bright's Disease—failure of the kidneys. She was forty-eight. Rollin was left with Edna, fifteen, Glen, thirteen, and Jeanne, eleven.

The family boarded the steamer S.S. *President*, bound for Seattle,

Louise Rosslow

Rollin Hyde's Royal Bank Building, Prince Rupert

to take Mary back to Spokane for burial. Rollin Hyde's grandson Bob Emerson recalls, "Family lore has it that a relative in Spokane—it might have been grandmother Hyde—after being informed of Mary's death, replied, 'I know it! I saw her! But there were two of them!'" As the ship approached San Francisco, Louise Rosslow died in her berth of chronic myocarditis—heart failure. She was forty-nine. The sisters were buried side by side at a double funeral in Spokane.

Devastated by twin losses, the Hydes headed north to begin anew. They went to Prince Rupert, British Columbia, another small town with potential. A transcontinental railroad promised to connect the vast grain fields of Canada with this port, thousands of miles closer to the markets of the Orient than any American city. Hyde began building again—two houses, one of which he rented, and a large masonry office building which he leased to the Royal Bank of Canada. Schooling was primitive. The "high school" consisted of one room in the grade school building. But Rollin Hyde was adamant about education for his children, regardless of his location or financial status at the time. To balance out the rustic learning of Prince Rupert, he sent Edna to Auburn, Massachusetts, to attend the Lasell Seminary for a year. Hyde encouraged all three children to study Spanish. Opportunities in North America, Hyde told them, were all but gone. His eyes were on South America.

Glen Hyde was now fifteen years old. He excelled in school, was a gifted athlete, and learned much of the building trade from his father. Jeanne Hyde later said it was in Prince Rupert that Glen first began boating, recalling family canoe trips on the Skeena River. Throughout their early years the Hyde children spent an inordinate amount of time out of doors, picnicking, hiking, and camping. When they lived on farms, they spent more time outside than in. When they vacationed—to New Mexico from California, to Alaska from Canada—they camped, fished, and hunted; explored caves, glaciers, deserts, and mountains; and in general eschewed urban attractions. By adolescence Glen Hyde's outdoor skills were well honed.

AS THE SIMMERING WAR in Europe erupted into a roiling boil, Rollin Hyde's finances collapsed once again. Although he was not forced to sell his holdings this time, he left for the lower forty-eight with little to show for his efforts. One reason he may have left, according to family lore, was to keep Glen out of the Canadian Army—the United States had not yet entered the war. Hyde went first to Los Angeles, where the children spent a semester in school. From there they returned to Spokane for another semester. Finances dwindling, Hyde picked a new destination and headed southeast, leaving Jeanne with her aunt and uncle in Spokane to finish school. Rollin Hyde arrived in southern Idaho in 1915 with two teenage children, and fifty cents in his pocket.

20

When the sun
Goes down,
Then I would rest.
For there is work
For me to do;
Tomorrow.

 ---- *Bessie Haley*

3

*T*HE BROAD SAGEBRUSH PLAINS of the Snake River in southern Idaho boasted little attraction at the turn of the century. Although rich earth covered the great lava fields, there was no way to water it. The Snake River had carved a deep gorge through the lava plains as it cascaded west toward Hells Canyon and its vast quantities of water remained inaccessible. That changed on March 5, 1905, when the Murtaugh Canal Company closed the gates of Milner Dam and canal systems began delivering water to 360,000 acres east of the tiny town of Twin Falls. By 1910, the population had boomed to five thousand and the Oregon Short Line Railroad was hauling record amounts of beans, wheat, potatoes, and sugar beets to distant markets.

In 1914, Rollin Hyde's brother-in-law, Henry Rosslow, bought a forty-acre tract of prairie five miles southeast of Kimberly, a small farming community east of Twin Falls. It was on Rosslow's land that Hyde and his children arrived a year later, destitute. Hyde borrowed money to plant, and spent the summer working the land with his children. After harvest he had enough to pay his debts, live through the winter, and plant again the following spring. Within two years he was able to buy the land from Rosslow, and over the next few years acquired additional acreage. Rollin and Glen built a small house on the land and surrounded it with trees and an orchard. They called it "the Home Place." From the outside it looked little different than any other shack, but inside were touches from "the good years" in Spokane—a set of crystal, a calendar

21

clock, and an ebony piano. Not far from the Home Place, Rollin's sister Mattie and her husband John Blalock were absentee owners of another ranch. There Glen built a dirt tennis court, the net stretched between two poplars. Although the Hydes' mail was addressed to the tiny crossroads village of Hansen, they went to school and shopped in Kimberly. In Edna Hyde Emerson's memoirs, she wrote of her dismay at moving to the bean fields of southern Idaho.

It was not beautiful. The streets and roads seemed to be dust holes in summer and mud holes most of the rest of the time. People who had cars usually stored them during the winter. Old Dobbin took us to Kimberly where he was tied to a hitching rack on Main Street. Yes, it was a duplicate of the western town of the movies except that we rarely saw cowboys on the street. This was a farming community. Those who wished to go to Twin Falls often took the train. The "Galloping Goose" in those days did a good business.

On our farm we had no telephone, no electricity, no plumbing. We got our water from a well (cistern) and carried out waste water which we threw a short distance from the house. Needless to say, this, in addition to the stock, brought flies, millions of them. I'm afraid that farm life was not my cup of tea.

As for schools, I seemed destined to find them a bit primitive. In Kimberly, the High School consisted of two rooms, and occasionally the principal's office in the grade school. However, they taught the

School busses at the new Kimberly High School

Glen in the fields

Glen at work on the Murtaugh Place

The Home Place

required subjects for college entrance. I got my diploma on graduation from the Kimberly High School in 1916.

Edna soon went to Spokane to begin college. Rooming with the
Blalocks, she completed two years at Whitworth College before earning
a teaching degree from the University of Oregon in Eugene.

ROLLIN HYDE had no complaints with his lot in life. He never said an
unkind word, recalled his grandson, and never swore. He was a kind
man, if extremely quiet. His boom-and-bust fortunes seemed to cause
him no bitterness. Edna Hyde's brother-in-law, pharmacist Leonard
Emerson, smiles when he recalls Hyde's economic travails. "Oh," says
Emerson, "he was a plunger."

Hyde made occasional shopping trips into Twin Falls, sometimes
by train, sometimes by buggy, rarely in his old Dodge. According to
neighbors, he never really mastered the motorcar. They told of a time
he approached a gate, pulled back on the steering wheel and hollered
"Whoa!" as he plowed it down. Likewise, the buggy sometimes got
away from him when he hitched it to one of the wilder young colts.
Neighbors prepared to get out of the way when they saw Hyde coming
in any conveyance.

Although he was well liked by all who knew him, he had few close
friends. Even fewer knew his given name. Among the things he left
behind in Spokane was the name Rollin. Leonard Emerson remembers
Hyde as a gentle, soft-spoken man who occasionally came into the
Twin Falls drugstore for a box of Hershey bars. Yet when asked what

Hyde's first name was, Emerson smiles and shrugs. "I just always knew him as Mr. Hyde." The few Idahoans who knew him as anything more than Mr. Hyde knew only that his initials were R.C.

R.C. and Glen continued to develop the Home Place and the neighboring Blalock farm, but felt they could use more land. At that time the Desert Land Act still provided irrigable land to those who would work it. Glen, being underage, had Edna file on a parcel fifteen miles east, near Murtaugh, which she later transferred into his name. The acreage was on a low winding ridge known as "the shoestring" and was irrigated by the Milner Low Lift Canal. It was a half-day buggy trip from the Home Place across Poverty Flats to "the Murtaugh Place." R.C. and Glen cleared and planted Glen's eighty acres and built a small bungalow.

Glen's high school career remains a bit of a mystery. He was in and out of several schools, perhaps taking semesters off to work on the farm. He began high school in Los Angeles. In the fall and winter of 1914, he was an honor student at Lewis and Clark High School in Spokane, and served in the school Senate. He attended tenth and eleventh grades at Kimberly High School, studying a liberal arts curriculum and excelling in public speaking. At the end of his eleventh year, his classification for next term read, "excused for work."

In keeping with R.C. Hyde's determination to better educate his chil-

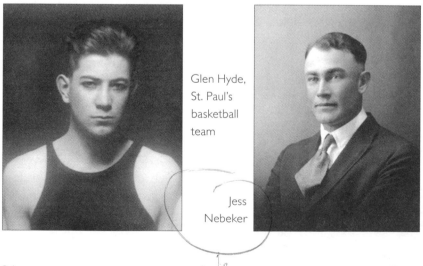

Glen Hyde,
St. Paul's
basketball
team

Jess
Nebeker

Friend

dren, he sent Glen to St. Paul's School, a private Episcopal school on Long Island, New York, for the winter of 1917–1918. Glen was on the St. Paul's swimming and basketball teams and boxed as well. "Vaughn proved no match for Hyde, the Man from the West," read the school bulletin, "in a three round match in the gentle act of sparring." Yet neither St. Paul's, nor Kimberly, nor Lewis and Clark has any record of Glen graduating.

Glen Hyde was spared two of the grimmer fates of his day. He turned twenty shorty after World War I ended, still a year too young to be drafted; and the Spanish Flu, which reaped more victims that the war, tread lightly in southern Idaho.

Leonard Emerson remembers Glen as a nice fellow, but had a hard time imagining him as a farmer. "He just wasn't that serious," says Emerson, "always joking around." Indeed, although strong, talented, and a good worker, Glen was looking for adventure early in life.

In 1919, he and Jess Nebeker, a tall affable Mormon boy from Kimberly, sensed a lifetime of responsibility ahead of them. They decided to launch on a grand expedition while they still could. They headed northwest. In Seattle they visited the new forty-two-story Smith Tower, the tallest building west of the Mississippi. After taking in the view from the top, the two of them returned to the elevator. The operator asked the two if they wanted a thrill. They nodded gamely, whereupon the operator set the elevator into what appeared to be free fall all the way to the bottom, where the air cushion in the shaft slowed them to a stop. Nebeker talked about the ride for the rest of his life.

From Seattle, Hyde and Nebeker took the ferry north to Prince Rupert and arrived to a cheering populace. The levity had nothing to do with the ferry—it was the first day the sun had shone in over six months. From there they headed inland. Acquiring a canoe, they launched on the Peace River for a six-month voyage, portaging from one drainage to the next as they worked their way east and south. Part of the draw to the area may have been Glen's cousin, John Gordon Olmsted, who had moved to the Peace River country. Hyde and Nebeker believed they were the first whites to pass through much of the area. The hunting and fishing were child's play, as if the wildlife had never before encountered humans. They eventually made their way down into Montana and from there returned to Kimberly. The trip had gone extremely well. The two young men were fast friends, and Hyde would later act as best man at Nebeker's wedding. The river, too, had found its way to Glen Hyde's heart and would draw him back for the rest of his life.

Glen Hyde apparently *did* graduate from high school, as he entered the University of Oregon, Edna's alma mater, in January of 1920. He was twenty-one years old. He studied liberal arts, including dramatics and public speaking. But in the middle of the fall semester, Glen withdrew. He took a year off, and in February of 1922 enrolled at the University of Idaho, in Moscow. His sister Jeanne, two years younger, was by now two years ahead of him in her studies there. Glen pursued a Bachelor of Science in Education, but after one semester switched to a Bachelor of Arts. He remained active in dramatics, literature, and debate, and in September joined the Sigma Nu fraternity.

The following February his team won a series of debates against the University of Washington and Whitman College. Before an audience of four hundred people, "Briscoe and Hyde melted the frigidity of the crowd and effectually answered the arguments of their opponents with well-timed humorous thrusts," stated the *Idaho Argonaut*. Glen Hyde in particular, "distinguished himself by his ability to meet the arguments of his opponents in a jocular but convincing manner."

With the Varsity Players, Glen played the supporting role of Fred Darcy in *Her Tongue*, a one-act comedy. In March, the school produced the first issue of a new literary magazine, *The Blue Bucket*. Glen Hyde's "Tomorrow" was one of three short stories featured. In light of Hyde's later disappearance in the trackless wilderness of western Grand Canyon, the story is particularly haunting. Set in the drizzling, sphagnum-floored swamps near Prince Rupert, it is the story of a thief trying to make his way to freedom through the interminable muskeg:

> Night was coming on, and that same peculiar grayness was settling. The lack of a single shadow made the dreary silence doubly unreal. The rotten, water-soaked log on which Dick was crossing a stream broke, and when he turned, after wading ashore, the stream was running the other way. Something snapped. Reason toppled from its throne, and the terror of being lost had him in its grasp. He screamed into the deadly silence. Unconsciously he tore the pack

from his aching shoulders, and stuffing his pockets with some of its contents, slung it into the stream. Then he ran—and unnoticed, four crows circled, and circled, and cawed their dismal cry.

…Reason pulled itself back on its throne. He laughed in nervous relief; then covered his ears to shut out the distorted echo that the mountains sent back. He glanced down at something white; then bent to examine the weather-stained skeleton of a man. The sight sent a cold chill up his spine and a maddening thought to his brain. There comes a time to all when they first come to think of death as something real. Like a flash it comes to them that death will reckon with them; as it does with all the world. But the loss of that inborn feeling of youth that death somehow does not apply to one's self was not alone what caused Dick to stand paralyzed and his hands to turn cold. It was the thought of death in that swamp. As his body would lie, forever, unseen by any human eye, the thought came of death without end, to the end of time, time without end.

During the winter of 1922–23, Glen met a boatman named Harry Guleke who was wintering in Moscow. Guleke told Glen of his many trips down the Salmon River at the helm of his huge wooden sweep scows. Enthralled, Hyde conceived a plan to run the Salmon from Salmon City, Idaho, to the Snake River, then down the Snake to the Columbia, and on to the Pacific Ocean. School work prevented the expedition, but the plan simmered for years.

The May, 1923, issue of the *Blue Bucket* opened with another short story by Hyde. "Flotsam," a love story, told of the fall and redemption of a ne'er-do-well in Skagway, Alaska. But by the time the story was printed, Hyde had again withdrawn from college and returned to Kimberly. At twenty-five, he quit school for the last time.

EDNA HYDE had returned to Kimberly after college to teach school, and in 1922 married Carl Emerson, operator of the local grain elevator. A year later they had a son, Robert. Jeanne remained at the University of Idaho until she graduated in 1924, an honor student. She took a teaching assignment in Hawaii before returning to Kimberly to teach.

Meanwhile, the extensive acreage of R.C. and Glen Hyde kept the two men busy. In early spring the land needed tilling and planting.

Beans, potatoes, clover seed, and sugar beets were local staples. During the winters the Hydes raised lambs. In the spring they sheared them and sold both the lambs and the wool. One of Glen's jobs was to stamp the wool down into the bins as it fell from the newly shorn sheep. He would emerge afterward stinking and sticky with lanolin. The Hydes also kept a number of horses for riding and farm work. Bob Emerson recalls when he was four or five years old, going out to the Home Place with his parents. When they turned into the dirt driveway, there was Glen, bounding up and down the tree-lined lane astride a young horse he was breaking.

Glen took the duty of secretary of the local irrigation district. But when not working the ditches, the crops, or the animals, he had time to play tennis or swim. His swimming prowess, in fact, was legendary. "Shortly after the low line canal comes out of the high line, there are some rapids that can be seen from the highway," recalls Bob Emerson, "and it's very, very swift, mean looking water. My mother said that Glen had swum across there several times. I have swum in the canal in *quiet* water—the current is strong enough that when I try to swim upstream I just float backwards."

Harvest came after the first frost set the crops, and was finished before the snow flew in November. But there was time before and after harvest to get away. In the winters the Hydes often traveled south to California—in the summers they might travel north to camp in the mountains. In late August, 1926, Glen and Jeanne went for a vacation in the Sawtooth Mountains. After an extended camping trip, Glen followed through with his long dormant plan. With his sister, he embarked on a journey down the Salmon River in what was, at least for Glen Hyde, a novel new craft: a sweep scow.

Jeanne and Glen Hyde,
Kimberly, Idaho

28

Seagulls; endlessly
Flying high and far
With strong wings made for adventuring.
Can it be that they
Too are in search of dreams,
Or is it just from the joy of living?

—— Bessie Haley

4

⌒ 1926 ⌒

GLEN AND JEANNE HYDE arrived in Salmon, Idaho, in late August
of 1926 to float the River of No Return. They went straight to the
river to look up Glen's old friend Harry Guleke. Guleke, known
as Captain, or "Cap," was the unquestioned king of Salmon River boatmen. He had arrived in Idaho in the 1890s and gone to work for the
Sandiland brothers, George and Dave, who were running sweepboats
on the river. First as a bailer and camp hand, then as a boatman, Guleke
soon mastered the craft and took over the business.

Sweepboats were little more than large wooden boxes, crudely built
from planks and steered with long, ponderous oar-like sweeps extending from bow and stern. The heritage of the boats and those who ran
them dates back to the 1840s when flatboats began to take over downstream trade from the keelboats on the Ohio and Mississippi. Flatboats,
too, were just giant wooden boxes, about eighteen feet wide and up to
ninety feet long that floated the rivers from Pittsburgh to New Orleans.
Hammered together from rough cut lumber, the flatboat was a floating
general store and trade center, manned by the scourge of every port,
the hard-drinking, hard-fighting, jolly, young flatboatman. Like the
scowmen that descended from them, flatboatmen led captivating lives.
"There is no wonder that the way of life which the boatmen lead," wrote
flatboatman Timothy Flint, "in turn extremely indolent, and extremely
laborious; for days together requiring little or no effort, and attended
with no danger, and then of a sudden, laborious and hazardous beyond

Jeanne and
Glen Hyde,
Cap Guleke

Atlantic navigation; generally plentiful as it respects food, and always so as it regards whiskey, should always have seductions that prove irresistible to the young people that live near the banks of the river."

The flatboatman steered his craft with a tremendous sixty-five-foot steering rudder, or "sweep," and occasionally propelled the boat with long "broadhorn" oars. Arriving in New Orleans, the flatboatman would liquidate his remaining cargo, sell his boat for lumber, squander his earnings in a dissolute spree, then tramp overland back to the upper reaches of the river to start again. "There is a charm about it that one can hardly account for," wrote another flatboatman, Thomas C. Collins, "unless it is because one is on the move nearly all the time. Almost every trip I took I would say, 'This is my last,' but, soon as I got home and rested a few days, I wanted to go again, and so it was with most of those who tried it."

On the Salmon, the first sweepboats, or scows as they were called, appeared in the 1870s. They were a scaled down, high-walled version of the flatboat. Like their predecessor, they were crudely built from rough-hewn planks, but only ranged from five to ten feet wide and sixteen to thirty-five feet long. The sidewalls rose three to four feet, and the bow and stern cantilevered up and out over the water. There were no broad-horn oars to propel the craft—instead the scowmen added a forward sweep to pry the bow of the barge into the proper thread of current.

The speed of the river provided the only propulsion, and the rear sweep aided in maintaining the proper heading.

The smaller sweep scows could be run by one man; the mammoth scows required two, one man for each sweep. The Salmon River was swift and shallow enough that the sweepboats excelled. Many were the miners that built scows and worked their way down the Salmon. The most prominent of the early Salmon scowmen was Johnny McKay, a Scottish hermit who worked the Salmon for more than twenty years beginning in 1872. After building a new boat in Salmon, Idaho, he would spend up to two years working from placer bar to placer bar, ending in Lewiston, Idaho, where he would sell his gold, scrap the scow, sell the lumber, and work his way overland back to Salmon.

By 1900 Harry Guleke had adopted sweepboating as his trade and, like the old flatboatmen, would work his way downstream buying, selling, trading, and delivering many tons of goods, always selling the boat for lumber at the end of the journey. Guleke took the trade a step farther by taking tourists through the gorge. One of them, a novelist named Caroline Lockhart, described him in 1911:

> There was Guleke, big as a bear and as strong, and with a bear's surprising agility as I afterwards learned—low-voiced, deliberate, with a slow, pleasant smile and a droll fashion of shaking his head and saying: "Well, well, I declare!"
>
> Many are the tales they tell of his strength—how, in an emergency, he broke a sweep in two, a tough green fir tree, to save a girl's life, and they chuckle over the story of how, upon an occasion, when attacked because he would not drink, he knocked the belligerent down three times and then said plaintively: "What's the matter with you? I don't want to fight," not being conscious that the fight had started.

Guleke was glad to help the Hydes build a scow, coaching and aiding them wherever he could. Guleke supplied the lumber from his small sawmill. Glen, an accomplished carpenter, had little trouble assembling the boat—the average time to build a scow was three days. On the afternoon of August 30, 1926, Glen and Jeanne Hyde launched on a paltry 650 CFS. (*Cubic feet per second*—the standard measurement of streamflow, as recorded by the United States Geological Survey, indicating the number of cubic feet of water that pass a given point each second.) Years later, in a short story, Jeanne described their departure:

> The boat was a flat-bottomed scow, measuring five by sixteen feet. A platform was built in the middle of the boat, where the boat-man, and boat-woman, in this case, were to stand. Nearly meeting here were the ends of the two sweep oars, each extending out into the water about four feet. The captain of the crew, my brother…, took the fore sweep; the mate, myself, the rear. The captain shouted orders; I obeyed, to the best of my ability.
>
> When we had stocked our boat with food calculated to last two weeks, thrown in our bedrolls, and other essentials, we started forth. Capt. Guleke went part way with us, just as sort of a send off. When he left I took over my position as rear oarsman. It was thrilling what a slight pull at the oar it took to turn the little scow.

Glen at the forward sweep

Glen at University of Idaho

Jeanne also kept a set of notes that Salmon River historian Cort Conley describes as "the most peculiar ever to come off the river; so sparse as to be almost poetic." Yet her spare phrases add flavor to the story of their trip. *People seeing us off—running along bank— horse looking at us, stupefied. First battle with oar—leaning on it—boat swerves—oar nearly knocks me out.* Below the town of Salmon, they passed the small community of North Fork. *First casualty—visor overboard. People watching us go by—"Goodbye, boys!"*

The Hydes had to learn quickly. Glen had learned to read the river's currents in his months on Canadian rivers. And they learned enough of the art of sweepboating in the first few miles with Guleke to survive the trip. They pried and wriggled their way between shallow rocks, hoping the river would deepen as tributaries joined the river. *"We're on a rock!"—wind holding us back! Taking wrong branch of river—stuck on low bottom—managing boat myself!*

Below North Fork a small dirt road paralleled the river as far as Shoup, where the Hydes arrived on their third day. They bought provisions and headed downstream to their first major rapid, Pine Creek. *Run onto rock—prying for an hour—bailing—waiting to swing—broken oar.* They eventually worked the boat free and replaced their broken sweep with a slender log. Later that day they broke their second sweep, and replaced it with another log. The weather added to their difficulties. *A fire on shore to dry out—raining—things wet—cigarettes—the candy melted to syrup.* In spite of the rain, Glen was enjoying himself. He shot a duck for dinner and assured Jeanne the weather was improving. *"It's clearing up!"—optimist.* It rained for another week.

Early morning beautiful—white mist rising from blue mountains. Feeling of being absolutely shut in—in the mountains. They had entered Black Canyon, a steep batholithic gorge, and home to Salmon Falls, a particularly steep, narrow drop. *Salmon Falls—highest—rocks—I on my back hanging to oar.*

"I was thoroughly scared just once," Glen later told a reporter from the *Lewiston Morning Tribune:*

> That was when the boat became half upturned against a huge rock at Salmon Falls in the Box Canyon of the Salmon River. There the river drops twenty feet in fifty as it boils over jagged rocks. I broke

Salmon
Falls,
Hyde
photo

two pike poles trying to pry the boat free and had to swim ashore to
get some more. The boat was filling with water and my sister was bailing out as fast as she could—we jarred the scow loose just in time.

After the wreck, Glen handled both sweeps in the larger rapids while
Jeanne perched in the bow, *riding 'em all on front railing—fell off—only
first time.*

They had lost much of their food in the wreck at Salmon Falls. The
next day Glen shot a deer, butchered it, and loaded the meat on board.
Below Mallard Falls they stopped to visit with Bill Jackson, "Genius
of the Salmon River." Known up and down the river for his mechanical wizardry, Jackson had crafted many of the mills, irrigation systems,
and mining setups of the other settlers. He told them they were now
past Black Canyon—*the bugaboo*, Jeanne called it. They traded venison
for vegetables and continued. *Everyone along the way telling us of others
who had been drowned just below.*

On September 8, the tenth day of their trip, the weather finally broke
and they dried their mildewed clothes around the fire. They christened
the sweep scow *Balaam's Ass*, after the recalcitrant biblical donkey. As
the story goes, Balaam was going to Israel, against the wishes of the
Lord, riding on his ass. The way was blocked by an angel, which only
the ass was perceptive enough to see. Terrified, the ass swerved into
the field, for which Balaam smote her. She thrust herself into the wall,

Jeanne Hyde

View from the scow, above Riggins

crushing Balaam's foot. He smote her again. Exasperated, she collapsed beneath him and was smitten yet again. "What have I done unto thee, that thou hast smitten me these three times?" she asked Balaam. And Balaam said unto the ass, "Because thou has mocked me: I would there were a sword in mine hand, for now I would kill thee." A more appropriate name for an unruly scow would be hard to find.

The next day they reached the small town of Riggins—*Cars again— looking queer to us—civilization unwelcome*—and continued on. *Rain— sun—desert country—great rolling hills, purple and blue and brown in the distance—looking like work of a child in a sand pile—looking also like great relief map—unreal—light blue sky and fleecy clouds—green rocks.* For two days below Riggins a road paralleled the river. At Whitebird the road veered off to the north and they entered the lower gorges of the Salmon. *Leaving road—relief…rapids at short intervals—getting used to them.* By this point tributary rivers had raised the water to around 3,500 CFS—still quite low and rocky.

In his Lewiston interview, Glen gave his impressions of the scenery:

> From Box Canyon in the Salmon River down to Riggins, the countryside, if it can be called that, is almost breathtaking for sheer

beauty. Great mountains of solid rock seem to sweep down into a trough for the riverbed. The great bare mountainsides were streaked with reddish gold and bluish colorings mingled with the slate gray of solid rock. In the early morning sun they stood out magnificently—a veritable "Grand Canyon" in Idaho.

Farther down, the valley opened and narrow table-lands spread out on both sides of the river. Here we saw several small herds of deer, grazing quietly, and here we looked in vain for the famous wild mountain sheep, said to be practically extinct except for these impenetrable regions of Idaho.

As we swept into the Snake River, the valley became wider, showing only the shadowy outlines of mountains in the distance. Here too, we noticed the nature of the rock changing. From solid granite-like stuff, the hills and canyon rocks became rounded and composed mainly of lava rock. From there on down to Lewiston, little boat trouble was experienced and the country steadily became more civilized in appearance.

When we sailed out into the Snake at the mouth of the Salmon, 50 miles up from Lewiston, we were thankful to find a broader smoother river, and one hardly less impressive to travel down. In fact in places the current became so sluggish that I improvised two sails of canvas over pike poles and thus speeded down the river in true buccaneer fashion.

Jeanne Hyde, *Balaam's Ass,* Snake River

There were rapids on the Snake as well, and with the greatly increased flow, the waves were the largest they had seen. *Enormous waves—sitting on top of one, looking at next—"We're going to swamp!"—but we didn't.* On September 15, 1926, their seventeenth day, they reached Lewiston, having traveled three hundred miles across the state of Idaho. *Grub left!—tears! Unloading Balaam's Ass—packing up—sad! Leaving boat under bridge—strange noises—strange land—seems unreal.*

Although running the Salmon in those days was not a highly unusual feat, the Hydes had the distinction of being one of few parties to run their own boat through just for the thrill of it. And although this trip does not establish Hyde as a world-class boatman, the fact that they made it through on their first attempt, and at such a low flow, says much for their innate skill and perseverance. Veteran western boatman Rick Petrillo observes, "To just go out and run the Salmon River—you've got to be a quick study, I would think. You'd have to be a real quick study. Like a handful of other people that I've run across in history, he just had

Glen Hyde

an automatic knowledge of how to read water. Nobody to learn from about how dangerous it was, he just knew where it was going and where he couldn't be. He had to have that instinctive idea about how to avoid those problems if he ever got that far. He had to." Jeanne Hyde added this detail: "As I say, the river has been run several times, but never once, so far as I know, with a woman at a sweep oar."

"The whole trip was a remarkable experience which my sister and I would not have missed for worlds." Glen summarized. "I think now that I'd like to come down again alone in a canoe."

Earl Helmick and Bessie Haley,
Parkersburg High School *Quill*,
February, 1924

The city streets
With noisy cars,
And many faces
Passing by,
Make the city
A place—
Of utter loneliness

— Bessie Haley

5

~ 1866–1926 ~

BESSIE LOUISE HALEY was born in Takoma Park, Maryland, on December 29, 1905, six miles due north of the United States Capitol Building. Of her family, nearly nothing is known. Her father, William Lindsey Haley, had been born in Maine in 1866 to Canadian parents. By the turn of the century he was a divorced wallpaper hanger in Takoma Park, then a new and thriving suburb straddling Maryland's border with the District of Columbia.

Bessie's mother, Charlotte "Lottie" Baynard, was born in 1880 of two pioneer families, the Baynards and the Jumps, from Easton, Maryland, on the eastern shore of Chesapeake Bay. Lottie's father, Daniel, had not been one of the prominent Baynards, however, but worked in the local brickyard and rented a small flat on the edge of Easton. By 1901, Lottie had made her way to Takoma Park.

Takoma Park had been carved out of the forest as an affordable and safe place for Washingtonians to live, several hundred feet above the malarial lowlands of the capital, a short train ride through the woods from the squalor and crime. There, on November 19, 1901, William and Lottie married. William was thirty-five, Lottie twenty-one.

Sometime after Bessie's birth, the Haleys moved to Saint Michaels, Maryland, a tiny fishing village near Easton. William was working as a salesman there when Bessie's only sibling, William Austin Haley, was born in 1910. By 1912 the family had moved to Pittsburgh, Pennsylvania, where they shifted from one shabby quarter of town to another for the next ten years. William Haley worked on and off as a painter and wallpaper hanger while Lottie raised the children. These were Bessie Haley's formative years.

It was a time of fabulous wealth and tremendous poverty in Pittsburgh. While Andrew Carnegie was giving away a fortune squeezed from the working poor of Pittsburgh, robber barons were still squeezing, busting unions, fighting their way to the top. Meanwhile the skies darkened and the river roiled with unprecedented amounts of pollution. "One month in Pittsburgh," said philosopher Herbert Spencer, "would justify anyone in committing suicide."

The Great War demanded night and day steel production at home, while abroad it killed off more than fifteen hundred of the city's young men. In 1918 the flu killed two thousand of the twenty-three thousand infected. The horrors of the war had disillusioned a whole generation of youth, and women in particular were ready to change the way the world worked. Prohibition became law and a year later women got the vote. It was the dawn of the roaring twenties, the birth of the flapper, and the debut of the heretofore unseen female knee. The shimmy, the Charleston, and the Age of Jazz were all about to sweep the nation. Bessie was poised to ride this wave of change.

right to left: Bessie's mother, father, and cousin Mildred

At PITTSBURGH, the Monongahela and Allegheny Rivers join to form the mighty Ohio, once the commercial freightway of the Midwest, and the river that dominated much of Bessie Haley's life. In 1922, the Haleys followed many other Pittsburghers two hundred miles downriver to Parkersburg, West Virginia. Parkersburg had become a mecca for money, as oil—and the new uses for oil—had been discovered nearby. The town grew rapidly, with turreted Victorian mansions and multi-towered office buildings sprouting on the east side of the Little Kanawha River and the burgeoning poor expanding to the west.

For the first time, the Haleys lived in a pleasant house, at 2317 Oak Street, a ten minute walk from the new high school. Sixteen-year-old Bessie immersed herself in school activities, made friends, and jumped a semester toward early graduation. She starred as Juliet in the class play, was in the Debating Club, and wrote for the high school annual, *The Quill*. She was an honor student in a college entrance curriculum. Her strongest creative interest, although her early efforts might make one cringe, was art.

Bessie Haley and Earl Helmick combined efforts to do the artwork for *The Quill*. Earl, the son of a mattress maker, came from a large Parkersburg family and was a good student in a commercial curriculum. An atypical high school male, Earl was in the gardening club, literature club, and the chorus. In *The Quill's* "Prophecy," coauthored by Bessie Haley, Earl was fated to tutor women in the art of blushing. He was a creative, if bashful, young man. Bessie and Earl graduated

Some of Bessie's *Quill* art.

William Austin "Bill" Haley, 1930

EARL HELMICK
Aug. 22

Gardening Club '19, '20; Lit. Club
'23, '24; Chorus '21, '22, '23; Quill
Staff '24.

Born under the Zodiacal sign Con-
stellation-Virgo. You are of a jeal-
ous temperment, especially of one
black haired member of the opposite
sex. You are capable of making
money and are in a direct line for
success.

BESSIE HALEY
Dec. 29

Let's Go Club; Debating Club; Class
Play; Class Prophecy; Regular Qui'l
Staff '23; Senior Quill Staff.

I find that you were born under
the Zodiacal sign known as Copri-
corn, and your ruling planet it Sa-
turn. I see a great future for you.
You will travel in foreign countries
accompanied by a blue eyed, brown
haired young man who pays the bills.
Disposition: Jolly, but baseful.

together in February of 1924, when Bessie was eighteen. On the Senior
Staff page, Haley and Helmick, artist and assistant artist, were pictured
in a sweetheart pose.

IN FALL OF 1924, Earl went a dozen miles upstream to work in Marietta,
Ohio, while Bessie moved ninety miles down the Ohio to Huntington,
West Virginia. There she enrolled in Marshall College and studied,
among other things, freehand drawing, design, and commercial design.
She was an A student. The 1925 yearbook, *Mirabilia*, carried two pieces
of Bessie's artwork, much improved in the two years since high school.
In her sophomore picture, with hair bobbed short, flapper-style, she
looked all of about fourteen years old.

From the 1926 Marshall College Yearbook

Regulations for young women on the campus were strict. "Listlessness and loafing are educational sins," admonished the school catalog. "Intense interest and hard work are essential to success." Marshall College required all women under twenty-one to room and take their meals in College Hall. Permission to attend a social function or stay out overnight could be granted by the Dean of Women only upon written request, signed by the girl's parents. Social functions ended at 11:30 P.M. sharp. Moreover, there were to be no intermissions at dances.

Bessie Haley turned twenty-one in December of her sophomore year and promptly moved off campus. To help support herself she took a secretarial job at the YWCA in town. Her studies were apparently going quite well when, in early June of 1926, near the completion of her fourth term, Bessie Haley's life took a strange and sudden turn. On Saturday, June 5, she and Earl Helmick traveled fifteen miles downstream to Catlettsburg, Kentucky, bought a marriage license, and wed. Two members of the minister's family signed as the legal witnesses. No news of the wedding appeared outside of Kentucky, but the *Huntington Advertiser* printed this discreet piece the following day:

Miss Bessie Haley, who has been a student at Marshall College, and an assistant at the Young Women's Christian Association here, has returned to her home in Parkersburg. She plans to spend the next year in California studying art.

The strange turn got stranger: by early August, less than two months after her wedding, Bessie Haley was living in San Francisco, alone.

Irene
"Eraine"
"Greta"
Granstedt

The model sat mid cherub clothes,
And thought about her many beaux,
The party where she'd go that night,
With cocktails, jazz and blazing light.

The artist stopped in deep despair
And almost tore his greying hair,
How could he paint an angel's face,
From a girl who thought of a dancing place?

— Bessie Haley

6

~ 1926–1927 ~

SAN FRANCISCO, then as now, was a Mecca for offbeats and individualists. In the 1960s the city gave birth to the Hippies. In 1926 it was a haven for Bohemians—nonconformists, artists, and poets. The California School of Fine Arts had just moved into its handsome new classical Spanish-Colonial building at 800 Chestnut Street, near Fisherman's Wharf. In early August Bessie Haley enrolled at the school. Immersed in the aromas of oil paint and damp clay, and surrounded by wild, creative young people, she studied Drawing and Life Drawing under the locally prominent painter Spencer Macky. She wrote verse as well. During her stay in San Francisco she gathered fifty of her poems into an unpublished volume titled *Wandering Leaves*.

Among the first people Bessie Haley met in San Francisco was Eraine Granstedt, a nude model at art school. Both women were attractive and tiny—Bessie was barely five feet tall, Eraine just over an inch taller. The two became immediate friends. Two years younger than Bessie, Eraine had already lived longer and harder than most nineteen-year-olds. So much so that she had already abandoned her given name and the infamy it carried.

Although she later claimed to have been born in Malmö, Sweden, relatives claim she was born Irene Granstedt in Scandia, Kansas. Her family later moved to Mountain View, California, thirty-five miles south of San Francisco. In the summer of 1922 Irene leapt from obscurity to the front page of the tabloids. "SCHOOLGIRL, 14, SHOOTS SWEETHEART!" Irene, said the papers, was having a troubled relationship with her boyfriend, Harold Galloway, seventeen. She borrowed a gun from a friend and on the evening of April 18 pointed it at Harold. He grabbed her hand; the gun went off. Harold lay dying, his guts stewing with peritonitis, while Irene languished in jail. For weeks headlines broadcast the story of the murderous maid and her dying beau, paired with side bars cursing the collapse of society. But Harold failed to die. Irene got off with juvenile detention and banishment from Mountain View.

Barely a year later she made the headlines again. Lying to a judge about her age, she married Robert Bleibler, twenty, of Menlo Park. The marriage was annulled in less than a year. Meanwhile, Harold Galloway, who had fully recovered, was being sought for statutory rape of his new fifteen-year-old girlfriend in San Mateo. Harold was a slow learner.

Irene went to San Francisco and immersed herself in the Bohemian atmosphere. She auditioned for plays and entered beauty contests. She remarried, this time to an artist named Lowenthal, but again with short success. She changed her name to Eraine and took a job modeling at California School of Fine Arts. When Bessie met her, Eraine was single again, rooming with her brother Theodore, who had run away from

Bessie, Eraine, and Theo's flat on Hyde Street

Greta Granstedt, 1928

home shortly after Irene shot Galloway. Theodore had worked the high seas under a pirate's pseudonym, Henry Morgan. He had now returned and, going by Theo, worked as a nude model at the school. "Those two were doing things that just weren't socially acceptable," recalls Theo's son Ted, "they were pushing the edge of society."

Bessie Haley could sympathize with Eraine's man problems. Bessie's short-lived marriage to Earl Helmick remains a mystery, although most attribute it to an accidental pregnancy. Bessie's brother Bill later stated, "Earl said Bessie was pregnant when she left the East and he sent her money for an operation." Whether this was a euphemism for terminating the pregnancy—or whether she carried the child to full term and gave it up for adoption—or whether she was really ever pregnant at all—may never be known. Bill was not entirely sure himself. Some historians have thought Bessie's poem, *A Visitor*, indicated Bessie had indeed had a child:

> *This soft bundle,*
> *So close to me,*
> *Is yours and mine,*
> *Come, love, and see.*
> *I'm glad the stork,*
> *In hurried flight,*
> *Took time to stop,*
> *In here tonight.*

If Bessie really was pregnant, the paternity, too, remains a mystery. Even if the child was not Earl Helmick's, he may have cared enough for Bessie to "make an honest woman of her." Regardless, it seemed a short, strange, and loveless marriage.

Bessie took a room with Eraine and Theo on Hyde Street. She got a job at Paul Elder's—the biggest and best known bookstore in town and a gathering place for the Bohemian elite. For the January semester, Bessie switched to night classes, perhaps in order to work days at the bookstore.

Eraine had her eyes on Hollywood. The current silent movie queens, the Talmadge sisters, poor girls from Brooklyn who had become millionaires, were easing into retirement. Their rags to riches story of glamour and fame forged dreams in young women across the country. Eraine wanted to head south, to be famous, to be on the big screen. She convinced Bessie to join her.

The most exciting way to travel to Los Angeles was by steamer. Two of the fastest and most luxurious passenger ships in the world, the *Harvard* and the *Yale,* were then running four trips a week each way along the California coast. At 376 feet long, the sleek white ships boasted over three hundred state rooms and twenty-five luxury suites. In the glass-roofed ballroom a fast jazz band played all night, and haute cuisine was included in the price of the ticket. Although Prohibition was in full force in the United States, the ships sailed in international waters for most of the voyage. On weekends the ships were packed with young people splurging on a three-day round-trip party. Dancing, fine food, and the romance of being on a luxury ship began at four in the afternoon and continued non-stop until arrival in port at ten the next morning. One could leave Friday evening, dance all night each way and return to work Monday morning exhausted. Toward the end of February, 1927, Bessie withdrew from night school and, with Eraine, booked passage to Los Angeles. They were only going one way, however, with no plans to return.

The band struck up that evening as the ship sailed out of the still bridge-less Golden Gate for a long and transformational night. When they arrived in Los Angeles the next morning, Eraine was no more. It was Greta Granstedt, the young starlet from Sweden, that stepped from the ship and went straight to Hollywood to begin thirty-some years of bit-part roles and another six marriages.

Bessie Haley, too, stepped ashore with a new destiny. At her side walked the tall, handsome farmer she had met on board the night before: Glen Hyde.

Delpha Jewell's home, Elko, Nevada

Hollywood
A place of make-believe,
And strange human wrecks
Who know broken hearts,
And disillusion.
With now and then
A break—
To spur them on
To utter hopelessness.

— *Bessie Haley*

7

~ *1927–1928* ~

GLEN HYDE and Bessie Haley's immediate attraction soon blossomed to love. Bessie accompanied Glen to Idaho, where she met the Hyde family and joined them for a camping trip to spectacular Redfish Lake, nestled in the Sawtooth Mountains north of Twin Falls. Later that summer, Glen and Bessie made a trip back to West Virginia. She introduced Glen to her parents as the man she planned to marry. There was only one glitch—Bessie was still married. Earl Helmick appeared at the Haleys to reclaim his wife. Bessie refused and asked him to grant her a divorce. Helmick refused in turn, insisting that she come back to him. Glen jumped into the argument, with dismal results. Bill Haley later said that Glen should never have come to Parkersburg at all, that both he and Helmick had made fools of themselves. Mildred van Siclen, a cousin of Bessie's, added that Mrs. Haley did not take warmly to Glen. She was fond of Earl, whom she described as a very nice boy with a bad temper. It had been a difficult summer for the Haleys even without this. In June, William Haley's small paint and wallpaper business had become insolvent and gone into receivership. With little resolved, Glen and Bessie returned to the West.

Bessie moved to Elko, Nevada, in November, 1927, and took a room with Delpha Jewell, a single woman seven years her senior. Nevada had the most lenient divorce laws in the country at the time, but a six-week residency was still required.

It was a particularly cold and snowy winter. "She stayed at our house the time she was in Elko," recalled Delpha Jewell in a 1949 interview with Colorado River historian Otis "Dock" Marston. "She was a good tenant. Her habits and morals were good. She kept to herself...very unhappy...limited funds...would almost faint from hunger. She did not work while she was here. She used to draw and would make things out of felt."

Although Glen Hyde lived only one day's travel to the north, it is not clear if he was able to visit her during that lonely winter. "I do not recall any visit from anyone in Idaho. She got mail," said Jewell. "She did not tell me her troubles."

"THE DIVORCE MILL continues to grind in district court here..." stated the *Elko Independent* in December. Regardless of grounds, few divorces were denied. On February 7, one was granted for nagging. On February 21, 1928, Bessie Haley Helmick filed for divorce on the grounds of non-support. She chose Milton Reinhart to represent her. Reinhart was a popular Elko lawyer and partner of Morley Griswold, who would later become governor of Nevada. Judge Edward Carville, who heard the case, would succeed Griswold as governor. It was an all-star cast, scripted to succeed.

The case went to court April 11. Carville stated that Earl G. Helmick had been served with papers in Ohio on February 29, but had failed

Bessie Haley,
circa 1927

Courthouse,
Elko, Nevada

to respond within the required forty days and was therefore in default. Delpha Jewell testified that Bessie had lived with her for the required six weeks. Reinhart then asked Bessie if, indeed, Earl Helmick, disregarding the solemnities of his marriage vows, had failed to provide her with the common necessities of life for the last year. Bessie, undoubtedly coached as to appropriate testimony, affirmed. Reinhart asked if this was due to poverty or lack of a job. Bessie said no, it was not.

MR. REINHART: Is there any community property?
MRS. HELMICK: No.
MR. REINHART: Are there any children?
MRS. HELMICK: No.
JUDGE CARVILLE: Did you ever live together as husband and wife?
MRS. HELMICK: Yes… For about two months.
JUDGE CARVILLE: Did you leave him or he leave you or what was the trouble?
MRS. HELMICK: I was going to school and it was perfectly all right with him; but he was totally indifferent; it didn't seem to make any difference after that time….
JUDGE CARVILLE: How have you supported yourself since that time?
MRS. HELMICK: My father supported me mostly… I supported myself part of the time…
JUDGE CARVILLE: Does he give any reason for not supporting you, or is there any reason why he shouldn't?
MRS. HELMICK: No, not that I know of. He just doesn't seem to care one way or another.
JUDGE CARVILLE: Does he drink?
MRS. HELMICK: No.
JUDGE CARVILLE: Or gamble?
MRS. HELMICK: Not that I know of.
JUDGE CARVILLE: How did you separate; did he just leave you and never send for you to come to a home, or what?
MRS. HELMICK: Well, I was going to school; that was the agreement when we got married that I should continue to go to school, and he just went to work and seemed totally indifferent whether I come or not.

JUDGE CARVILLE: Did he ever ask you to come?

MRS. HELMICK: No. He suggested that I might come up there and work later on.

JUDGE CARVILLE: You didn't feel like going up there and supporting yourself?

MRS. HELMICK: Well, it seemed a peculiar arrangement.

JUDGE CARVILLE: Yes, it seems rather peculiar to me.

MR. REINHART: After school you returned to your home in West Virginia?

MRS. HELMICK: Yes, I was home.

JUDGE CARVILLE: It seems rather peculiar to me, if he doesn't drink or gamble, unless he didn't seem to care for you.

CARVILLE granted the divorce, and Mrs. Helmick took back the name of Bessie Haley, the only name she had ever used anyway. No mention was made of Bessie having moved to California, nor her engagement to Glen.

Helmick's side of the story was never told. Although he married again in 1930, had four children and lived to be ninety years old, neither Helmick nor his family ever again discussed his marriage to Bessie Haley. In spite of the court testimony, it is hard not to wonder if Bessie Haley used Helmick in time of need, then discarded him. In 1985, when researcher Martin Anderson phoned to ask about Bessie, Helmick, then eighty-two, said simply, "I don't want to discuss it. She is dead." Click.

Bessie
on the farm

When I was rather young,
Men thought me strangely cold,
But, I saved my love,
And I'm glad now I am old.

Some girls fling a little love,
To many lovers, friends, and all,
Until they can no longer hear
The wondrousness of love's real call.

— *Bessie Haley*

8

∼ *April – October 1928* ∼

BESSIE HALEY left Elko that afternoon, divorce decree in hand, and traveled over the high sagebrush country of northern Nevada and down into Twin Falls. Bob Emerson remembers his parents getting dressed up the following morning, April 12, 1928, hiring a baby sitter, and heading into Twin Falls for Uncle Glen's wedding. It was a small affair, held at the Rector Ascension Episcopal Church. Inasmuch as divorcées were not allowed to be wed in the church, they spared Reverend W. Hewton Ward the details.

The newlyweds settled in at Glen's place in Murtaugh. Bessie, with her flapper's *à la garçonne* hairdo, soon had new overalls, a dog, Mickey, and a horse, Terry. Bessie's brother Bill, in and out of high school with bad health, came out to Idaho for the summer. The three of them worked both the Murtaugh and Home Places throughout the summer and Bessie learned to ride.

Glen and Bessie had a tremendous amount in common. Both were extremely bright, had been active in drama and debate, and were talented writers. Both of them were uncommonly good looking. Each had a yen for the extraordinary, for adventure, for travel. Bob Emerson remembers, as a preschooler, being horrified when his parents mentioned that Bessie was "a Bohemian." He was sure that must be something dreadful. Perhaps their tone of voice betrayed a disapproval of the faster, looser mores of the 1920s. Yet Glen, too, was cast in the new mold. As the old model of the staid, straightlaced Victorian man crumbled, a newer, more sensual, and more egalitarian male began to emerge. There was less emphasis on dignity, honor, and responsibility; more demand for the exciting, the enticing, the here and now.

Glen and Bessie were young, intelligent and progressive. Neither had any interest in spending the rest of their lives on an Idaho spud farm. And most likely they were very much in love.

As the summer went on, they came up with a plan for escape. Glen had already been smitten by the lure of life on the river and the thrill of whitewater and had proven himself an adept boatman of the Salmon River. Over the past year another river had been in the news. Two expeditions on the Colorado had brought the whitewater of Grand Canyon to national attention, and had reawakened Glen Hyde's longing.

ON JUNE 27, 1927, perhaps the most bizarre Colorado River expedition to date launched from Greenriver, Utah. It was the whimsy of World War One veteran Clyde Eddy, who had since made good in the pharmaceutical business. He wanted fame and adventure and chose a river trip as a way to achieve them.

Glen and Bessie Hyde, Bill Haley

Bessie
and
Mickey

Bessie
and
Terry

Ignoring the great leaps made in whitewater boat design during the past sixty years, Eddy commissioned three boats—oversized, overweight replicas of the original wooden boats used on Major John Wesley Powell's exploration of the Green and Colorado in 1869. He recruited a dozen college boys for the adventure, keeping secret their destination until the last minute. Even more peculiar, he bought a bear cub from the New York Zoo, and added a dog to the crew shortly before launching.

For the first 120 miles down the Green River, things went smoothly, as there were no rapids. Unfortunately for Eddy, though, he was on the tail end of one of the largest floods of the decade. Cataract Canyon nearly destroyed them, and had Eddy not had the wits to hire a professional guide, Parley Galloway, they likely would not have made it.

The floodwaters had subsided by the time they reached Grand Canyon and, although they had calamities daily, they pressed on, the bear chewing at their ankles, the dog yapping, and Eddy awakening them with a shrill tin whistle each morning, barking orders. Eddy was barely able to keep control of the men and figured the best way to maintain morale was to shave daily. "A more humorless man," said historian David Lavender, "never ran the Colorado." They sank one of the boats at Dubendorff Rapid, but salvaging much of the gear, floundered

Eddy crew losing boat
at Dubendorff Rapid

Pathé-Bray trip in ice jam
at Hermit Rapid

on through Grand Canyon, arriving in Needles, California, by early August. Eddy returned home to New York to write his book and edit his film.

THREE MONTHS LATER, another expedition left Greenriver, Utah. The Pathé-Bray film company of Hollywood planned a feature film of river running, but went with the more modern Galloway-style wooden rowboats and only one mascot, a dog named Pansy. The water level was far lower than the flood that had abused Eddy in June, allowing the Pathé-Bray folks to work their way down though Cataract Canyon with less danger. But it took far longer than they had hoped, or at least that is how their ground crew portrayed it. The film company had established a land-based control center on a barren mesa southeast of the river and were broadcasting daily news updates as to the progress of their expedition. By the third week in November, they announced that the expedition was late in arriving at Lee's Ferry, the midpoint of the trip, and called for a search. Newspapers around the country carried the story. An army plane was summoned to fly the river, and a reigning river expert was brought in from the east coast to lead rescue efforts—none other than Clyde Eddy. By the time Eddy and the plane had arrived on the scene, the trip had arrived safe and sound at Lee's Ferry. But Pathé-Bray achieved the true goal of the search: America was now quite aware of the expedition.

As December's chill temperatures descended into Grand Canyon, the men worked their boats through the rapids and along the icy shores.

They arrived at Phantom Ranch, midway through the canyon, nearly frozen. The trip continued on downriver another nine miles to Hermit Rapid, where they spent nearly a week filming rapid shots and dragging the boats back upstream for additional takes. Ice floes were beginning to clog the eddies and the stunt photography was absolute torture. The trip ended there at Hermit Rapid. The movie died on the cutting room floor, but river running was now, at least marginally, on the public's mind. It was certainly on Glen Hyde's.

AFTER THE COSMOPOLITAN excitement of San Francisco and Los Angeles, the novelty of bean farming in Murtaugh, Idaho, soon wore thin. Throughout the summer of 1928, the Hydes looked hopefully toward autumn and the end of the harvest, and began to plan their honeymoon escape. They may well have been planning even farther, plotting a life that could break their ties to the hard dusty life of farming.

The primary form of evening entertainment in those pre-television, pre-talking movie days, was vaudeville. In 1928 it had reached its peak of popularity with some thousand theaters across the country. Song, dance, stunts, and humor dominated the fare. W.C. Fields, Eddie Cantor, Harry Houdini, and George M. Cohan were household names. Equally popular were traveling lecturers, who would travel from town to town, often utilizing the same theaters, showing their magic lantern slides and enthralling the populace with their glorious, often hair-raising, expeditions to obscure parts of the globe. Although billed as educational, they were, like vaudeville, primarily entertainment.

It was still the age of record setting and explorations. In June of 1924, George Mallory, attempting Mount Everest "because it's there," disappeared with his partner near the clouded summit. Three years later Charles Lindbergh flew the *Spirit of St. Louis* nonstop across the Atlantic and became the darling of the Western World. A year later, in June, 1928, Amelia Earhart became the first woman to cross the Atlantic by airplane, and returned to a cheering America.

Scarcely the day went by that the papers did not banner a story about another aviation record being smashed, another distant land being reached, another extraordinary stunt being pulled. With each feat, another name leapt from obscurity to headline news.

Glen had read of the Pathé-Bray trip in the Twin Falls papers the previous winter; Bessie had seen similar stories in the *Elko Independent*. Throughout their courtship and marriage, Glen often spoke of his journeys on the Peace and Salmon Rivers, the richness of outdoor adventure, and the thrill of whitewater. As summer passed into autumn, rough plans and thoughts coalesced. Glen and Bessie would run the Colorado River.

Using a scow such as Glen and his sister Jeanne had used on the Salmon two years earlier, they would be able to make good time and possibly set a speed record. Better yet, Bessie would be the first woman to traverse this all-male river. It would be a thrilling honeymoon. The opportunities the trip could bring were limitless. With their combined literary and artistic talents, they could produce a best-selling book. With their abilities as public speakers and performers, they could go on the lecture circuit, maybe even vaudeville. The couple began devouring every book they could find on the Colorado.

Jeanne Hyde later said Glen had not been intent on just Bessie and himself going. Glen's father had hoped to join them but, as he could not swim, was ruled out. Glen had asked Jeanne if she would like to accompany them. She would have loved to, she said, but did not want to be the odd one out on a honeymoon trip. In the end, it was settled that it would be just Glen and Bessie.

When the first frost set the beans and potatoes, the family began the harvest. Once finished, Glen and Bessie assembled supplies and bought train tickets to Greenriver, Utah, the small desert whistle stop where both Clyde Eddy and the Pathé-Bray trips had launched.

Dellenbaugh Butte,
Hyde photo

58

The flaming sky,
Against which
The purple hills
Were silhouettes,
Has faded.
And there is something
In the blue-grey light
That breathes
Of romance.

9

~ *October – November 1928* ~

GREENRIVER, UTAH, was not much—a busted boom-and-bust rail-road town set on the yellow-gray Mancos shale of central Utah. From the 1890s into the 1920s a riverboat industry on the flatwater between Greenriver and Moab, Utah, achieved halting success and ulti-mate failure. The river trip—120 miles down the Green to the confluence, then another sixty-four up the Colorado to Moab—was far more diffi-cult and time consuming than the fifty-mile overland drive. Besides, the river was usually too shallow and sand-barred to be reliable.

What remained of Greenriver survived by farming alfalfa and water-melons, although a few old boatmen still lurked in the area. Two of them, Harry Howland and Bill Reeder, wandered down to the waterfront where Glen Hyde was sawing and hammering together his scow. One of the Magarrell brothers was giving Glen a hand with the carpentry.

Harry T. Howland had quite a bit of experience on the flatwater between Greenriver and the confluence with the Colorado. He, his son Harry Jr., and the Galloway brothers, Parley and John, had run the flat-water of Glen Canyon the previous March. Although he had no rapid-water experience, Howland was concerned about the boat Glen was building. "It looks like a floating coffin," he said to Reeder. "Maybe you can tell him something."

59

Bill Reeder, an oil driller, had been to the confluence several times twenty years earlier. He had also been through Cataract Canyon in 1914, when he joined Charles Russell and A.J. Tadje on an ill-fated movie-making trip. Of the five boats the expedition used, four went to the bottom of the Colorado. They abandoned the last one halfway through Grand Canyon. Reeder had quit when the second boat sank, and left the trip at Hite, Utah, at the head of Glen Canyon.

Bessie was back at the hotel. Reeder mistook Hyde's trip to be with a few other men. He did not hit it off with Glen. Twenty years later, at the bidding of the indefatigable river historian Dock Marston, Reeder wrote down a sour recollection of his conversation with Glen, recalling him as "surly, conceited and stoopid."

> REEDER: You going down in that?
> HYDE: I've run the Salmon River. I can run anything!
> REEDER: You aren't going to cover it?
> HYDE: Nope!
> REEDER: Life preservers?
> HYDE: Nope! Won't need them.
> REEDER: Water bag if you have to walk out?
> HYDE: Won't have to.
> REEDER: Well, you might. Better take a pistol to shoot rabbits. Food's awful scarce around there.
> HYDE: We've got enough.

Although the local boatmen did not know much about sweep scows, they did know the hazards of the Green River. The water had been so low ten days earlier that a government survey trip scheduled to launch by motorboat had switched to canoe. Led by boatman Elwyn Blake, they were currently being picked up at the confluence by a motorboat coming down the Colorado from Moab. After Blake's launch, rains had brought the flow up to 5,000 CFS—enough to float a scow—but the water was falling again.

Glen finished his scow in two days at a cost of fifty dollars. By four o'clock on Saturday, October 20, 1928, they were packed and ready. With little cheer or encouragement from the locals, they pushed off. Glen took the forward sweep, Bessie the rear. They drifted out of sight. The

only swift water in the first week lay in the first five miles—a series of
S-curve riffles culminating in the Auger, which contains a stretch of
foot-high waves. It was a perfect way to introduce Bessie to the art of
the sweep scow. They camped beneath the cottonwoods that night, on
their way at last.

It was not a Spartan camping trip. A sweep scow can carry a tremendous amount of gear, and there was little reason to pack light. Idaho
spuds and crates of canned produce from home lined the floor. In the
corner stood Glen's 1894 .30-30 long-barrel Winchester—a classic lever-
action deerslayer. In the stern of the craft stood a small sand-and-ash-
filled barrel. By pouring kerosene on the sand and lighting it, they
could make a cooking fire on board. The real luxury however—the
first of its kind to go down the Colorado—was a set of bedsprings.
The Hydes were equipped to camp cozily aboard if the water was calm
enough. If not, they could make just about any terrain comfortable.

For the next two days they drifted south, at first through open
farmland, then into the red sandstone cliffs of Labyrinth Canyon. The
Navajo sandstone rose to engulf them on one side of the river, then
the other, finally both at once. The river continued to meander slowly.
Noticing several inscriptions on one rock face—a 1909 steamboat group
had signed in, as had two of Clyde Eddy's men, Bartl and Carey—the
Hydes added their own.

Glen shot a duck on October 24 which, with homegrown potatoes,
made a fine dinner. The canyon deepened, then spread out into a weird
pastel plain that Powell called Tower Park, dotted with buttes and
spires. The river level continued to drop, to 4,000 CFS, then to 3,500.
The walls closed in and grew higher as they entered Stillwater Canyon.
Shortly before noon, October 27, they reached the confluence of the

Labyrinth
Canyon,
Tower
Park,
Hyde
photos

Below Mile-
Long Rapid,
Cataract
Canyon,
Hyde photo

Green and Colorado. Here the combined flow doubled to 7,000 CFS, a low flow for Cataract Canyon, but enough to get them through. The current quickened in the next four miles, then with a sharp bend to the east, the dull roar of Cataract reverberated upstream to meet them.

With more than a hundred miles of flatwater above and below it, Cataract Canyon had long been known as the "graveyard of the Colorado." Many of the boaters that entered it were not prepared for the sheer violence of the rapids it contained. Trappers and prospectors arriving on or in a variety of floating contraptions were dashed to their deaths before they had a chance to realize what they had done.

Glen Hyde had done his homework, however, reading all he could find about previous trips. Major Powell and Frederick Dellenbaugh had each written of the Powell expeditions; Robert Brewster Stanton had told of his troubled railroad survey expedition in 1889–90 in *Scribner's Magazine*. The Kolb brothers had published a popular book of their 1911–12 photography expedition. Lewis Freeman wrote a book about the 1923 government survey trip through Grand Canyon. In addition, both Freeman and Dellenbaugh had published excellent histories of the Colorado. There was no dearth of information about previous successes and failures on the Colorado.

All previous explorers, however, had attempted the trip by rowboat— none had even considered the Idaho scow. From Powell onward, each

Top of Big Drop
One, Cataract
Canyon,
Hyde photo

had gone with a craft they had some familiarity with, a craft in which, for one reason or another, they had faith. This, too, was true of Hyde. He had begun boating in canoes, but switched to the scow for big water on the advice of none other than Captain Harry Guleke, the foremost boatman in the Northwest. With what Guleke taught him on the few miles of the Salmon, Glen had been able to navigate three hundred miles to Lewiston with but one significant wreck. Naturally Hyde chose the scow for his next whitewater adventure. Although he may not have mentioned it to Hyde, Guleke, too, had considered running a scow down the Colorado as early as 1920.

River historians have long faulted Glen Hyde for not bringing life jackets. But this, too, Hyde had learned in Idaho. None of the Idaho sweepboatmen wore life jackets, and none were available. "Here we never thought of such a thing," recalled Jeanne Hyde. Cap Guleke himself had lost his rear sweepman when George Sandiland, one of the brothers who had taught Guleke the art of sweeps, was knocked overboard and drowned in 1897. Even so, life jackets were not adopted in Idaho until much later. Although most Colorado River boatmen had donned life jackets before the turn of the century, Idaho sweepboatmen simply didn't wear them. Nor did Glen and Bessie.

Bessie might have gotten a feel for the rear sweep during the smooth currents of Labyrinth and Stillwater Canyons, but she got an abrupt awakening in one of Cataract's first rapids. A wooden sweep weighs more than one hundred pounds, with a good twenty to thirty pounds of counterweight affixed to the handle. With an eight-foot blade in the river, there is a tremendous amount of leverage available to the boatman—or against the boatman if things go wrong. Ninety-pound Bessie had no sooner sunk her sweep into the current than she found herself airborne, then waterborne. Glen caught her foot and pulled her back aboard. After that Glen sometimes took both sweeps in the roughest rapids, although Bessie ran the rear sweep in many of the large rapids, and occasionally ran the scow herself.

Whitewater hazards include not only the small riffles, where shallow rocks are most often the problem, and the larger rapids where huge waves add to the threat, but several other features as well. In rapids, water can pour over a shallow boulder and form a violent "hole" behind it where the water explodes to fill the void. "Lateral waves" often break diagonally off the shore, knocking a craft on its side, or herding it across the river's channel. Rapids are usually caused by constrictions in the current, and below those constrictions, the river expands and flows back upstream along the shores in "eddies." A strong recirculating eddy can trap a boat—especially a cumbersome scow—for exasperating amounts of time. The Hydes would encounter all these phenomena and more.

Lower Cataract Canyon; note logs for counterweights, bedsprings; H9$% 0(/4/

With Bessie back on board they ran another ten rapids and three riffles. The last rapid of the day slammed the scow into an eddy. They recirculated for some time before getting stuck on a midstream rock as they exited the eddy. Glen pried the scow loose and they made camp below.

The next morning found them in the heart of Cataract Canyon. In her small pocket journal, Bessie made a note of one particularly steep rapid, but recorded no troubles. After eleven rapids and one riffle they camped for the day. On October 30 they ran another twenty rapids, among them some of the tougher drops in Cataract. Modern-day boatmen are left to puzzle how the Hydes found paths through the rocky mazes of Mile-Long Rapid and the Big Drops. The Hydes recorded no problems, but did spend the following morning in camp doing repairs. After lunch they launched in a steady rain that increased throughout the afternoon. They ran the remaining eight rapids of Cataract Canyon without complications, although the last two were difficult and long. They had made it through the "graveyard of the Colorado" unscathed—quite a feat considering that nearly every trip before them had portaged a few if not all the major drops. One can either credit them with unprecedented pluck, or simply acknowledge that they had little choice, as the waterlogged scow weighed more than two tons. With Cataract under their belt, Grand Canyon began to sound less intimidating.

They found a beach and put into camp for two nights. It poured throughout the first night, with lightning and thunder crashing and echoing about them all night and most of the following day. The Moab newspapers called the storm one of the worst in memory. Their tarp leaked and the Hydes woke up soaked. By late afternoon the sun poked through and they began drying around a raging bonfire. A brief double rainbow graced the canyon sky, then the clouds returned with a finale of hail. Sometime during the storm they named their scow after one of the great Sioux warriors and prophets—said by some to be the man who killed Custer: *Rain-in-the-Face*.

The river rose, and on November 1 they launched on twice the pre-storm flow. The runoff—high, muddy, and reeking of earth—boosted their speed. At the head of Narrow Canyon was a showy inscription

Hyde inscription, Narrow Canyon, now beneath Lake Powell, Nevills photo

Olympia Bar, Glen Canyon, now beneath Lake Powell, Hyde photo

with the names of the Eddy party of a year earlier. Glen and Bessie pulled ashore and chiseled "HYDE 11-1-28" along beside.

Mount Ellsworth had a fresh dusting of snow as it soared majestically above the red rock vista to the west. They passed the Dirty Devil River, spewing a muddy, malodorous flood into the Colorado. The walls of Narrow Canyon parted and they slid into the calm waters of Glen Canyon.

PLACER MINERS had worked the gravel bars of Glen Canyon since the 1890s, but most had moved on by 1928. The Hydes visited several cabins in various stages of decomposition. One was occupied. They spent the afternoon touring the prospector's placer works. Nearby, Anasazi Indian ruins overlooked the river and petroglyphs covered the walls.

The next day they passed the monumental wreck of the *Hoskaninni*, a gigantic but unsuccessful dredge built to extract the fine flour gold from the river floor. A day later they passed the Escalante River spewing in from the west. From the east the San Juan River, still swollen from the storm, heaved in another 2,000 CFS of desert mud. Glen, spotting a deer high on the slopes above, rebuilt the broken gunsight on his rifle with a splinter of wood, took aim, and shot it. After a difficult clamber over the cliffs, he returned with a deer hide and a good supply of venison.

On November 6 headwinds—something sweepboats are defenseless against—slowed them to a crawl. Turning the boat sideways, they attempted to use the sweeps as oars to push downstream. Finding that to be futile, they sat out the storm. The wind diminished the next day and they ran fourteen riffles. The following morning they floated out of Glen Canyon. Here the rust, lavender, and gray Mesozoic-age rocks of Utah parted, and the dirt tracks of the Honeymoon Trail reached either side of the river. Less than a mile downstream, the buff Paleozoic cliffs that form the rims of Grand Canyon rose sharply on either shore.

> Lee's Ferry
> November 8
> Dear Dad,
>
> Arrived two days ahead of schedule. We were much surprised when we came around the bend and saw the cluster of houses. There are six people here and about that many houses.
>
> We had a fine trip so far and are enjoying it immensely. Bessie is feeling fine and eating everything but the boat. The cataracts were rather fierce. In the first one Bessie fell out, everything but one heel. I don't think the cataracts are any worse than some places on the Salmon; that is, any more drop; but they are faster and the waves dash higher.
>
> It was great sport.

They had reached the small outpost of Lee's Ferry, founded originally by the infamous Mormon, John D. Lee, who was later executed for his part in the Mountain Meadows Massacre. Lee passed the ferry and ranch on to Warren Johnson, another Mormon, whose family continued to operate the ferry and the adjacent Lonely Dell ranch for many years. When Glen and Bessie arrived, Lee's Ferry was in decline. The ferry boat itself had been lost on June 7 in a high water crossing, killing Dolph Johnson, Royce Dean, and Lewis Nez Tsinnie. With Navajo Bridge nearing completion four miles downriver, the ferry had closed for good. A few souls remained to operate the ranch and run the government gaging station.

Throughout the history of whitewater boating, townsfolk have invariably come down to the river to advise boaters of their imminent doom. Lee's Ferry was no exception. Warren Johnson's sons, Jeremiah and Price, and Price's son Owen, tried their best to convince the Hydes of their foolishness.

"I tried to talk the Hydes out of going on," recalled Jeremiah. "We told them they were playing with death. He had been told he couldn't get this far and now thought he had passed the worst. His boat was not good for this water. She had been swept off by the sweep two or three times and he had gotten her back." With the retrospective knowledge of having been correct in his warnings, Johnson may have multiplied Bessie's mishaps in Cataract, as the Hydes freely mentioned one, but only one, dethroning.

Owen Clark, who worked as a government water gager at Lee's Ferry, met them as well. Clark's opinions of the Hydes' boat and their chances of survival were, if no more optimistic, at least more credible. Clark had been on the Pathé-Bray movie expedition the year before, running boats down through Marble and part of Grand Canyon in the dead of winter. Clark had nearly identical river levels to what the Hydes were about to encounter. Historian Dock Marston made notes of a 1948 interview with Clark:

> I was at Lee's Ferry when Hydes went through—they stayed overnight—when they landed he showed me how he manipulated the boat—to me it didn't look very adaptable to that kind of water—real hazard was going with one boat and I warned him about "Having all eggs in one basket." His wife couldn't help much—she was too light—think they did have a rifle—they could sleep and cook on raft—she was enthusiastic about going on—he had enough confidence to go on—he asked about river—I warned him about danger if anything happened to his boat—it was surprising the way he could handle the boat—he could push raft sideways.

The following morning the Hydes took time to explore the area. "At Lee's Ferry we walked about a mile up a gulch," wrote Bessie to her mother, "to see an Indian who makes moccasins and bracelets. The Indian girl was herding sheep. The Indian was squatting inside a mud hut cutting leather and the squaw was outside sewing it. He could only speak a little English."

They met a reporter from the Flagstaff weekly newspaper, *The Coconino Sun*, who wrote a small, richly misinformed tale of the Hydes called "Through Canyon On a Flat Boat." He mentioned the Hydes

Bessie and Glen
departing Lee's Ferry

having a wonderful trip in a flat-bottomed punt. "There are no oars, only paddles," he explained. "They drift with the flow, using the paddles for lading…" For the Hydes, fame would have to wait a bit.

Back at the scow, Price Johnson continued his harangue as the Hydes prepared to head downriver. He told them about the recent drownings at the Ferry, and how difficult the climb out of the Canyon was. Some of his family had recently scaled the cliffs at Soap Creek after searching for the bodies from the ferry accident. It had been a struggle. Johnson felt Glen took his advice with a grain of salt, but that Bessie showed some concern. As Johnson watched them head into Paria Riffle downstream, Glen lost his balance and nearly fell overboard.

Four miles later the honeymooners pulled *Rain-in-the-Face* ashore and scrambled five hundred vertical feet up a gulch to the Navajo Bridge project. Crews were pouring the cement roadbed on what would soon be the highest highway bridge in the world. David Crockett "Buck" Lowrey was operating a small trading post on the east side of the river at the time, while he raced to complete a lodge across the river before the new bridge opened. The Hydes bought a small Navajo blanket, food, and a few supplies. Marston's notes from a 1959 interview with Lowrey are so terse that they more nearly resemble haiku:

> I saw Hyde's
> I supplied them from post
> I tried to stop them
> She showed no inclination to quit
> They had old scow

> Told of being knocked over by sweep
> I have some pictures

Before leaving, Glen Hyde concluded his letter to his father with a few enigmatic lines:

> I'd quit river here, (not on my own account tho) but from what they tell us we are over all the worst water. I didn't find any mail. Have ordered it to Grand Canyon but I'm afraid it won't get there. We expect to be there in five or six days.
> Give my regards to Barney,
> Glen.

It is easy to explain that Barney was Glen's favorite horse, and almost as easy to explain his repeated insistence at being over the worst water: either he truly believed it in spite of the local doomsayers, or he chose not to worry his father unduly. What has kept historians bickering, however, is the line: "I'd quit river here, (not on my own account tho)." It can be argued that either Glen, or Bessie, or both, or neither of them, had cold feet at this point. Exactly what Glen meant is anybody's guess.

As to what Bessie Hyde thought of all the doom saying: "Everyone was very nice to us at Lee's Ferry," she wrote home, "and several people stood on the bridge and waved to us until we turned a bend in the river as we left in the scow."

Bessie on a rock,
24½-Mile Rapid,
Marble Canyon

Ambition
If it pause by you,
Will taunt you night and day.

Resistless
You will be its slave,
For it always has its way.

—— Bessie Haley

10

IT WAS LATE AFTERNOON of November 8, the twentieth day of their expedition, when the Hydes reached Badger Creek Rapid. Navajo Bridge had disappeared behind them an hour before. Glen and Bessie were now fully committed to Marble Canyon—the sixty-mile introduction to Grand Canyon. Badger Creek is a particularly rocky rapid and in the dwindling light Glen misjudged it, slamming onto a rock from which they had to pry the scow loose. No damage done, they pulled in and camped for the night.

The first rapid the next morning was Soap Creek, long said to be unrunnable. The Kolb brothers, river running photographers, had scouted it one evening in 1911. Ellsworth, the older brother, had given it his best shot only to be thrown from the boat in a near flip. After climbing back aboard and rowing ashore, he convinced his brother Emery to let him try again in Emery's boat. This he did, overturning in the failing light and swimming into the darkness.

The rapid may have been first run successfully in 1927 by Clyde Eddy's crew. Slightly lost and thinking they had already portaged Soap Creek—they had actually portaged Badger—they ran Soap Creek, bear cub and all. It was not until Eddy returned that fall on the Pathé-Bray trip that he realized he had accidentally run Soap Creek Rapid. His chest swelled.

The Hydes took a quick look, threaded their way down the right

Bessie,
27-Mile
Rapid

side, and continued on unfazed. That afternoon they plowed down the middle of North Canyon Rapid, huge waves breaking into *Rain-in-the-Face*, bailed her out again, and camped.

River mileage was originally laid out by the 1923 Geological Survey trip, using Lee's Ferry as Mile Zero. North Canyon is at Mile 20, and the next ten miles—the so-called Roaring Twenties—contain a dozen rapids, one after the next. In the morning Glen took two pictures of Bessie sitting on a boulder gazing into the froth of 24½-Mile Rapid. A few hours later they made portraits of each other at 27-Mile Rapid. For the next two days they sailed along without incident, passing the beautiful springs Powell named Vasey's Paradise, and cutting ever deeper into the spectacular red-walled Marble Gorge. On the night of November 11, they drifted past Nankoweap Canyon and into Grand Canyon National Park. Misreading the channels in the poor light, Glen ran aground again. After a great deal of muttering and prying, the scow shifted free.

At midday on November 12, the Hydes passed the mouth of the Little Colorado River, marking the end of Marble Canyon and the beginning of Grand Canyon proper. In the next few miles the canyon rims rose another thousand feet above them and spread several miles apart, towers and spires jutting up in the gigantic open abyss. The brilliant immediate colors of Marble Canyon dimmed with the haze of distance.

Glen,
27-Mile
Rapid

After running another thirteen rapids and nine riffles, they camped in the great open corridor hikers refer to as Furnace Flats, and were beset with a howling rainstorm. Bessie wrote to Jeanne Hyde:

> The wind is blowing so much that everything is just about covered with sand, including Glen and I. We should be nearly to Grand Canyon [Village], but of course it is hard to tell.
>
> The scenery, since the Little Colorado came in, is really more majestic but it isn't as beautiful or as fanciful as Stillwater and Cataract Canyons.
>
> We've had lots and lots of riffles, large and small, and have been gliding along at a great rate.
>
> We've had all kinds of camps—from beach to rock shelves.

Glen added this:

> The rapids we have come over have no straight drops higher than the Salmon (about eight feet) but are longer, much faster, and bigger waves. They get up more speed and the water has more power. I looked everything over that showed a big drop—after we hit the rock. Hope we hit no more rain. The tarp lets the water through pretty badly.
>
> The river appears straighter now and ought to make good time to

Grand Canyon. It seemed we would never get to the Forks, but from there to Lee's Ferry broke all records.

We sure have lived high as to grub—or at least it all tasted good. Rice with raisins, baked squash, good spuds, ham, eggs, "doe dads" (my own bread), oatmeal. We have a little kerosene can stove in the boat now, though in Cataract and Marble Canyon it was not used. We get lunch on it often.

This is windy camp. Last night it was rainy camp. Have been bothered by headwinds hardly at all so far. Is blowing like the Devil now, and Grand Canyon should be very close. The Grand Canyon is sort of disappointing after what we have seen. It is no grander than any of the other canyons we have come thru.

How is Terry and do you ride any?

The wind is getting worse. I may try rowing. Am anxious to get to Grand Canyon.

The Hydes packed up and pushed off, but finding progress impossible selected a more sheltered spot and pulled in just a hundred yards below. Glen wrote to his father:

How it can blow so hard in this canyon I don't see. We have run the Marble Canyon. It was not so bad as I expected. It was almost as bad as the Cataracts but not as many bad rapids for the distance. We hung up once in a bad place. It was getting late and in the poor light I got mixed. Now we should be over all the real bad water. There are rapids ahead, of course, but not so bad. We made quite a flurry at Lee's Ferry and at the bridge, where there is sort of a trading post.

From Greenriver to the Forks we had still water, not even a riffle. It was a beautiful canyon. Took us almost seven days. The Cataracts took three and a half. From there no real rapids to Lee's Ferry, where we must have made time. The way we traveled to Lee's Ferry we should be to Needles in three weeks or even less. Are a little over half way, I figure.

Saw mountain sheep twice. Once they stood and looked at me not over two hundred feet away. Saw several beaver…

The wind abated by morning and they pushed on. Glen's optimism about smaller rapids ahead proved drastically wrong. Hance Rapid was long, rocky, and difficult, but they were able to snake *Rain-in-the-Face* through. At the foot of the rapid the river enters the most forbidding stretch of the river as a black schist gorge suddenly looms up over a thousand feet, so steep that the upper four thousand feet of cliffs are often lost from view. Within a mile is Sockdolager Rapid, named by Major Powell's men for the knockout punch it delivers. True to form, Sockdolager drenched them in the first wave. Glen struggled to regain control. "I don't know just how it happened," Glen wrote in his letter to his father:

> The oar cracked me under the chin, and got away. I remember getting ahold of it again—next I was going into the river feet first. I don't recall clearing the boat. The first time I came up I missed the edge, but the next time, after being down some time, made it, and after getting my strength, climbed in. Bessie took my oar as soon as I went out and was doing her best, but afterwards was pretty well shaken up.

Bessie threw Glen a rope, helped him aboard and they continued on. "I was ready to climb the canyon wall right then and there," wrote Bessie, "but Glen laughed at me." They ran a few miles farther, but as the wind and rain picked up again, they camped and built a roaring fire.

First thing the next morning they hit Grapevine Rapid, the twin sister of Sockdolager. The waves were enormous but did not abuse the honeymooners as Sockdolager had. At noon they landed at Bright Angel Creek, at the foot of the newly completed Kaibab Trail, and heaved a sigh of relief.

After a quick lunch, they began the five-thousand foot climb to Grand Canyon Village on the South Rim. Broken clouds blew in as they climbed. Wrote Bessie: "You could see for miles—wonderful cliffs that changed all the time as the light changed. We ran into a snow storm (our sweaters were plenty warm on the river) and then could see clouds below us. The snowstorm was short but lovely."

They had not realized that the new Kaibab Trail, unlike the old Bright Angel Trail, hit the rim at Yaki Point, well to the east of the village. Wrote Glen:

And the tramp up! It was worth it but some climb. We got to the top just as it was getting dark. Thought the hotel and town would be there, but there was nothing but a stable, and snow, and trees—and a road. We followed the road—and saw nothing. The hotel, etc. is six miles from the top along the rim. We walked about two or three miles and a car came along, which I hailed. It was a "God send." The canyon certainly is a grand sight from the top—and trail. It was warm at the bottom. Coming up it snowed about half an hour, and up here there are about two inches of snow, and cold—certainly is cold. Had dinner in the big hotel, but was too "steep" to sleep in.

The El Tovar Hotel was fancy and famous, but well beyond the reach of the common man. To a large extent, touring the parks in those days was the province of the wealthy—traveling by rail and making extended stays at the luxury hotels at each park. The Hydes found affordable quarters a few hundred yards west at the Bright Angel Camp tent cabins, and collapsed into a real bed.

On the morning of November 15 the weather cleared and the view from the rim was crisp and stunning. The Hydes went about the business of buying groceries and arranging to have them packed down by mule. They spent an hour with Assistant Superintendent Preston "Pat" Patraw, telling him of their adventures thus far, and their plans as far as Needles. More significantly, they talked to a reporter from the *Denver Post*—the first real step on their road to national fame. The resulting Associated Press story made news as far away as Kansas City, where the *Times* carried the full half-column:

DARES RAPIDS FOR THRILLS
IDAHO WOMAN ON PERILOUS JOURNEY IN BOAT

Daring the swirling reaches of the Colorado River, a homemade scow is carrying a slight woman in search of a thrill over a course that no woman has ever dared before and that men have conquered only a half a score times.

Through foaming rapids and whirlpools, sometimes between towering sand cliffs and sometimes between sheer walls of rock rising thousands of feet on both sides of the stream, the frail craft has been bobbing along for a month.

And so on. The Hydes had been right—Bessie was making an otherwise passé story into headlines. Although Glen was dismissed as "a rancher, not a professional boatman," Bessie was quoted at length. She described Glen's accident at Sockdolager:

> We carried no life preservers. I admit, I was scared to death. I can't remember clearly all that happened. All I know is that I managed somehow to hang onto the sweeps by which the boat is guided and managed to keep the boat as straight as possible in the current until my husband could grasp the sides. Then I helped pull him aboard.
>
> Our main object in taking this trip is to give me a thrill. It's surely been successful so far; I have had the thrills of my life and I've been thoroughly drenched a dozen times; but I'm enjoying every minute of the adventure.

Grand Canyon Superintendent Minor Tillotson wrote a separate story, totting up statistics on the Hyde voyage:

> At least two records will be made by the adventure, the first being the running of all the rapids, the method of descent on previous Colorado Expeditions being by lining the boat down the more dangerous rapids. The second will be made by Mrs. Hyde as the first woman to descend the length of the canyon of the Colorado. Probably a third record will be running time.

Interestingly, the *Prescott Courier*, published just 125 miles south of Grand Canyon, ran an entirely different story based, they said, on a forest service bulletin. "SHOOT RAPIDS IN BOAT WITH BOTTOM OF WOOD," ran the headline. The Hydes, they reported:

> …in completing a successful trip from Green River, Wyo., down the Green and Colorado rivers to Needles, Calif., have done something that even the lumberjacks marvel at. Even lumberjacks contemplating driving lodgepole pine ties down the Duchesne and Green Rivers to Greenriver, Utah, for treatment and shipment over the Rio Grande Western, maintained that only a steel-bottomed boat could weather the rapids of Green River canyon.

Later that morning the Hydes called on the best known river man at

Grand Canyon, Emery Kolb. He and his brother Ellsworth had begun a photography business at the rim at the turn of the century, long before Grand Canyon had been declared a national park. After their 1911–12 river trip they began showing their movie four times a day in their studio. Emery and Ellsworth signed on as boatmen for a government survey trip in Cataract Canyon in 1921, and Emery had been lead boatman in a subsequent survey of Grand Canyon in 1923. A year later, business differences caused Ellsworth to leave Grand Canyon for California. Emery remained, running the studio with his wife Blanche and daughter Edith. Edith had since married Carl Lehnert, a ranger, and in the last year had given birth to a son.

Emery Kolb was always delighted to meet river people. He drove the Hydes around the village, lunched with them, and invited them to his lecture. Afterward he presented them with a signed copy of his brother's book, *Through the Grand Canyon From Wyoming to Mexico*. He took two portraits of them standing outdoors against the studio's chimney—one formal, the other with the couple smiling broadly. That evening, Bessie finished her letter home:

Emery and Ellsworth Kolb after a bad day in Waltenburg Rapid, 1911

The Honeymooners, Emery Kolb photo

Our trip is half over and we should be to Needles in a little over three weeks, and we're supposed to have run all the bad rapids. I won't be able to write again until we get to Needles.

We're going to get a few supplies in the morning and climb back down and start off once more.

This place is run mostly for the wealthy tourists and they go on pack trips with guides all around the country. Of course there are only trails as it would be impossible to build a road anywhere's along here.

I just had a nice hot bath and I'm pretty sleepy 'cause this has been a big day.

Give dad a big hug for me.

Love and kisses

Your loving daughter

Bessie

Glen echoed Bessie's enthusiasm in closing his letter to his father…:

At any rate, we are over all the worst rapids, so will go on.

Hope you and Jeanne are fine.

…and sister:

We will tramp down again in the morning—and it is *down*. We're anxious to be on the way again.

Hope you are feeling fine.

Glen

Emery Kolb, 1928

The mass of people never know
The fullest meaning of this life,
They jog along the even way,
Always avoiding thought and strife.

So placid and content they seem,
Existing ever on and on;
I'd rather have my blackest night,
That I may see the bright red dawn.

— Bessie Haley

11

∼ November 16–18 1928 ∼

MUCH OF THE MYTH of Glen and Bessie Hyde stems from what did, or did not, take place between their arrival at Grand Canyon Village the evening of November 15, and their final departure from Hermit Rapid three days later. Many people later claimed to have met them, seen them, heard them say certain things, or act in a particular way. The stories vary widely, often contradict, and have evolved with the passage of time. Primary sources of information are as rare as rumors are plentiful.

In a letter to river man Dave Rust, written two months after the Hydes departed, Emery Kolb wrote:

> ...you asked if the Hydes deserved to get through. They were a very nice couple, he about 28, she 23 I would guess. College folks, he a farmer or irrigator. She intended to attend Bingham College in Utah, I believe that was the name, to study art. We had them to luncheon while here and were a very modest decent type. I did my best to get them to take some kind of life preservers, but they would not. Had they done so, they probably would have been alive today.

In 1940, Kolb wrote to Barry Goldwater, who had asked him about the Hydes:

I entertained them and offered them life preservers and every assistance. They refused the life preservers. I then tried to persuade them to go over to the garage and get some inner tubes but all they did was to look at each other and smile. We believe the bride was ready to quit here. She told us of her husband being thrown into the water on two occasions and said she just barely got a rope to him.

My wife and daughter drove them to the head of the trail. Mrs. Hyde looked at my daughter's shoes and said "I wonder if I shall ever wear pretty shoes again."

Ray Tankersley, a guide for the Fred Harvey Company, recalled: "I had the pleasure of meeting them. Very nice and quite [quiet?] people. On their trip down they tied up near Phantom Ranch and went to the top of the rim for supplies. I packed some chuck down for them." Bob Francy, the corral boss, said they packed in two five-gallon cans of coal oil (kerosene for the stove) and supplies. He recalled the "scow was nothing but a mortar box," but said Glen "was quite a strapping boy," and "was a wizard at handling that raft." Francy's packer gave Glen an additional fifty feet of rope.

The Hydes returned to the river on the afternoon of November 16 and made a visit to the small tourist facility under construction about half a mile up Bright Angel Creek. Originally founded by river runner and guide Dave Rust, as Rust's Camp, it was now being

Rain-in-the-Face at Bright Angel Beach, Sutro photo

greatly expanded by the Fred Harvey Company and had been renamed Phantom Ranch. The Hydes signed the guest book: "Going down the river—Nov. 16–28 in a flat bottomed boat."

Back at the beach, the Hydes found a portly, balding man looking over their scow. His name was Adolph Gilbert Sutro. He was not just another wealthy tourist—he was an *extraordinarily* wealthy tourist. His grandfather was the famous Adolph Sutro of San Francisco, who had drilled the Sutro Tunnel into the Comstock Lode and had made several fortunes in San Francisco investments. Nor was Adolph G. Sutro a stranger to adventure. As a young man he read of the Wright Brothers' experiments, and in 1910 went to Dayton to work with them. After learning to fly he returned to California, went to engineering school, designed his own seaplanes, and earned Hydro-Aeroplane Pilot License

Adolph
Sutro
aboard
the scow

Bright Angel Beach, Sutro photo

number one. During one flight over San Francisco Bay in September, 1913, Sutro set world records for seaplane flight altitude, duration, cargo load, and distance, while one of his passengers crawled out onto the wing and squirmed forward to stem an oil leak in the failing engine. Two months later Sutro retired from flying, after twice being plucked from his wreckage in San Francisco Bay. Since that time he had busied himself managing the family's vast holdings in California.

Sutro was now touring the Southwest and lodging at the El Tovar. With his personal mule packer, Whitey Chamberlain, Sutro had ridden down to the river to visit Phantom Ranch. After Glen and Bessie explained their craft and their journey, Sutro made them a proposition. He would like to join them for a day's run, shoot a few rapids with them,

Glen at the sweeps;
Bessie below, right;
Sutro photo

and leave at the next trail. The Hydes were willing. Sutro had a better camera than they did and perhaps the Hydes saw him as a route to more publicity. "I knew Sutro went with the Hydes," recalled mule wrangler Ed Cummings. "I was at Phantom. I remember Sutro to have been about thirty-five. I know he was not an old man."

The trio pushed off around noon on November 17 against stiff head-winds, and immediately entered a long series of fastwater riffles and rapids. Sutro took a magnificent portrait of Glen standing at the sweep oar, and made a photograph of the two Hydes leaning into the sweeps as they swooped around the bends. Within a mile they ran into trouble, however, as they were sucked into a tight recirculating eddy on the north shore.

Glen in his jodphurs and tennis shoes, Sutro photo

John Baer, a tourist from Port Huron, Michigan, was on the trail at Plateau Point, thirteen hundred feet above, and later reported seeing trouble to the *Coconino Sun*:

> The Hydes were trapped in a whirlpool some hundreds of feet below, according to Baer, when he saw them. They sought to bring their flatboat into the main current of the river. But the swift water, making a bend, created a whirlpool and the couple appeared unable to manage their scow.
>
> Several times the Hydes tried to free their craft, Baer stated. They hauled the boat from the shore upstream to a point where the main current entered. Then the couple leaped into their craft and attempted to pole into the stream, only to be snatched again by the bordering whirlpool.
>
> They were still in the grip of the eddy when Baer left to secure help.
>
> "Returning to my party," Baer declared, "I informed the guide what I had seen. I told him I thought the people in the boat needed aid. He was unconcerned, and stated that the Hydes had been up Bright Angel Trail the day before, and that he guessed they knew what they were doing."

Although Baer does not mention Sutro, he must have been in the boat, as the only stretch Baer could have observed was that immediately below Phantom Ranch. The Hydes eventually made their way out of the eddy, floated another mile or so and dropped into Horn Creek Rapid.

THIRTY YEARS LATER river historian Marston tracked down Sutro for an interview. Considering what a unique view Sutro had of the couple in action and in camp, and the fact that Sutro *was* one of the last men to see them alive, Marston's cryptic notes give a frustratingly vague picture of what went on. Of the sixty clipped lines Marston jotted down, printed here in their entirety, many may be answers to questions we shall never know. But placed in some sort of order, a story begins to appear:

They came in afternoon
I was curious about fastwater work
I would leave next exit
I bought them groceries
They had nothing to eat

She was very petite
I recall she was on bow sweep
He stood in stern and handled the stern sweep
I have considerable experience in rough water
I was scared in the rapid
The girl was terrified
She registered stark fear
After riding with them I didn't blame her
I am a good swimmer
I don't think swimming was any good
I have seen much rough water experience

I was skeptical of their outfit
It shouted of no money
It was most inadequately equipped outfit I had ever seen
I think of Chinese Junk before I criticize naval architecture
I couldn't understand how they got to Bright Angel

We did stay one night
Recollection on S Side
on sand bar at a side canyon
They shoved oar into sand at acute angle
what would have happened had the boat got away
They only used one line
was frayed with Irish pennant
With the exception of the mooring, nothing impressed me

We had quite a few conversations
They made trip hoping they could get theatrical showing
Emphasis was on money that would be made in show business
Obvious whole object of trip was to make money in show business
The feminine angle is always essential

Glen and Bessie

He kept talking about the money they'd make on vaudeville

He was materializing spirit
She would never have run the river
He wasn't type that was going to settle down
He had no money
He was decent—not domineering—irresponsible

They brought me down one mile
I sent Chamberlain around with stock

Much better to be a live coward than a dead hero
I waved them goodbye and climbed out on the mule
Father came to see me

Sutro had signed on for the most horrifying seven-mile stretch he could possibly have picked. Not only did they manage to get trapped in a nasty eddy that afternoon, they had to run Horn Creek Rapid at its steep, violent, low-water worst. Most rapids in Grand Canyon are of a character called pool and drop. Long periods of relatively calm water—pools—are punctuated with abrupt rapids formed by rocky debris at the mouths of side canyons—drops. At Horn Creek, in the dark Granite Gorge, the fall is spectacular and leads into a series of large crashing waves at the bottom right, which in turn hurl the water toward the left cliff face. Although much of this can be missed in a light rowboat, doubtless *Rain-in-the-Face* took the worst of it in a violent inundation.

They camped on a small beach below and, too exhausted to drag their bedsprings up the beach, slept on the sand.

The following morning, with bad headwinds still plaguing them, they hit Granite Falls—a long, steep, screaming set of waves dashing along the right-hand cliff. Again, there is little doubt they had a wild and wet ride. When they pulled in at Hermit Creek to let Sutro off, they were at the head of another of the ten biggest drops in Grand Canyon—Hermit Rapid. It is no wonder both Sutro and Bessie were horrified.

"My unfailing guiding light in life," Sutro later wrote to Marston, "has been the precept that it is better to be a live coward than a dead hero. This has permitted me to avoid many perils such as wing walking on aeroplanes, running for political office or committing matrimony. So, in accordance with the foregoing, may I point with pride that I disembarked permanently at the very first possible landing spot. A rather comprehensive experience in sailing small boats in the North Pacific assisted me in formulating my judgment."

The crudely built Idaho scow had not impressed Sutro, nor had Glen and Bessie's slipshod mooring habits. What comes across as particularly baffling, though, is what appears to be Glen's near obsession with how much money the trip might make. It is the first, and only, mention of the commercial aspect of the voyage in any account. It could well have been that Glen, always the optimist, was trying to find a silver lining for an especially dark-clouded few days. But although Sutro seems to have little respect for Glen Hyde's river skills, equipment, or motivation, he did—and this seems significant later—think him a "decent, not domineering" man.

It was fully twenty years from the Hydes' visit to the South Rim until Dock Marston began interviewing people who might have met them there. By then the story was beginning to take on darker overtones. While talking to Kolb, Marston jotted: "Hyde was not at ease at the Kolbs. He seemed anxious to go. She said 'I realized how dangerous it was when Glen was thrown out and I had difficulty getting a rope to him.' We thought she wanted to quit the river."

Marston interviewed Bert Lauzon, long-time constable and later ranger at the South Rim. Lauzon knew the river—he had accompanied the Kolb Brothers on the final leg of their 1911–12 Grand Canyon trip—and had apparently met the Hydes on the rim: "The little woman was sick of it when she reached this far. He wanted to make a record—taking the first woman thru—she would have quit long before if she had her way—she just had no enthusiasm—she was dejected... Mrs. Hyde had enough of the canyon and went on only because Hyde insisted."

Marston's notes on an interview with Michael Harrison had this tantalizing fragment as well: "Bride had premonition she would not come out of Canyon—gave clothes to Edith Kolb." Another uncredited note in the Marston files says: "The old packer with the dome hat packed two mules loads to Hyde. Says she was sick." Still another dubious story

emerged of Emery Kolb offering them his house for the winter, and Bessie wanting to take him up on it.

But by far the most damning testimony came from mule-packer Bob Francy, who delivered their goods to Phantom Ranch, and later boated from Bright Angel Creek to Diamond Creek searching for the lost couple. He related the following anecdote to Marston: "The Hydes stopped at Hermit Camp and stayed overnight. The keepers and some dudes went down to the river and heard argument between Hydes which ended by his forcing her into raft." By the 1970s Kolb was telling a similar version, also based on second or third-hand information. One variation on the story has the altercation taking place at Phantom Ranch—doubtful, as Sutro launched with them and such behavior would undoubtedly have colored his impression of Glen. If something happened, it happened at Hermit.

Although Hermit Camp remained a popular resort destination until it was closed in 1930, November 18 is late in the season. It is doubtful many people were there. The managers, Mr. and Mrs. George Pifer were there, but only two signatures were in the guest book around that time. One was Mr. & Mrs. Glen R. Hyde. The other, dated the day after the Hydes,' was Paul Galtsoff of Washington D.C. Although Marston made every attempt to track down the Pifers and Galtsoff to corroborate Francy's statement, he came up empty-handed.

One problem with Francy's story is that the Hydes did not, as Francy attested, spend a night at Hermit Camp. Rather, they stopped for lunch and, after saying good-bye to Mr. Sutro, continued downstream into Hermit Rapid. But their signature in the guest book indicates they at least made the one mile hike up the creek to Hermit Camp. And it is almost certain that anyone at Hermit Camp at the time would have been curious enough to walk the mile back down to the river to watch them run Hermit Rapid. Their departure, then, was very likely witnessed, but by whom? And how many retellings had it gone through before Francy told Marston twenty years later?

What tells as much about the Hydes' state of mind as the fragments of oral history are Sutro's last two portraits. Gone are the smiles of two

On the river near Granite Falls, Sutro photo

days before at Emery Kolb's. In their place, Glen wears a look of grim determination, Bessie a haunted, unsmiling stare. There is little doubt that they were spooked, tense, apprehensive. Even today, many experienced river runners wear that same gripped look at the head of the rapids of the Upper Granite Gorge. All sense of humor vaporizes. One can only imagine what it was like for the Hydes. Glen had tackled many things in his life, and tough as those tasks may have been, he had not yet been defeated. They were 375 miles into their journey, with 430 to go. It is possible that Glen's eternal optimism was failing—that for once he felt they might not really be past the worst of it. But given what we know of his character, it is almost certain that, apprehensive as he may have been, Glen still wished to press on.

It is certainly possible that, as many stories indicate, Bessie wanted out at that point; but there was no indication of such at the time. Bessie's letters were consistently upbeat, and on November 24, 1928, Park Superintendent Minor Tillotson wrote, "Mrs. Hyde...admits to being scared but did not seem reluctant to resume the voyage." Jeanne Hyde recalled, "She was keener on the trip than he was. She was plucky." "Bessie," said her brother Bill, "should have been a man." It was not until memories were tapped some twenty years later—memories of a small group of people that had told and retold the story among themselves for two decades—that Bessie's feet turned cold. A difference of opinion above Hermit Rapid is not unlikely, but the use of force to resolve it contradicts everything known of Glen, his family, and his marriage. Just how that tension manifested itself can never be known.

Back at the scow, one way or another, the Hydes untied, cast off, and dropped into the haystacking waves of Hermit Rapid—a tall, angular man and a delicate, fine-featured woman aboard a coarse and savage scow. They blasted through the waves and slipped downstream into the black schist gorge. It was November 18, 1928. A wintry breeze shuddered upstream and darkness came earlier each evening.

The last photograph of the Hydes, Hermit Camp, Sutro photo

Rollin Charles Hyde at Diamond Creek, Emery Kolb in background

Part Two

Rollin Hyde's Search

Cha cha cha

My church
Is made of
Rocks and sand,
With clear, blue sky
And pounding waves.

— Bessie Haley

12

~ *1996* ~

HOUSE ROCK RAPID had shaken us. With the current hurtling us toward the hazards on the left, it was imperative to maneuver the scow to the right. We couldn't, we didn't, and we got clobbered. The Hydes had no problem there. House Rock is a relatively recent hazard, having intensified greatly in the 1960s. Few early river runners mention it. Most Grand Canyon rapids are relatively straight shots, however, and things were not likely to be that jagged for us every time. Or so we hoped. In fact, we were counting on it. The next rapid that required a similar cross-current maneuver would be Hance Rapid, which was several days off. We hoped we would learn something before then.

Later that morning we entered the Roaring Twenties—ten miles of intermittent rapids—all abrupt but relatively straightforward. The Hydes do not mention having much trouble there. Nor did we. What we did find, however, was that although the dance floor was designed to accommodate two boatmen, in major rapids the larger person (me) usually knocked down the smaller (Jeri). Thereafter we took turns in the big rapids, dancing and cowering. In the biggest rapids I usually took the sweeps—being taller, heavier, stronger, dumber. One of us would wrestle with the sweeps while the other would cringe in the back corner of the boat. But in the extreme rapids, the sweeps would take control. They became hundred-pound bludgeons careening through the boat, slamming down on the dance floor deck. Jeri made the analogy to the arcade game Whack-A-Mole, where a contestant with a large rubber mallet tries to bash the mole as he sticks his head up out of moleholes. We were the moles.

At such times the only safe place for a passenger was down on the bottom of the boat, below the level of the dance floor. And when things got completely out of hand, with both sweeps gyrating, the sweepman would have to dive to the floor as well. In the tailwaves we would scramble to regain control of the sweeps. This became our *modus operandi* in the very biggest waves. How Glen and Bessie dealt with the situation, we can only guess.

By midafternoon we were nearly through the Twenties. As I pried my way along the boiling current line at the foot of 27-Mile Rapid, the forward sweep caught a wayward current with its far tip and my stomach with the near. A moment later I was ten feet from the boat and spiraling down into a whirlpool. I was not that worried initially. Although I am a poor swimmer, unlike Glen Hyde, I had always put ultimate trust in my life preserver, and had survived accidental swims in most of Grand Canyon's major rapids without incident.

Wherever the fast jetting water of a rapid hits the slow, pooled water below, it dissipates its velocity by spinning both horizontally—as eddies—and vertically—as upthrusting boils and down-sucking whirlpools. Although the whirlpools are quite short lived, so are people under water. I came up sputtering only to see the boat at least fifty yards upstream, retreating up the eddy, as I was being swept downstream into the next rapid. Then another whirlpool pulled me down, this time with empty lungs. I came up choking and scared and saw the scow still receding. But by then Brian had his sportboat on plane, heading my way at a good thirty knots.

The water in Grand Canyon comes out of Glen Canyon Dam at a steady forty-eight degrees year-round, about forty miles upstream from where I was floundering. In such frigid water, it is hard to maintain any energy for more than a minute or two. I was spent. As Brian and Cooper plucked me from the river, I thought of the Hydes. In November of 1928, the water was far colder. Within a few weeks of their disappearance, the shorelines were icing. I had gotten sucked under with my life jacket on. The Hydes had none.

I climbed back aboard the scow, shaken. The river gave us another respite and we sailed down through the relatively easy riffles of Marble Canyon toward camp. Jeri was running most of the rapids. After my dunking, Brian had presented us with a long aluminum pole with a large plastic hook at the end—a people retriever he had acquired on a movie shoot. We placed it handily alongside the gunwale.

By late afternoon we were exhausted. We were both on the sweeps, and began to pull into a beach below a small riffle. But once again I was dancing out of step. In slow motion the forward sweep handle pushed into my gut and backed me, slowly and irrevocably, across the dance floor and over the side. With images of the morning's whirlpools, I dropped into the river screaming "Get the hook!"

When I surfaced seconds later I was a foot from the scow in calm water. Jeri was on her back on the dance floor, convulsed. "Get the hook!" she gasped, laughing. "Get the hook! Get the hook!" We were in the eddy, drifting slowly in to camp. My sense of humor was still inoperative.

TWO DAYS LATER we exited Marble Canyon and the rapids picked up again in earnest. At Unkar Rapid, a long sweeping curve to the right with a mammoth set of waves crashing down against the left wall, we crept down the right shore and threaded through the shallow rocks. It worked magnificently. The scow actually seemed to like the shallows. Two miles later in Nevills Rapid we ran the big waves down the right side, diving to the floor in the biggest of them. We were surviving, but with little grace. And I was sick to my stomach about the next rapid: Hance.

Hance Rapid is long, large, rocky, and rated among the toughest to navigate. Its waves are not as big as many others, but the rapid is far longer and the obstacles are very inconveniently placed. The water all pushes to the right. That's where the rocks and crashing holes are. There is often an easier run on the left, but the water was too low that day. Any craft that ran Hance would have to enter on the right and make some sort of move to the left—some sort of move that we still did not know how to make.

We parked a good half mile above Hance and took the sportboat down to scout the rapid. It looked awful. I imagined a dozen scenarios, each ending with a wreck in the rocks on the right. When we got back to the scow I made a proposition to Jeri. It seemed to me that one victim and three rescuers made a lot more sense than two victims and two rescuers. She understood. I was not just scared for her. I was scared for me. I wanted help below Hance. With resignation, she agreed to go with Brian and Cooper.

I entered the rapid where I wanted to, on the very right edge of the center rockpile. Once past there I began prying hard toward the left. Not surprisingly, the scow ignored my efforts and bounded down the right. At the first hole I dove to the bilge and the sweeps bashed the dance floor. I jumped up, grabbed a sweep, and tried to straighten the boat. Another hole, back to the bilge. Back to the sweep, back to the bilge. While I was busy panicking, the scow was hurtling down between the rocks, plunging through the holes, and making what turned out to be a fine run. But it certainly wasn't my fault. Brian motored up below and Jeri got back in. "I'm not doing that again," she said. "I'm staying in the scow." I nodded, apologized, and we bailed.

The next rapid was Sockdolager, where a sweep had clocked Glen in the chin and flung him overboard. Groggy, he had caught a line from Bessie and hauled himself aboard. By now we were painfully aware of such hazards and our big-water procedure had evolved accordingly. Rather than waiting for things to get out of control, we began retracting

Blasting
through
a wave
in the
Granite
Gorg%

the forward sweep in anticipation of the big hits. If we pulled it about six feet inboard on its thole pin, the bulk of the sweep would lie placidly on the dance floor while we steered with the rear sweep. This worked better, although in the true monster rapids we both still dove for the bilge.

We thundered on through Sockdolager and Grapevine without incident and pulled into a small cove a few miles short of Phantom Ranch. I crawled under a ledge and collapsed in the sand. Jeri, eyes glazed, stared downriver. The scow had thrashed us, soundly and repeatedly. And tomorrow was going to be much, much worse. Four of the most violent rapids on the river lay in the next fifteen miles. I hurt everywhere.

The next morning we stopped at Phantom Ranch, made a few phone calls to concerned relatives assuring them we had not perished—yet— then pushed on. Below Phantom, the gravel outwash from Bright Angel Creek forms a long series of gravel bar riffles. We were negotiating them when we got sucked into a fast, tight, swirling eddy on the right side of the river. I tried several times to break out of its grasp, only to be sucked back in and swirled back up along the cliff. Looking back on it now, I realize we were very likely caught in the exact whirlpool the Hydes had been in when they were spotted by tourist John Baer. The Hydes had tried everything they could think of and somehow finally made their way out. One note in Bessie's journal indicates they used a rope. I was stymied.

On about the tenth ride around the eddy Brian reappeared from downstream and looked at me questioningly. In boating, much is communicated with eyes and gestures. I nodded. Within minutes Brian had pushed us back into the main current and vanished downstream. A mile later we braced for Horn Creek Rapid.

Horn Creek is abrupt. As we entered, I had already retracted and dropped the forward sweep, using the rear sweep to keep the boat aimed slightly to the right. The first of three humongous waves wrenched the rear sweep from my hands and I dove to the safety of the floor. This was the plan. I hoped the scow would hold its angle through the next three giant waves and enter the tailwaves still heading right. The cliff on the left had a history of drawing in and wrecking boats—and those boats had maneuvering power. We had none.

Once again, things didn't work out. Each wave nudged the bow farther left, and by the time the violence subsided enough to regain the forward sweep, we were freight-training straight into the left cliff. I had seconds to make a move—either attempt to miss the cliff and continue downstream, which was obviously not going to work—or aim for the small eddy just above the point at which the current slams into the cliff—the same small eddy Brian was filling with the sportboat as he waited for us—the small eddy that there is no way out of. At the last moment I placed the forward sweep in the eddy and pulled with everything I had, staring into Brian's wide eyes and screaming "Incoming!"

It worked. The scow snapped into the eddy and stopped, docile as a kitten, while Brian rocketed full-throttle out the top end. One thing we were learning: it was only in the most critical of situations that the scow seemed to respond—near cliffs, or in fast shallow rocks. This makes sense, as water is non-compressible. When the huge sweep blade, or the huger flank of the scow itself, approaches something solid, the water between cannot escape and the boat responds by buffeting off the water cushion being formed. But in the deep water, where the river swirls in three dimensions, the water simply accommodates the momentum of the two-ton scow and there is little the boatman can do to alter it. Grand Canyon, then, composed chiefly of deep water hydraulic rapids, is not the best place for this type of boat. We wondered when Glen Hyde figured that out.

In the flatwater stretches upstream we had worked out two methods of attaching the motorboat to the scow, and practiced quick set-up and release procedures. One method we called "T-Bone," which was simply Brian ramming us broadside without tying on, and goosing the engine. Although quick, it was not always terribly effective, as scows just hate to move sideways. Yet it had worked well enough to get us out of the eddy below Phantom Ranch. The other method we called "I-Beam." For this we retracted the rear sweep and Brian motored up snugly behind us, whereupon we attached two high tension lines along either side of the boats to hold us straight. This was a far more maneuverable set-up, much like operating one of the big pontoon rafts he and I had run commercially.

Brian was in the eddy seconds after he left, pulling in behind us. He glanced at Jeri and me, held a conference of the eyeballs, and shouted,

At the mercy of
Hermit Rapid

"I-Beam!" Again, within a minute we were peeling out of the eddy and
heading downstream.

Two of the largest rapids in Grand Canyon followed in quick succession. Granite Falls shot us down along the right cliff, slamming us from
either side, rolling us alarmingly to the left at one point, before shooting us out inundated.

Hermit Rapid was astonishing. We had a flow of around 20,000 CFS,
over twice what Glen and Bessie had. At that level the river forms over
a dozen mountainous haystacking waves down the middle. We considered trying to miss them, realized we could not, shipped the sweeps
and dove for the floor. We porpoised through, the scow alternately
diving and standing on end. As we climbed the largest wave, the rear
sweep slid back into the river, then slammed the deck so hard that it
broke the oar grip off the end, sending splinters whizzing over Jeri's
head.

The ride was so amazing we allowed ourselves a few moments of
exhilaration before the dread returned. We were drifting out of sight
of Hermit, the last place the Hydes were ever seen. Just ahead lay the
toughest rapid on the modern river, Crystal Creek, formed by a debris
flow in 1966. It was not there when Glen and Bessie ran, but they had the
dread of an unknown river instead. We had helmets and life jackets—I
was now wearing two jackets in the big stuff. We had full knowledge of
the river ahead, and a red-hot rescue boat. The Hydes had none of that.
They had wool clothes, leather jackets, and each other.

Feared Lost in Shooting Rapids

GLENN HYDE and his wife, Bessie Haley Hyde, above, were sought by rivermen and government aviators after the young couple made a daring attempt to shoot the rapids in the Grand Canyon of the Colorado in a small boat. Mr. and Mrs. Hyde resided at Hansen, Idaho. Mrs. Hyde's parents live in Parkersburg, W. Va. She formerly attended school in Pittsburgh. So far attempts to locate the couple have proved fruitless although their scow has been found lodged on the rocks of Separation rapids.

Seated at the piano, I softly touch the keys,
And plan such wondrous songs
Of dream-like melodies.

Hopelessly, slowly rising,
I by the window stand,
For such songs can never come,
From my old, untrained hand.

— Bessie Haley

13

"*I* DID NOT WAIT until they were late for I have been afraid all of the time," wrote R.C. Hyde to Bessie's father. "When they did not telegraph on the day they set to arrive, I left..."

Glen Hyde had told his father to expect a telegram from Needles on December 9, his thirtieth birthday. From Needles, the honeymooners planned to take the train to Los Angeles, where R.C. Hyde and Glen's sister Jeanne would meet them to spend the holiday season.

December 9 came and went. No word, no sightings, no clues had come from the Colorado River since that dark afternoon at Hermit Rapid, twenty-two days earlier. Glen had set December 11 as the outside date they should arrive in Needles. On the morning of December 12, R.C. Hyde boarded a train for Las Vegas, Nevada. In the next week he made what even today is considered an astonishing inventory of the lower Colorado River.

Glen and Bessie had last been seen at River Mile 95, some 375 miles above Needles. From Hermit, the river is tightly hemmed by Grand Canyon for another 180 miles, at which point the Grand Wash Cliffs break away to the north and south. There the river leaves the Colorado Plateau canyon country and enters the jagged Basin and Range terrain that characterizes Nevada. For nearly two hundred miles the river—nowadays beneath Lakes Mead and Mojave—winds through the craggy peaks and barren basins of the Mojave Desert. Much of this country is inaccessible today in anything but a rugged four-wheel-drive in the hands of someone who knows the territory. In the late 1920s it was far more remote.

R.C. Hyde assaulted the landscape. In the lower two hundred miles of the Colorado he found there was but one spot where anyone lived by the river: Grigg's Ferry, an obscure outpost some fifteen miles below the end of Grand Canyon. There the Smith brothers, Tom and William, were running the ranch, mines, and ferry of their late stepfather, William Grigg. Hyde went by railroad to the town of Saint Thomas, Nevada, and from there by horse over the high, jagged limestone ridges, and down the Scanlon Dugway to Grigg's Ferry. He asked the Smiths if they had seen his son. They had not.

"I cannot describe the country," continued Hyde in his letter to William Haley:

> I can only say it is unlike any other. The river runs in a canyon from four to six thousand feet deep. In nearly one thousand miles only one road crosses the river. No one lives on it except in a few places—no one within many miles. I spent two days finding anyone on the river. Old settlements marked on the map had been abandoned and no one there. The country back from the river is so rough that only in a very few places is it possible to get down to search the river.

R.C. Hyde figured Grigg's Ferry to be a week upstream of Needles, making Glen now, instead of just a few days late, *very* late. His concern escalated to alarm. He returned to Saint Thomas and took the train into Las Vegas, where he launched a barrage on the federal government, pleading for an air search of the river. He telegraphed Governor William Borah of Idaho, and Jeanne Hyde began a network of telegrams to everyone she could think of. Even Sigma Nu, Glen's old fraternity at the University of Idaho, telegraphed Borah.

Although he regretted alarming Bessie's parents unduly, R.C. Hyde alerted William and Lottie Haley to the couple's tardiness, described his search efforts, and asked them to seek the support of their governor. The first national press coverage was an Associated Press story dated

December 16: "Pair In Canoe Feared Lost In Grand Canyon." It was posted in Parkersburg, West Virginia, and told of William Haley's plans to ask Governor Howard Gore for an airplane search.

Haley met with Gore, who called Secretary of War Dwight Davis to request a search. Governor Borah made a similar call and Congressmen Smith and French of Idaho met with President Calvin Coolidge to press for a search. On the morning of December 17, 1928, Secretary Davis ordered Major General John Hines, Commander of the Ninth Army Corps in San Francisco, to commence an air inspection of the river.

Hines, reluctant to send his small single engine planes into such rough terrain, requested the new Fokker Tri-Motor plane from Crissy Field for the search. Single-engine planes were far from reliable at that time, and one had plowed into the trees at the South Rim a year earlier in the search for the Pathé-Bray river trip.

Hyde notified the Mojave Indian tribe, on their reservation seventy-five miles north of Needles, to be on the lookout for any trace of the trip, posting a thousand dollar reward for information leading to the recovery of Glen and Bessie.

Still only four days after his departure from Idaho, Hyde moved operations eastward to the tiny town of Peach Springs, Arizona, headquarters of the Hualapai Indian Reservation. In the past week a thick blanket of snow had covered the high country surrounding Grand Canyon. This would make travel on the rim more difficult, but make tracking far easier—if there were any tracks to be found.

Peach Springs lies along the Santa Fe Railroad, and a rough dirt track leads twenty-one miles northward down Peach Springs Wash into Diamond Creek and meets the river some 130 miles below Hermit Rapid, fifty miles upstream of the Grand Wash Cliffs. Hyde checked into the Harvey House, the hotel adjacent to the train depot. He began negotiating with a man to start a river search from Diamond Creek.

"I wanted this man to take lumber down Diamond Creek build a boat there and go on down the river," Hyde wrote to Haley:

> but I could not get him to do it. He would not say so but I know
> he was afraid to run the two bad rapids below Diamond Creek. All I

could do was to get him to run the lower and safer part of the river. He is to build a boat about fifty miles below Diamond Creek and run from there to Needles, Cal.

The newspaper the next day announced a party of two men was preparing a boat to search from Pierce's Ferry, below Grand Canyon, to Needles. Hyde did not expect them to find anything of interest. He had already confirmed with the Smiths, who lived just ten calm miles below where the men would begin, that Glen had not passed. But Hyde had to cover all bases. "While I am sure they are not there," he wrote to Haley, "there is a possibility."

Deputy Sheriff John Nelson was quick to offer his services. Nelson, a former rancher who had recently moved to Peach Springs with his wife and ten children, was the town's sole legal authority—a position he carried well. A teetotaling man of average build, he commanded the respect of Anglos and Hualapais alike. "He was a frontiersman from the word go," recalls Bob Goldenstein, who arrived in Peach Springs in 1938. "If there was anyone missing, he was the one who went looking. In fact, when I was young and failed to come back from a hike to the river, he found *me*." With Charles Taylor and another man, Nelson made his way down Peach Springs Wash to the river to search for any trace of Glen and Bessie's passage.

Hyde telegraphed Emery Kolb at South Rim: "COULD YOU BE INDUCED TO SEARCH RIVER WITH BOAT ELTOVAR TO DIAMOND CREEK OR FARTHER." Hyde received no reply, as Kolb was two hundred miles south in Phoenix. A week earlier the *Coconino Sun* had reported: "The health of Mr. Kolb is not very good and upon the advice of doctors they plan on spending most of the winter in the south."

"I also telegraphed the Manager of the Hotel," Hyde wrote to Haley, "asking if he knew of anyone, and got a telegram from a Mr. Francy that he would go and that he had a boat. He got there in a few hours and I arranged with him to look over the lower river." Hyde caught the next train east to Williams, Arizona, and took the spur line to the South Rim.

BOB FRANCY was the corral boss for the Fred Harvey Company at the South Rim. He had been involved with the Pathé-Bray river trip during the filming of the final scenes at Hermit Rapid. Of the three boats the trip possessed at Hermit, one had been sawed nearly in two, then crashed into a rock for a dramatic wreck scene. Another had been hauled by mule out to the Hermit Camp tramway, sent out to the rim, and from there to Hollywood for studio filming and promotion. The third boat had been spirited away by Francy. That winter he and friends had dragged, rowed, winched, and portaged the boat, named *Bright Angel*, upstream to Phantom Ranch. There they used it for flatwater work above Bright Angel Creek, taking dudes for rides, and retrieving firewood. In fact, during the time Glen and Bessie were at the South Rim, Dick Mueller and Ray Tankersley had rowed and dragged the *Bright Angel* nearly to Clear Creek, three miles upstream, with a group of power and water surveyors. Upon their return to Phantom Ranch, Mueller had taken a photograph of Tankersley standing in the Hydes' scow with Glen's hat on.

Francy got hold of his friend Jack Harbin, a brakeman for the Santa Fe Railroad, a former barnstormer in small planes, and an aspiring boxer. Three weeks earlier the two had won the six-shooter division at the annual Turkey Shoot. Harbin was the physical opposite of his brother "Fats" who also worked for the railroad. "There wasn't an ounce of fat on him," recalls Michael Harrison, who sang in a trio with Harbin. "I don't know anyone who disliked Bob. Jack was something else again. He was arrogant, had a swelled-head and thought of himself as the handsome Lochinvar of Grand Canyon. Hell, he couldn't have been that—I was." Harbin had helped Francy retrieve the *Bright Angel* the previous winter and was, said Francy, "a fine boatman."

Francy and Hyde worked out a deal. Hyde would pay Francy five hundred dollars to go the seventy miles to Havasu Creek, where the National Park ended. If, after calling Hyde from the Havasupai Indian village, Hyde wished him to continue on, Hyde would pay an additional five hundred dollars. Over and above that was Hyde's reward of one thousand dollars for anyone who found the lost couple, dead or alive.

Superintendent Tillotson felt the rescue trip should have a Park Service representative along as far as the park boundary. He chose his Assistant Superintendent, Pat Patraw who, a day earlier, had joined Scenic Airlines pilot Dean Buford in a search of the Inner Gorge below

Phantom Ranch in a huge Ford Tri-Motor plane. They had found nothing. On December 17, R.C. Hyde discussed plans and eventualities with the river team. Late that afternoon, Francy, Harbin, and Patraw gathered food, clothing, and equipment and headed down the trail.

The next morning they set about packing the *Bright Angel* and found they had an overabundance of gear. Some of the rear decking had been removed over the previous winter in order to better facilitate firewood retrieval, but making for less stowage and buoyancy. Heavily overloaded, they departed, only to swamp in the first set of rapids. From there on, they portaged gear and lined the boat at nearly every drop. Harbin took the boat through smaller rapids alone. The river, which had been low when the Hydes passed through, had dropped even further to a brutal 5,500 CFS, making for slow current and violent rapids. At the major drops they lowered the boat through the rocks along shore. By that evening the party had made it as far as Hermit Rapid, and hiked up to Hermit Camp for the night.

ON THE CANYON RIM, Hyde telegraphed Emery Kolb in Phoenix, telling him of Francy's search and asking if Kolb would build a boat at Diamond Creek and search from there down. He added, "THE TIME WE CAN HOPE TO FIND THEM GROWS SHORT I CANNOT EXPRESS THE IMPORTANCE TO ME YOU MAKING THIS RUN."

Francy and Harbin preparing for departure

"I was in Phoenix when the father wired wanting to know if I would go on a search," recalled Kolb nearly fifty years later. "We were down there to see a friend who was dying with cancer. My wife gave this man blood. The doctor asked me if I wanted to give him blood and I told him I had pretty low blood pressure. He said 'Well you better let me examine you and see what's the matter with you.'"

"Finding my blood pressure so low," Kolb wrote Dave Rust, "they would not take my blood but insisted that I have some X-rays made. I didn't wait for the report, but left for the trip. My pressure…should be 130 to 140. It was down to 80. My wife saw the doctor who said I had an appendix which should come out at once." Kolb received Hyde's telegram the morning of December 18 and was back at South Rim that night.

In Flagstaff, Arizona, private planes were scheduled to fly to Grand Canyon to aid in the search, but foul weather had the local airport at Koch Field socked in. In California, Major General Hines learned there would be delays with the Fokker Tri-Motor. Reluctantly, he sent two small Douglas 0-2 single-engine observation planes to begin the search of the lower river. Piloted by Lieutenants John Quincy Adams and William G. Plummer, the 400-horsepower biplanes sped across the Mojave Desert to Needles. Each plane had a mechanic on board, as well as food and clothing to drop in case they spotted the Hydes in dire straits. Refueling in Needles, they headed upriver, flying low, following each bend. Below them dozens of Mojave Indians were working their way to the river along various trails to aid in the search. By nightfall the pilots had searched as far as Las Vegas and landed for the night.

"NO SIGN OF MISSING PARTY," they radiogrammed back to Hines. "REFUELING AT LAS VEGAS. EARLY TOMORROW WILL RECONNOITER REMAINDER OF CANYON AS FAR AS EL TOVAR HOTEL."

Late that evening, as he waited for Emery Kolb, R.C. Hyde finished his letter to William Haley:

> What I want of [Kolb] is to build a boat at Diamond Creek and run the rough water below there. I am quite sure he will do that. If so we will soon have the river searched as there will be three boats at different places going down. I had thought to go down myself but I

find it is necessary to stay along the Railroad to look after the different things that come up...

I have made inquiries from every source imaginable and the information...I have gotten was useless and often wrong. The people here with a very few exceptions know no more about the River than do people living a thousand miles away. I had asked for help from the Indians. In the North they know the Trails and can go around better than the white men. I also found that these Indians living within twenty or thirty miles of the river know nothing of it, most of them have never seen it, and none of them have ever been on it. They do not hunt and know nothing about getting anywhere...

I have very far from lost hope of them. After Glen wrote me that he expected to be out by Dec. 6, they lost four days that I know of and two they stayed at Grand Canyon. If they were held up by headwinds yesterday they would only be seven days late. They could easily be that without anything serious having happened. Every time I am called to the telegraph office which is about thirty times a day I go expecting a telegram from Glen. Even if they have lost their boat I am confident that they will be found along the shore, trying to make it down on foot.

Michael Harrison

The small, brown, shack-like cottage
Hung close to the top of the hill,
The door lamp gave a pale, dim light,
And the leaves and wind were still.

—— Bessie Haley

14

～ *December 19–20 1928* ～

LINING A BOAT DOWN A RAPID is treacherous work—lowering a boat along the fast currents, straining on heavy wet ropes, slipping on muddy, icy boulders as the current yanks the boat into the fast-water, ankles twisting, palms burning, shins bleeding. It can test the strongest nerves. But Bob Francy and Jack Harbin were irritated even before they began the morning's work. They were mad at Pat Patraw.

"You have to remember this," recalls Michael Harrison who, at 102 years old, still remembers well his years with the National Park Service:

> When Grand Canyon was set up as a National Park in 1919, *we* were the interlopers. We came there long after the Harvey Company and the Santa Fe Railroad were there. And Emery Kolb hated both of us. And for the almost ten years that I was there, I was never, *never* in the home of a Harvey employee, or a Santa Fe railroad employee. And by the same token, there wasn't a Harvey or Santa Fe employee that was in my house. And that was true, I think, of everybody in the Park Service. We were friendly enemies.

It was true. The Fred Harvey Company, who ran restaurants and hotels in partnership with the Santa Fe Railroad, had been going out of its way for years to run Emery Kolb out of business, diverting and distracting tourists from the Kolb Studio whenever possible. When the Park was established, Park Service personnel immediately ran into regulatory conflicts with all existing operations. So when Francy and Harbin, who felt they were risking their necks in this search, found out they were taking a Park man along, they were not overjoyed.

Early the morning of December 19, when the three men were break-fasting at Hermit Camp, a Phoenix newspaper arrived by tram. It carried a news release announcing that not Francy and Harbin but the *National Park Service* was launching a search expedition with *P. P. Patraw* in charge. When the Hermit Camp manager read it aloud, Patraw left the mess hall without finishing breakfast. Harbin hit the roof, shouting that they ought to just cut Patraw's throat and toss him overboard.

On the river things got worse. At Boucher Rapid they began lining the *Bright Angel* down through the boulders. Francy was in the boat, pushing it off the rocks, while Harbin was on the downstream line holding the boat against shore. Patraw, on the upper rope, slowly let out line and lowered the boat. Just as the boat was getting into the worst part of the rapid, Patraw slipped and fell. The boat swung into the current and slammed a rock. Francy was thrown from the boat and sucked under water. As he floundered ashore he saw Harbin blow up. He recalled: "Jack put fear into Pat right there—he abused him terrible. 'I'll cut the end off this rope and tie it around your neck and the other around a rock and throw you over! I'll drown you! Bob will never tell!'"

Once Francy convinced Harbin that killing the Assistant Superintendent was poor etiquette, they continued downstream, still overloaded and increasingly grumpy. The weather was clear but horribly cold, and the sun rarely hit the river. At night the calm eddies iced over and the water buckets froze solid. The river level continued to drop. Progress was slow and agonizing.

IN THE WORLD ABOVE, the search for Glen and Bessie Hyde was headline news across the country. In just one week, R.C. Hyde had initiated three river searches, dozens of land searches, and now a federal search by air. On the morning of December 19, Lieutenants Adams and Plummer had, along with their mechanics, boarded their 0-2 planes and left Las Vegas for Grand Canyon. Meanwhile, the lumbering Fokker Tri-Motor left Crissy Field in California to join the search. Adams and Plummer flew low, winding up the river, entering the four-thousand foot high walls of Grand Canyon at the Grand Wash Cliffs. Thirty miles farther they began seeing major rapids and a few minutes later spotted a boat adrift in the river. They circled and swooped, getting as good a look as they could at the boat. They scanned the shorelines for people but saw no one. Continuing to search the river, they sped for the South Rim.

R.C. Hyde and Emery Kolb were awaiting them when they landed. From the pilots' description, Hyde was certain they had found Glen's scow and was elated to hear the boat was intact, right-side up, fully loaded, and in calm water. This could bode nothing but good for Glen and Bessie. Hyde was more certain than ever they must simply have lost the boat and were scaling the cliffs or holed up on a ledge or in a cave, somewhere near the river. "BOAT FOUND EVERYTHING IN DRY HOPE TO FIND THEM UNHARMED," he telegraphed Haley.

To get a positive identification of boat and location, Emery Kolb climbed into the rear cockpit of Lieutenant Adams's plane and they took off again, screaming downstream amid late afternoon snow flurries.

Near Mile 237 they spotted the scow, in the same place it had been before, apparently stuck. Diving to within fifty feet of the water, they could look not only at the boat but at the contents, to the point of being able to describe the gear on board to Hyde afterwards. Recalled Kolb: "Pilot Adams...played like a kitten, diving over the ridges and peaks, giving me two hours of thrills. He took me into the inner gorge up and down and over the boat many times, so close that I could see the bed and knew there was no mistake." At one point Kolb took off his seat belt to peer over the side of the plane just as Adams banked the ship on its side in a steep turn. Kolb nearly tumbled from the plane. There was no question it was the Hyde scow. They returned to the South Rim, landing in near darkness and five inches of snow.

ON THE MORNING OF December 20 the planes began their return to Riverside, California, dipping into the canyon immediately after leaving the South Rim. They spotted Francy, Harbin, and Patraw approaching Bass Camp, some fifteen miles below Hermit, and dropped them a message, telling them the scow had been found empty and to carry on without delay. One of the planes was so low, recalled Harbin, he nearly hit William Bass's cable car crossing, strung just thirty feet above the river. As the planes neared Diamond Creek, they spotted Deputy Sheriff Nelson's party on foot, working along the Tonto Platform, a broad, shale bench atop the Granite Gorge that affords hiking throughout much of Grand Canyon.

"John and I had followed a wild burro trail up on the first rim above the river," recalled Charles Taylor. "We were on this rim when the plane dropped the information about the location of the boat. It was written on pasteboard like the back of a Big Chief tablet, and it tore in two coming down. After receiving it we went back to Peach Springs, as there was no way of us getting to the boat."

Continuing downriver, the planes found the boat R.C. Hyde had dispatched from Pierce's Ferry to Needles. The pilots dropped a message advising the party of the progress of the search. Pilots Adams and Plummer were back at March Field before Major General Hines's Fokker Tri-Motor was even able to join the search.

Back at the South Rim, Superintendent Tillotson called a meeting of his staff. Tillotson had risen through the ranks of the National Park Service after starting out as a civil engineer. Before becoming superintendent, "Tilly," as he was known, had overseen the construction of the new rim-to-rim Kaibab Trail and the completion of the new Kaibab footbridge over the Colorado. An egalitarian official, he befriended and socialized with everyone in the Park, from Navajo road worker on up. To him, they were all family. Michael Harrison, who had come to the park shortly after it was formed, was working as chief clerk, which meant he did a little of everything. He recalls:

> The first I knew of Glen's father was when he came to the park...to see if we would put a boat on the river, to hunt for his son and daughter-in-law.... We held a staff meeting consisting of Minor Tillotson, the Superintendent, Jimmy Brooks, the Chief Ranger, Clark Carrel, the Park Engineer...and me. That was the staff. Glen Sturdevant was also there—he was the Park Naturalist.
>
> Sturdevant wanted to go on the party. Jimmy Brooks, of course, was to be in charge. I objected to Glen's wanting to go because he was married and had two kids. And I had just been divorced, so I was all by myself. In addition to that, I was a champion swimmer and had

a trunk full of medals. So the next morning, a party of four left the park. Jimmy Brooks in the official car—he had an Essex—I swear it was made of tin cans. I was driving my own Buick coupé. With me I had Mr. Hyde. Jimmy Brooks had Emery Kolb. The four of us drove...to Peach Springs, and that was the closest point to the river.

And we stepped into the little fleabag of a hotel at Diamond Creek. The gentleman who ran the hotel said "Which one of you is Mike Harrison?" I said "I am." He said "I have a telegram for you." And it was a telegram from Tillotson. I was not to go beyond Diamond Creek. I was to return to the Park immediately. See, I was also the paymaster. [laughs] I was the only one who could write checks and it was close to payday. They wanted me back there, so I just stayed overnight—and turned around and went back to the park the next day.

"I read of the incident in the Los Angeles papers," recalled Ellsworth Kolb, "which stated that Emery would go to Diamond Creek via Peach Springs to organize a search. I sent a wire to Emery and said to call on me for supplies from L.A. and said I would like to join him." Before leaving the South Rim, Emery telegraphed Ellsworth to catch the next train east and meet the party in Peach Springs.

Peach Springs, Ariz.
Dec 21, 1928
Dear Mr. Haley;

The airplanes found the boat as I wired you. So far as they could see from the planes the boat was not damaged and the entire outfit, bedding, food, etc., was on board. I am going down to Diamond Creek and will take lumber to build a boat. When we reach the river that will be 12 miles above the stranded boat. The boat is not drifting as the planes first stated but stationary in the river about 30 feet from the shore.

We will have to carry the lumber for the last [four] miles so it will be all we can do to get there today. I have four men and hope to have the boat ready by noon tomorrow, then it will be only a few hours run to the stranded boat. I will telegraph you as soon as the boat is reached or rather as soon as I know. I cannot go with them down the river much as I would like to as I have to be where I can look after the other searchers.

After these men reach the boat they will have to go down the river quite a way before they can get on land. I will have horses for them there and a couple of days ride will bring them here. The planes made another search yesterday but found nothing new. I have asked that they return tomorrow and search both banks.

I have thought it possible that Glen and Bessie landed above the rapids to look them over before running them (They always did) and that the boat slipped away while they were looking. If that should be so, right at that spot is one of the few floors of the Grand Canyon where it is possible to climb out. They would do that as there is nothing else they could do as one cannot get by the Rapids on foot, nor can they get down to the river again below.

It is an uninhabited country but timbered and at this time of the year some snow so there will be water. Glen carried matches and is used to life in the woods. I am notifying all of the Indians and advertising a reward. I can only say that there is hope.

Yours truly,
R. C. Hyde

A cigarette
May be a ritual,
After a day
Of accomplishment,
Then the thin smoke
Drifts upward
Like incense.

— *Bessie Haley*

15

~ *December 20–23 1928* ~

GRAND CANYON, DEC. 20 — (U.P.) — Officials of Grand Canyon
Park tonight issued a warning to all thrill seekers to hunt
elsewhere than the Colorado River for their adventures…

Emery Kolb, only living man who twice has negotiated the
river rapids, declared that no one who has not experienced the river
trip can realize the treachery of the stream and the perils of the
rugged country.

The river has often caused disasters, park officials said, but the
Hyde episode has magnified the dangers and caused them to issue the
warning.

"THE SULLEN COLORADO guards its secret closely," wrote the Associated
Press. "Kolb thought the Hydes might be found under the canyon rim
near the wrecked scow. There is a possibility, however, that the pair may
have been swept to their deaths by the torrent." The *Twin Falls Daily
News* reaffirmed R.C. Hyde's belief that they would be found along the
shore. Quoting Glen's brother-in-law, Carl Emerson, an article stated
that before Glen left Idaho, "he had advised that in the event that he and
Mrs. Hyde should be compelled to leave their scow at any time on their
trip down the river, that they would remain in the canyon until found."

"The tedious process of wrenching from the Colorado River some
clue to the fate of Mr. and Mrs. Glen Hyde was progressing today…"

read another report. "Indians and volunteers from Grand Canyon were mushing through the snow on the canyon rim in an effort to find some trace of the couple who may have climbed the cliffs and begun a dangerous journey southward toward habitation." Another told of Havasupai runners being dispatched to meet the Francy trip. "It is noted by those acquainted with the country that the couple could not be more isolated if they were in the Arctic regions, or the interior of an unexplored continent."

The biggest headlines throughout the country that morning were about the Colorado River as well, but not about the Hydes. After a contentious passage by Congress, President Coolidge signed the Boulder Dam Act. The untamed Colorado was to be dammed at last, and within a decade, Lake Mead would flood every bit of the river from where the Hyde scow was found to Las Vegas.

DECEMBER 21 was the first day of winter and the shortest day of the year. In Peach Springs, Emery Kolb, Jimmy Brooks, and R.C. Hyde finished buying lumber to build a boat, and loaded it into general store owner Ancel Taylor's Model-T truck. They lashed it down securely for the rough drive down Peach Springs Wash. Hyde dispatched two Hualapai Indians with a horse-drawn wagon to carry the lumber over the last few rough miles to the river.

It was day ten of Hyde's search, thirty-three days since Sutro waved goodbye to the couple at Hermit Rapid. Hyde telegraphed Secretary of War Dwight Davis for further air searches and received word that the planes would be sent out again. Based in Las Vegas, the planes would make daily flights up and down the river corridor, scanning the shore and cliffs for signs of life.

Before Hyde, Emery Kolb, and Brooks left Peach Springs, Deputy Sheriff John Nelson and his men returned from their search of the river. They had found no sign of the Hydes, but they did notice a beat-up old boat that Kolb might be able to repair. Nelson turned around and drove back toward the river with Kolb's party. They walked the last four miles to the river to assess the old boat. Kolb deemed it salvageable, and Nelson returned to Peach Springs to cancel the lumber delivery, only to find Ellsworth Kolb getting off the train. Turning around the following morning, he made a third trip to the river.

Diamond Creek is unique in Grand Canyon. With its tributary, Peach Springs Wash, it descends at such low gradient that an automobile track was pushed through to the river as early as 1912. It was then that James B. Girand, a dam builder from Phoenix, applied for a permit for a 450-foot dam on the Colorado at Diamond Creek as part of a private water and power operation. He built an extensive camp by the river and began drilling test holes. He worked the site again in 1922 and won preliminary approval for the dam but was defeated three years later on the grounds that his dam would interfere with federal plans to build a dam downstream at Bridge Canyon. Girand left nothing but a cluster of wooden shacks, tent cabins, and a very dilapidated flat-bottomed boat.

The Kolbs and Brooks began patching the boat on the morning of December 22. Using wooden floors and doors from the shacks, they decked over the fore and aft of the hull. In a burst of inspiration that nearly proved to be fatal for Ranger Brooks, Kolb fashioned two tall wooden posts sticking up amidships for Brooks to hang on to, as "he was not a river man." Brooks did have some river experience, however. While Glen and Bessie had been visiting Emery Kolb in November, Brooks, Park Naturalist Glen Sturdevant, and Ranger Art Brown had departed on a twelve-day trip into Grand Canyon below the Little Colorado River, crossing and recrossing the river in a collapsible canoe, and running several miles of flatwater.

Building a boat to run the rapids of the lower gorge of the Colorado, however, was not a quick task. Although the Associated Press stated hopefully that Kolb would "avoid all rapids, keeping to the river's edge," Kolb knew better. The job ended up taking a full two days.

Word arrived in Peach Springs on the 22nd from the search party on the lower river. They had found nothing. Nor had footprints been found in the snow along the South Rim. But an eerie story came in from farther downriver that day. Murl Emery, one of the best known boatmen of the lower Colorado both before and after the creation of Lake Mead, contacted the *Las Vegas Review*. He told them a prospector from the Black Hills area, six miles from Boulder Canyon, saw a leather jacket float by in the river. The current had been too swift to retrieve it,

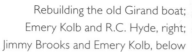

Rebuilding the old Girand boat;
Emery Kolb and R.C. Hyde, right;
Jimmy Brooks and Emery Kolb, below

but a lookout had been posted to watch for further flotsam.

By the evening of December 23, the Kolbs deemed their remodeled boat seaworthy. They loaded it with what provisions they could, outfitted it with a good set of oars that Emery had brought from the South Rim, and prepared to launch the following morning. Hyde, meanwhile, was arranging for Deputy Sheriff Nelson to head an overland horse trip to the mouth of Spencer Canyon, some nine miles below the point where the scow had been sighted. With any luck, the Kolbs could be there in a few days with word of what they found, possibly even bringing the scow that far. And it was still possible, although Hyde was reluctant to say it aloud, that they might find Glen and Bessie holed up somewhere along the way. They had been missing thirty-six days now, yet perhaps somewhere, somehow, they were still alive. Early on December 24, 1928, Emery and Ellsworth Kolb and Jimmy Brooks launched. R.C. Hyde and John Nelson pushed them off. They wallowed through Diamond Creek Rapid, overloaded and, in spite of their efforts, ill-equipped.

THAT AFTERNOON word finally came to the South Rim from Francy and Harbin's search of the upper river in the form of Pat Patraw himself, who staggered in after three days of hell on foot. Things on the river had not improved between him and Harbin. "I didn't care for him," recalled Harbin. "He could eat more than any man I ever saw. I ran him off at Bass' mine."

"Jack," added Francy, "made him glad to go." Yet it may be that Francy and Harbin had let their memories of strife build up over twenty years of telling the story. Patraw's memory reflects no bad blood:

> I'll tell you right now, I never worked harder than those days on the Colorado River... We had all this stuff loaded in the front, in the water-tight compartment, see. Unload that boat and then carry all that stuff and scramble up over the ground where it comes to the bottom...
>
> We were getting practically no sunlight at all. In fact, the only sunlight would be in a very few and very short places. All the rocks exposed in the river and on the shore of the river had ice, oh, probably an inch thick. Just a few minutes after you'd start in the morning your feet would be numb.
>
> But anyway, it took us four days to get to the Bass Trail. By the time we got there, the folks asked me to leave. We were overloaded. We were going to have to speed up.... I did try to get Bob Francy to leave because he had a bad knee and furthermore he was frightened of water. I was very familiar with water and I never had the slightest fear of water at all... But it was their expedition...they asked me to leave, so I did.
>
> That was quite an experience. I enjoyed it.

But Patraw's hike out did not go well. "It took me the better part of two days to hike out, principally because of a considerable delay in finding the Bass Trail where it started up from the Supai, as the ground was covered with snow." Once on the rim he was still many miles from Grand Canyon Village. Half starved, he arrived at the village on December 24. "When I came off that trip I couldn't get enough to eat. I gained so much weight around the shoulders that I broke out the stitching of two uniform blouses."

Patraw told the press of his thirteen-mile river trip, and of seeing Hyde's footprints where he scouted major rapids—Ruby Rapid and Bass Rapid in particular. The tracks appeared to be Glen's, scouting his run. They had found no further clues.

Francy and Harbin planned to reach Havasu Creek early the following week, where Havasupai Indian runners were scheduled to descend thirteen miles to the river to meet them. Relieved of both Patraw and cargo, they made haste downriver into the darkening gorge as the temperatures, and the already meager river level, continued to drop.

Back in Peach Springs: Ellsworth Kolb, Charles Taylor,
John Nelson, Jimmy Brooks, R.C. Hyde, Emery Kolb, Ancel Taylor

Broken dreams hurt me so,
I sometimes pause to wonder,
If dreaming really is worthwhile
And not a foolish blunder?

— Bessie Haley

16

~ *December 24–29 1928* ~

EMERY KOLB was at the oars. At this point he was the senior boatman of the brothers, having led the 1923 USGS survey trip through Grand Canyon while Ellsworth minded the studio. Emery was the younger and smaller brother, and the more outspoken as well. "He was the cocky bantam, always fighting… Like a piece of emery board," recalls Michael Harrison. "Ellsworth was the type anyone can get along with. He was a gentle gentleman. Very much a loner, very shy. He would keep in the background, would almost only speak when spoken to. Emery was always out front."

Ellsworth rode on the decks and Brooks sat amidships, grasping the upright posts Emery had built for him. The river level, which had dropped from the Hydes' level of around 8,000 CFS, down to 5,500 when Francy and Harbin launched, had now dropped below 4,000. At that level the rapids literally become rock gardens, and the current between rapids all but disappears.

Looking for footprints as they worked their way downstream, hollering now and then in case the Hydes might be alive on a ledge somewhere, they arrived at 231-Mile Rapid, a long sinuous cataract. After scouting the route, Emery rowed them safely through and they proceeded to the next one. Ellsworth had been itching to row a little after all these years, and Emery reluctantly agreed to let him try 232-Mile Rapid.

At low water levels, 232-Mile Rapid is a tough run, consisting of a series of sharp waves throwing the boat into a nest of sharp, bedrock fangs at the foot of the rapid. Ellsworth gave it his best shot, but was rusty enough that he missed the run. He recalled, "I took 232. I was being carried into shore. I put hand out and pushed away. Others were worse scared than I was—I haven't sense enough to be scared when I should be. Emery would scramble out and on top like a squirrel." Ellsworth piled into the fang rocks in the lower right corner of the rapid. The three men worked the boat out of the boulders and back down to the river below. Emery took back the oars. It was too late in the day to reach the abandoned scow and the men holed up for the night, lighting a tremendous driftwood fire for warmth.

Christmas morning dawned cold and somber in the Lower Granite Gorge. The men warmed up around a fire and began working through the remaining rapids toward the scow. "The rescuers hoped to find a message at the abandoned scow," wrote the papers, "or some indication of the route the adventuring couple intended to take when they left their homemade craft." There was still hope that the Hydes were alive somewhere.

The Kolbs found the scow just above Mile 237, eerily silent in a calm pool of water some thirty feet from shore. Ever aware of their movie business, the Kolbs pulled first to shore so that Emery could film the other two boarding the scow. *Rain-in-the-Face* sat low in the river, with over a foot of water in the low end of the boat. The sweep oars were still in place, floating in the river off each end of the craft as if Glen and Bessie had just paused to rest for a minute. All their gear was stowed in place. Glen's .30-30 stood in the corner. On the gunwale of the scow the Hydes had carved forty-two notches—one for each day of the trip, with a cross for each Sunday. They had left Hermit Rapid on day thirty. The bowline stretched from the front of the scow, taut, into the river. "The rope was fastened in a crevice in the rock," recalled Brooks. "We gave it a good stiff pull and there was no give to it—don't know how deep the water was." But as for Glen and Bessie? They had vanished.

It was hard to tell if the bilge water was from damage, from waves in the Hydes' last rapid, or simply from three weeks of leakage. The men began unloading gear, looking for clues. Some of the lower gear was soaked, much of it frozen to the boat. They found Glen and Bessie's hiking boots and warm coats. Bessie's camera was there, with six rolls of film. "There was a baked ham, untouched," recalled Ellsworth Kolb. "Also a full sack of flour. An old bed spring and blankets. A small suit-

Scow as the Kolbs found it

case which held some of Mrs. Hyde's better clothes. I wore a fur lined moleskin coat of his and some laced boots myself for ease of carrying."

They found the copy of the Kolbs' book Emery had given them. Tucked into the side of the boat where it could be quickly reached was Bessie's small red journal, wet, but readable. A hasty look at her final jottings showed the men little. Bessie's notes were terse and cryptic, but it appeared the last entry was Friday, November 30. That tallied with the gunwale notches. A quick attempt to decode Bessie's notations for rapids lead the Kolbs to think the Hydes had passed Diamond Creek before they vanished.

Ellsworth stood on the sweep deck for a while and hefted the sweep blades. He was amazed at how well-balanced they were, how easy it was to pivot the boat. Unable to dislodge the bowline, the Kolbs finally cut it. In later years Emery was criticized for cutting the rope. Perhaps, some thought, there might have been a body on the end. Emery, too, later felt remorse for the act. If the Hydes had been alive, somewhere out of earshot, working their way toward the scow, the Kolbs had just severed their best means of resupply and escape.

Ellsworth maneuvered the craft through the next riffle, still impressed with how well it handled. He told Emery he'd like to take it on downriver. Emery, remembering Ellsworth's performance at 232, and recalling the magnitude of the rapids still downstream, was adamant. No. They would take what gear they could carry and abandon the scow. Ellsworth did not press the issue.

"We would like to have investigated a little more," recalled Emery, "but with the sponge of a boat we had, and the extreme cold, made it terrible as our beds were wet and so frozen we could scarcely get them out of our hatch."

They took the gun, the diary, Glen's deer skin from Glen Canyon, and as much else as they could stow in their small leaky boat. What clothes they could not stow, they wore. Then they let the scow loose. In the first rapid it smashed a sweep on the wall, then wedged inextricably between two rocks.

Three miles downstream, they pulled to shore to scout the biggest rapid of their trip, Separation, named when three of Major Powell's men decided to leave the river and take their chances hiking out to the North Rim and the Mormon settlements beyond. After portaging the first drop of the rapid, Powell and his remaining five men ran the remainder with little worse than a good dousing. The three who left were never seen again. Emery picked his run and returned to the boat.

"Ellsworth was swept off in the upper end of Separation, but soon got back," recalled Emery. Dock Marston's note on an interview hints at Ellsworth's feelings about what happened next. "Emery ran up on rock—Emery was so sure of himself—I warned him."

The boat, said Emery, "must have weighed about fifteen hundred, and very hard to maneuver... I could not pull the heavy thing clear of a big rock and over she went."

Emery then illuminated why Ellsworth may have been a bit sore about the flip. In spite of the fact that the Kolb brothers and many others were quick and unrelenting in pointing out what an inexcusable mistake the Hydes made in not carrying life preservers, Emery stated, "I had a life preserver on and Brooks had a life preserver... My brother had a five-gallon can on his back for a life preserver."

Brooks vanished beneath the boat. Fortunately he was a resilient sort. "He had been a soldier in Yellowstone Park, before the troops were turned into Rangers," recalls Michael Harrison. "so he was an old-timer in the Park Service. A man of very few words. He was a thorough-going gentleman, a man I admired very much. But I always felt he was tough as a piece of old rawhide."

"I pulled my brother up on the boat when I got on," continued Emery:

> He said, "Where's Jimmy?" No Jimmy in sight. Finally his head popped up beside the boat and I grabbed him by the collar. And he said "Let me go!" and I let him go and down again he went. And for a long, long time I couldn't understand it. Finally his head come up again and I grabbed him again. He let me pull him up on the boat that time. What had happened—I'd put two standards [wooden posts] up on the boat for him to hold to—he was not a river man—he was a good outdoorsman but not a river man—and one of those standards found the only hole he had in the back of his overalls, and pinned him under the boat through that entire rapid.
>
> It was so cold when we got that boat uprighted, in a very short time all the stuff under the decks was frozen that got wet. From then on Brooks and my brother would climb over the walls if possible as I run the boat.

Darkness came early; the temperature plummeted. Their clothes were frozen solid by the time they made camp, and firewood was scarce. Upstream near Moab, Utah, it was so uncommonly cold that the Colorado had jammed solid with ice.

Frozen boaters: Jimmy Brooks, Ellsworth and Emery Kolb; John Nelson holding bowline

Spencer Canyon; standing: Jimmy Brooks, Emery Kolb,
John Nelson; seated: Ellsworth Kolb, Ancel Taylor

DEPUTY SHERIFF JOHN NELSON had been working on the search from the time R.C. Hyde first arrived in Peach Springs over a week earlier. No sooner had he come out of Diamond Creek from launching the Kolbs, than he left overland to retrieve them. Nelson, one-armed Hualapai guide and horsepacker Joe Weapu, Charles and Ancel Taylor, and a group of horses worked their way out past Milkweed Canyon, down the pack trail to the old Spencer Ranch in Meriwhitica Canyon, and down into Spencer Canyon to the river. "I ate Christmas dinner under a tree in the snow," said Nelson. The descent took longer than they had hoped. "It was a welcome sight," recalled Ancel Taylor, "to see them come around the bend of the river a short time after our arrival." Around a huge fire the shivering men thawed their clothes and bodies. "It was glorious," said Emery, "to sleep in dry clothes that night."

The debris fan of Spencer Canyon, before it was inundated by Lake Mead in the 1930s, formed one of the more infamous obstructions on the Colorado, Lava Cliff Rapid. There Major Powell had seen one of his boats break away from its lining ropes with George Bradley aboard. Powell and others chased after him in the other boat, only to swamp and be rescued by Bradley. The Kolbs had portaged through icy boulders there in January, 1912. They had few regrets about leaving the river this time. Nor had they grown overly fond of their boat. Before they left the river they sent the cumbersome, leaking craft into Lava Cliff unmanned.

The party met R.C. Hyde back in Peach Springs late in the evening of December 27, 1928. They turned over Bessie's journal, Glen's gun, and the few other remnants that had survived Kolb's flip in Separation. The Kolbs took Bessie's film back to the South Rim to develop. They had little encouragement for Hyde. They had seen no tracks whatsoever, not a trace of Glen or Bessie. Worse, whatever hiking gear the honeymooners owned was still aboard the scow when the Kolbs found it, as was their food and money. Whatever had become of them, they had certainly not left the boat intentionally. The last notch cut in the scow's gunwale was twenty-seven days old.

Hyde had been busy keeping tabs on the various searches, haranguing the Army for more airplanes, still hoping to find his son alive. Hope had flared briefly on the day after Christmas when an airplane from the Air Touring Line, sent out to look for the Hydes, sent a message back to

Kolbs
unloading
at Spencer
Canyon

Emery Kolb
exiting
Spencer
Canyon

The Girand boat's last run: Emery and Ellsworth Kolb, Jimmy Brooks

their home office: "PARTY SIGHTED FROM PLANE." The main office, jumping to conclusions, notified the press that the Hydes had been found. It was a short-lived story. When the pilots returned they clarified their message—they had seen Francy and Harbin, not the Hydes.

The next day another story flashed across the wires. Beulah Roth, an old friend of Bessie Hyde's from her YWCA days in Huntington, West Virginia, had just received a package in the mail from Bessie. "With the exception of a small greeting card with Mrs. Hyde's name written on it in her own handwriting, the package was not accompanied by any communication. It contained an ornament," said the *Huntington Advertiser.* "Miss Roth believed the couple might have gotten out of the canyon safely and returned to their homes unknowingly to the searchers," stated the *Parkersburg Sentinel.* By that evening the mystery was cleared up. Jeanne Hyde had mailed the parcel, along with several other Christmas packages that Bessie had prepared prior to her departure.

Still hungry for misinformation, newspapermen raced for a story from the Kolbs. On December 28 the Associated Press (AP) posted two conflicting stories out of Peach Springs. One stated that Emery Kolb felt "Hyde and his wife had perished in the swirling waters of the Colorado River," and that examination of the scow "indicated that disaster had overtaken them not far above where the scow was found lodged in the rocks which clog the tortuous canyon riverbed... It was pointed out," the story went on, that "both might have been thrown from their bounding boat while throwing their weights upon the long sweeps to steer the scow away from the rocks in the perilous rapids."

"Belief was expressed by the Kolbs," stated the other AP story, "that Hyde and Mrs. Hyde had deserted their scow and had set out to scale the walls of the canyon and attempt to reach civilization afoot. It appeared almost certain, the searchers said, that the couple had come to their deaths because of freezing weather and lack of food." Moreover, the article went on to describe "the finding of footprints in the snow at points along the rim above Diamond Creek by searchers who believed the prints were made by the Hydes."

Although the first story errs only in saying the boat was found in the rocks instead of calm water, the second appears to be complete fabrication. It is the only story that ever mentions footprints in the snow. A third AP story came out of Peach Springs that afternoon. "Despite evidence found by Emery Kolb, veteran river man...H.C. Hyde [sic], father of the missing man, has not given up the search... Unwilling to abandon the search without further evidence that the sullen river has taken its toll, the elder Hyde planned to start for Diamond Creek today to make an intensive search on foot. He is pinning his faith on the possibility that the young couple, possibly thrown out of their scow, or forced to abandon it, were unable to get back to it to obtain their supplies, and are attempting to walk out of the canyon."

The Kolb brothers left for Grand Canyon Village on the afternoon of December 28. Scarcely had they left when Hyde scrawled a letter to Emery. "Since you left I have been studying the diary and the map and best I can figure they could not have reached Diamond." Hyde felt that their journal did not allow enough time to make the forty miles from Lava Falls, which they had run on Day 39, to Diamond Creek by Day 42, when their journal ended. He directed his gaze upstream.

Hyde begged the Army for yet another air search of the shore and cliffs of the lower canyon. Major General Hines refused, said the newspapers, citing "the extreme hazard to army fliers from the air currents and the remote possibility of success." "The Hydes," the story concluded, "are believed to have perished."

Not according to R.C. Hyde. Barely allowing Deputy Sheriff Nelson time to brush his teeth, Hyde dragged him back to the river at Diamond Creek to begin a trek upstream. Hyde hoped to go ten or twelve miles looking for tracks, planning to meet Francy and Harbin two days hence. Although the cryptic notes in Bessie's journal hinted they had passed Diamond Creek, Hyde could not be sure. Despite increasingly dismal indications, he was unwilling to admit they could be dead. On the afternoon of December 29, the eighteenth day of the search, Hyde and Nelson reached the mouth of Diamond Creek and headed upstream. It was Bessie's twenty-third birthday.

R.C. Hyde

Waves
(Unlike mere men)
With ever different,
Endless song,
Send praise
To heaven.

—— Bessie Haley

17

⌒ December 20 1928 – January 1 1929 ⌒

WHEN HARBIN AND FRANCY ousted Patraw at the foot of the Bass Trail, they abandoned more than three hundred pounds of gear—nearly half their load. Greatly lightened, they found the going much easier, the *Bright Angel* less prone to swamping. With one less person, however, they did not have the manpower to line the boat around the rapids and Harbin took to running them. Although Francy rowed a good deal of the flat water, he had no desire to attempt a rapid, and would build a fire and watch from shore. "Handling a rapid," said Harbin, "is strictly coordination." Francy had somehow acquired top-notch life jackets, and they were fastidious about wearing them in rough water. Recalled Harbin, "I used to swim a lot but would have no chance in a rapid."

While scouting one rapid they found a set of oars—possibly those jettisoned by the Eddy party a year earlier when they lost a boat at Dubendorff Rapid. It was a lucky find. Shortly afterward, Harbin hit a rock, spun, and snapped an oar. A fragment of the oar shot back into Harbin's right side, fracturing his rib as the boat rocked up on edge and flipped over. Harbin vanished. "I stood on [a] rock and watched," Francy recalled. "I didn't think he'd come up but he had [a] life preserver on. He caught [a] life line and came up with the boat. After that I rode forward—would rather go with the boat than freeze to death in Canyon."

Francy rode through the rapids after that, bailing out the boat at the foot as Harbin kept rowing. Once they got to camp, Francy would sprint up the beach and light a fire while Harbin secured and unloaded the boat. They wore long red flannels, Levi's, heavy cloth jackets, shoes, and heavy socks. Nothing is much colder than wet cotton, and each night they would change into dry clothes as they stood around a raging bonfire drying their gear. The cold spell did not ease. The eddies continued freezing over at night, and their water buckets froze solid.

On Christmas Eve, Harbin came up to the fire and found two socks hanging and a bottle of whiskey sitting beneath. "We're celebrating," Francy said. The socks were still empty in the morning. So was the whiskey.

Their river trip nearly ended soon after. Even with their lightened load, the open back compartment acted like a scoop in waves, filling the stern and cockpit of the boat. "About two or three in the afternoon we got hung on a rock," remembered Francy, "right in the middle of the river and wedged boat so tight you couldn't shake it—front end raised and lower end went down. Were both in boat. I got out and went to bank, fifty feet to shore, taking rope with me and anchored it to a big rock. Got eats and beds out of hatch and ferried ashore. I went out to boat until dark—couldn't move it—water running into hatch and after compartment."

Bob Francy, left; Jack Harbin, right

With the *Bright Angel* totally swamped, the men spent a discouraging night on shore. The next morning the river had risen six inches, worsening the situation. Using cottonwood logs to raft out to the boat, the men took the hatch lid off the forward compartment and braced it vertically on the upstream side of the cockpit to prevent water from pouring in. They bailed as quickly as they could with a gallon bucket—until it slipped out of their numb fingers and sank. Desperate, they fashioned a scoop out of a piece of metal and kept bailing. The change of buoyancy caused the boat to shift suddenly and, recalled Francy, the "boat shot out and ran to end of rope and it jerked both of us out of boat. It was the happiest moment I've ever had."

They finally arrived at Havasu Creek and camped for the night. Early the next morning they hiked the thirteen miles to the Havasupai Village, crisscrossing Havasu Creek and clambering around the huge, spectacular waterfalls. "We walked up to Supai and talked to Hyde by phone," recalled Francy. "Havasu took all day long and was hardest work. Hyde urged us to go on and make all speed we could." Hyde told them of his hunch that Glen and Bessie might have lost the boat somewhere above Diamond Creek and become stranded. Telling them to look everywhere for tracks, he agreed to meet them at Diamond Creek on New Year's Day. Harbin and Francy each carried forty pounds of supplies back to the *Bright Angel*, arriving at the river late that night.

The next day they scouted Lava Falls. They felt it would be impossible to line around it with just the two of them, and the boat was too big to portage. With no choice, Francy and Harbin became the third known party to run the cataract, George Flavell and Ramón Montéz being the first in the winter of 1896, and the Hydes being the second. Dock Marston's notes on an interview with Harbin are unclear, but indicate a wild and very painful run. "Francy said it seemed like hours—I looked at wave—water boiling so I didn't bail out—I shot loose—breaker board struck spine and I still have to have treatments—for a long time I couldn't straighten up."

On the morning of December 30, 1928, Francy and Harbin scouted 217-Mile Rapid. Glen Hyde's tracks were there, as they had been at nearly every major rapid. The storm that had inundated the Hydes on Halloween, temporarily doubling the flow of the river, had coated every

Harbin and Francy at Diamond Creek

sand bar with a slimy layer of mud. Slow to dry, the mud preserved the Hydes' tracks perfectly. "We checked every creek—thought once I saw his tracks going up canyon—we found no further trace—we found no trace of fires," Harbin recalled seeing both Glen and Bessie's tracks until the last few rapids. Only Glen's tracks were visible at the last few. "Last time I saw footsteps, could see footsteps going down and back to scow marks—saw where he tied scow."

Harbin and Francy had been making especially good time below Havasu. After scouting 217, they ran it and stroked for Diamond Creek, just eight more miles downstream. A few river bends above Diamond Creek and a day ahead of schedule, they surprised Hyde and Nelson.

Harbin and Francy were "about done up," Hyde wrote to Mr. Haley. "One of them said that he would not make the trip again for $5,000. They had gone 140 miles."

The four of them rowed down to Diamond Creek. The *Bright Angel* was in rough shape. They had punctured it in several places, with one hole, Francy recalled, the size of a plate. Harbin said the bottom needed replacing—that he could push his thumb deep into the rotten wood. Both men had had about enough of river boating anyhow, and they bequeathed the boat to Nelson. The four men dragged it high up on the shore above flood level and tied it to a mesquite tree. Nelson guessed it to weigh at least half a ton.

"I was ready to quit," said Harbin. "We came out by flivver. We got to Peach Springs, I ordered ham and eggs. Then second order. Then two pounds of candy. By the time we arrived at Williams I had consumed all the candy."

"Bob and I went through river for thirty days and we never had a cross word."

IT MUST HAVE seemed like thirty days, even though it had only been two weeks. Francy and Harbin's little-acclaimed trip through lower Grand Canyon was a remarkable feat, in extreme conditions. The haggard team returned to the South Rim, arriving on New Year's Day, ready for a break. But Nelson, who still had not had any time off since the search began, had already succumbed to another of Hyde's requests. They gassed up Nelson's Ford and headed west to Needles, California, then doubled back northwest to Utah.

It was January 1, 1929, and R.C. Hyde was entering the third week of his search. "...ALMOST SURE THEY ARE IN THE HILLS I GO TO SAINT GEORGE UTAH NOW WILL GET SEVERAL SEARCH PARTIES OUT HORSEBACK," Hyde telegraphed to Haley. In a letter to his daughter Jeanne, he elaborated:

> If they lost the boat where the tracks stopped and got out on the South Side they could make their way down to Diamond Creek by climbing over one hill. They could have made Diamond Creek in one day and as Kolb had told them all about Diamond Creek and that it was only 22 miles from the railroad it would seem sure that they would go out there.
>
> If they were left on the North Side it would be different. It is 100 miles north and northwest before they could reach anyone. They could not follow down the river but would have to climb up to the first bench. Then they could follow on a long way but could not get down to the river or out. But after a while they could reach the second bench and also the third. If they got out on the third bench they could go on North and likely find someone before long.

In a letter to Emery Kolb, Hyde confessed, "I realize this is likely of no avail but I wish to leave nothing undone that can be done." With Nelson's help, the indomitable Hyde would now launch an all-out search of the north side of Grand Canyon.

Some people,
Are ambitionless;
And only,
Now and then,
Catch a
Glimpse of it—
Through others.

— *Bessie Haley*

18

*T*HE AMERICAN PRESS took Emery Kolb at his word—Glen and Bessie Hyde were dead—and moved on to new stories. The Hydes had provided papers with thirteen days of sensational news, but with the exception of a few summaries in local papers, the honeymooners were already history. Few papers looked beyond the immediate story for a purpose, a moral, a meaning.

The *San Francisco Chronicle* ran a small editorial on Christmas Eve, describing the peril of Major Powell's 1869 journey, and concluded:

> Mr. and Mrs. Glen Hyde, now lost in the canyon, certainly could not have been advised of the perils of such a honeymoon voyage. An anxious country watching the search with hope that they will be found and rescued also hopes that the advertisement they have given of the desperate character of this adventure will deter others. The Grand Canyon voyage is not one to be undertaken without pressing reason.

Jeanne Hyde was outraged and fired back a rebuttal.

> ...Mr. and Mrs. Hyde were not a couple of foolhardy youngsters who decided on a trip down a river of which they knew comparatively nothing in search of a peaceful honeymoon. They had read all available material concerning the river before they started, including

the account of Major Powell's trip. They knew just what they were attempting....

Mrs. Hyde shares my brother's love for adventure and, knowing his skill with boats in the past, was anxious to go on the Colorado River trip. She did not go for notoriety and neither did he. There happen to be some people in the world who do such things for the love of it. There happen to be some people who retain enough of that love of roughing it and living, if only for a short time, after the manner of our ancestors, to attempt such a trip. Such are Mr. and Mrs. Hyde. They cared enough for that sort of adventure to take a chance....

People in Idaho, on the other hand, understood the adventure's significance. In a farewell editorial on December 30, the *Lewiston Sentinel* described Hyde's Salmon and Colorado River trips and summed up:

> It is difficult to believe that Glen Hyde is dead. Men of his stamp like life too well to give it up easily. He liked life and he also dared it. Few were more experienced in navigating wild rivers, as witness his exploits in Idaho and Canada. Few men were braver, more resourceful or resilient to prolonged and bitter hardship. But his skill and endurance were not enough to conquer the Colorado...
>
> Lewiston people will hope that the river experts are wrong, that the Hydes have in some way made their way to safety. Men of the west like him are too rare, too courageous to be lost overnight.

But certainly the most eloquent tribute was in Glen Hyde's home town paper, the *Idaho Evening Times* of Twin Falls. On December 19, in the heat of the search, the *Times* ran the following editorial:

> CHALLENGES WE MEET
>
> Old Mother Nature still has challenges for us to meet. As this is written government planes are whirring over the yawning seam in the earth that is known as the Grand Canyon of the Colorado that traces of Mr. and Mrs. Hyde of Hansen may be found.
>
> In their attempts to conquer the turbulent stream in their home-made scow, relatives fear that the Idaho couple may have met disaster. So a search is made in an effort to discover just what has happened

and to lend succor if it is needed. Their daring may have brought them death, or they may have been marooned. In either event the world, along with relatives, will want to know the result of the adventure.

Of what use are such daring exploits? we can hear timid souls asking. Of what use indeed? No one will be the richer in dollars and cents by the success of their attempt to ride the treacherous river through its box canyon. The exploration was not made in the interest of science as we understand it. Yet we hold firmly to the belief that these bold young people have added to the richness of life by the daring they have displayed.

Life is not a cut and dried proposition. It may be to some few of us who live by rule and rote. There are others who demand the more spectacular, even the dangerous, before their lives can be lived. We of sedentary habits may decry their daring and the risks they take—unnecessary by our standards—but life would be a sorry spectacle if all of humanity were cast in the mold of the commonplace.

We ardently hope that Glen Hyde and his wife are safe. He grew to manhood on farms on this Twin Falls tract. Quiet in his deportment, slow speaking, in no sense a seeker of the short-lived fame we know as notoriety, his is of that mold that sees Mother Nature's big spectacles as obstacles to man's control that challenge him. The canyon of the Snake River intrigued him as a boy, we happen to know. Even so did the canyon of the Colorado. He answered the challenge.

The desire to fly, the desire to scale mountains never before conquered by man, the desire to make speed in vehicles propelled on the earth have all been challenges. They were answered by venturesome souls, some of whom lost their lives. The claim that the exploit down the Colorado had slight possibility of utilitarian benefit to humanity might be made as an argument against it. Such argument would be true enough, but the studied courage displayed in carrying out the exploit is of a sort that humanity needs, even though death be the price that is paid in exercising it.

Mouth of Grand
Canyon at Grand
Wash Cliffs. Now
beneath Lake Mead

Deserted town;
With crumbling shacks.
Where once men drank,
And played for yellow dust.
Then a whisper came,
And the gold-crazed horde
Moved on.

— Bessie Haley

19

~ January – February 1929 ~

Saint George, Utah
Jan. 1, 1929

*D*EAR JEANNE;

Just arrived Saint George where I came to get pack train to search the country north of the River. I got a Mr. Nelson to bring me over from Peaches [sic] Springs… I am sending men who know that country just like we know the ranch. One of them lives there. I haven't all arrangements made yet, but will in the morning. Mr. Nelson a former cattle man in this country got the men for me…

Next day. We did not get off today. The old Ford that we came in had a bad cough and Nelson thought it best to have it fixed up before starting as it will be bad road, almost no road at all. We start in the morning Nelson and I and three others, two more men will join us at the stock camp which we hope to reach with the cars. It will likely take all day tomorrow to reach the camp 90 miles, then we will take saddle horses and separate into three parties of two each and search all of the benches first, then the country on top. I have no idea how long we will be. It may be ten or fifteen days, but maybe not so long. There will be no way for me to get telegrams or letter but if such a thing should happen, always possible, that you hear from Glen, telegraph proprietor of the Liberty Hotel in Saint George and tell him to send word. Anything else don't send word as it would likely cost 25 or 50 dollars to send a man to tell us. I have arranged for him to do that if necessary....

Papa

Deputy Sheriff John Nelson was back on his home turf. He had cowboyed on the north side of the river for years before crossing over to Peach Springs. Called the Arizona Strip, the territory encompasses an isolated tract of Arizona, squeezed between Grand Canyon and the Utah border. It was a relatively lawless area, being hundreds of miles via California and Nevada from the county seat in Kingman, Arizona, and peopled chiefly by renegade Mormons who had broken off from the Utahans. There were rumors that Nelson had been run off for rustling cattle, but there were rumors like that about nearly anyone who moved on, and about many who stayed.

Nelson enlisted four rugged ranch hands: Ross Mills, Jack Spencer, Charles Walters, and Jim Hudson. Within a year Hudson would have to leave the Arizona Strip country after killing a man known as "The Greek" over a water dispute.

Hyde and Walters drove southwest to Grand Wash and followed its course down toward the Colorado. At Tassi Springs they borrowed a horse and worked their way east toward the Grand Wash Cliffs where the river debouches from Grand Canyon. Tassi, wrote Hyde to Haley a week later:

> is just a squatter place ten miles from the river and about 40 miles from where Glen's boat was found. Here we got a pack horse and going to the river followed up as far as we could, looking especially for tracks in the sand. I thought they might have tried to make it down river as Glen said he would stick to the river because of no water on the desert.
>
> We found no sign of anyone having been there. Finally we were forced to climb up on a bench on the cliffs. We went as far as the pack horse could go and I went on a way farther but found no sign. Feeling certain that they had not endeavored to come out that way we came back to St. George last night.
>
> The other party did not come in. I do not expect them for several

days. All I can do now is to wait. These are all men who have cattle running between here and the river. They know all of the country and if they do not find any trace of them I feel sure that they are not there. I can only wait until they come in.

Glen and Bessie would not starve nor die of thirst on the upper benches. There is a little snow and things enough to eat to keep one from starving especially cactus. Glen took a water proof match safe with him and they would have matches. While they should have been out before now if ashore, it is hard to say. From the river to the rim is up 4000 feet and so many places you think you can get through and finally come to a wall. There are several places through which one can get out all right. All I can do now is to wait for these men to come in.

Hyde and Walters had worked their way nearly thirty miles upriver from Tassi but, when forced to turn back, they were still ten miles below where the scow was found.

Nelson, Mills, Hudson, and Spencer left Saint George in Nelson's Ford on the morning of January 3, heading one hundred rough dirt miles south toward cattleman Slim Waring's winter camp. There, on the Shivwits Plateau, the most remote part of the Arizona Strip, the road ended. Nelson enlisted Waring and one of his cowboys, Roy Dickerson, and the men broke into three mounted parties.

Hudson and Dickerson went south to Kelly Point, at the very tip of the Shivwits Plateau. They worked their way off the rim and down as far as the top of the Redwall Limestone—a prominent cliff barrier throughout Grand Canyon. Unable to find a way off the Redwall, they worked their way upstream several miles to a point overlooking Mile 227, then returned to Kelly Point. Waring and Mills descended the Snyder Trail to the river at Mile 219. From there they worked their way downstream along the Tonto Platform, a few hundred feet above the river, to around Mile 228. Finding nothing, they retraced their tracks upstream.

Nelson and Jack Spencer worked their way down an old Indian trail, known locally as the Spencer Trail, reaching the river near Mile 206. He described what they found in a letter to Emery Kolb:

We hit the river about four miles above a large island.... About half a mile below the island on the West Side we found one of Hydes' camps. Just above a small rapid.... We found in the camp a four pound Swift Jewell lard can, top on, and one baby lima bean uncooked in it. Also a empty can of fruit or tomatoes as the label had come off. He also throwed a empty Prince Albert can in the fire. Also had eaten eggs as the shells were laying there.

You could see her track very plain in the sand as she had changed shoes and wore the slipers [sic] that were in the boat. He had not changed shoes and his tracks were very dim, could just tell. There was a big track where the wet sand had stuck to the shoes. The next morning she walked down the river below the rapid and a little rifel [sic]. You could see her tracks once in a while in the wet sand. Could not see no sign in the blow sand.

They found several more lima beans on the ground and pocketed them. About a mile below the camp they saw a "bad little rapid," most likely the drop at Mile 212, that only manifests itself at very low water. Across the river they saw Francy and Harbin's fresh tracks and a stake they had driven into the sand to tie up their boat. Nelson and Spencer met Waring and Dickerson near Mile 219, and the four men returned to the rim in a snowstorm. Back in Saint George, Hyde identified the fruit can and lima beans as coming from his farm in Hansen. Hyde paid the cowboys and thanked them for their work.

Nelson's two parties had covered the north shore from well above Glen and Bessie's last camp at Mile 210, to Mile 228, well below Diamond Creek, nine miles upstream of the scow. Hudson and Dickerson had traversed the Redwall for an additional six or seven miles downstream. Hyde and Walters had come upstream to within ten miles of the scow. And the Kolbs had scanned all the sandbars, looking for tracks, from twelve miles above the scow to nine miles below it. Yet other than the Hydes' last campsite, Glen's tracks at Mile 217 Rapid, and the scow itself, no one had found a trace of Glen or Bessie. Although evidence pointed ever stronger to their death by drowning, Hyde could not accept it until he was sure. Absolutely sure. Deputy Sheriff John Nelson was heading back to Peach Springs. Hyde, twenty-three days into his search, accompanied him.

When they reached Peach Springs, Hyde made plans to go back to the river and work his way up the south bank as far as their last camp. Because no tracks had been seen below there, Hyde had reasoned they might well have lost the boat at that camp. Nelson, who had searched longer than anyone except R.C. Hyde himself, finally declined to go on. He wrote to Kolb, "Mr. Hyde…went in today to spend three days or two weeks on the river, he would not state any length of time. I tried to talk him out of it…. I can't just figure him out."

"The old man seemed to be throwing his money away," Nelson later recalled. "I wired his daughter to get him to come home—he wanted to do more."

HYDE WAS NOW ALONE in his belief that anything could still be done. Alone and broke. He had spent everything he had on the search, had borrowed money from his son-in-law Carl Emerson, and was in debt to several others. Francy and Harbin had not yet been paid.

When Hyde had contracted with Francy for the search, he had made out two checks, for five hundred dollars each. The first was to be cashed if Francy stopped at Havasu Creek. The second was contingent upon them going all the way through Grand Canyon. In addition, had Francy and Harbin actually found the Hydes, they would have collected the thousand-dollar reward. Both five-hundred-dollar checks were held at the Williams Arizona Central Bank. Later, when Francy and Harbin met Hyde near Diamond Creek, they offered to give him back one of the checks, but Hyde refused it.

Yet after they returned home, Francy and Harbin found that Hyde had inexplicably stopped payment on both checks. Herein appears to lie one of the few aberrations in Hyde's boiler-plate integrity. Bob Emerson, R.C. Hyde's grandson, knew Hyde until his death. "My grandfather was very honest, and a humanitarian. He would never have reneged on anything. Unless maybe he didn't have it—maybe he'd spent all he had and couldn't cover the checks."

Francy consulted County Attorney Tom McCarty in Flagstaff, who filed suit against Hyde. Francy claimed he was out two hundred dollars in cash and had worn out his five hundred dollar boat. Grand Canyon residents were appalled at the crassness of the lawsuit. South Rim resident L.A. Bailey upbraided McCarty in a letter for filing suit "against that old man who, I am reliably informed, is fast losing his mind over the loss of his son..." Francy settled for seven hundred dollars which, prorated for a trip ending at Diamond Creek instead of the Grand Wash Cliffs as contracted, was just about right. Yet the blemish on Hyde's character remains.

"All the officials have helped in every way they could," Hyde wrote Haley, "all excepting the sheriff." Apparently the sheriff in Saint George, shying from the enormity of the task or sensing ultimate futility, had refused to help.

"I sure have a line on human nature," Hyde wrote to Jeanne, "some are anxious to graft, others will do all they can and very reasonable, and the two Kolb brothers would not take a cent. Emery Kolb from Grand Canyon put in ten days time and would not accept anything. His brother from Los Angeles would not even let me pay his fare from Los Angeles, but I gave the money to Emery Kolb to give him after they would be on the way."

"I gathered that funds were limited with Hyde," recalled Ellsworth Kolb, "but told him nothing doing when he offered to pay my expenses. Later, he complained that the two men who kept a lookout at Pierce's Ferry charged him plenty."

R.C. HYDE doggedly returned to the river and headed upstream toward Glen and Bessie's final camp. It was January 17, 1929, and Hyde had now been hunting for his son for thirty-seven days. The terrain was rough and he took no pack animal, carrying his scant supplies on his back. In three more months he would be seventy years old.

"Now he has gone back to the river," Jeanne Hyde wrote Mrs. Haley:

> ...to go over again the ground between where the tracks were last seen and where the boat was found... Had I known that Papa was going over that ground again alone I should have gone down to go with him. He has probably covered the territory by now. I hate to think of him being alone on that tramp but perhaps he prefers it that way and he writes that he is well.

R.C. Hyde wrote to Mrs. Haley:

> It was mainly in the hope of finding them that I went back to the River alone at the last. But I could do very little walking along shore and could only reach one side. I had planned to run the river with the boat that was left at Diamond Creek and reach the other side. But when I got there I found that I could not get up the river from where I would land on the other side and it was impossible to get the boat up river.
>
> It was impossible to get anyone to go with me. All the people in this country are afraid of the river and none of them are boatmen. The only ones I could have gotten to go were the Kolbs and the two who came down river and I could not ask them to go again.…
>
> I am glad that I went back to the river and made my way on foot all the way along where the accident happened. I made certain that if Glen and Bessie had gotten ashore they would have gotten out. The people in this vicinity tell such stories of the country and that there are few places that one can get out. This was my worst worry, that they were trapped between the river and the rim. I satisfied myself that this could not be…

When he returned to Peach Springs, Hyde received word from Nevada that put his heart in his throat. "Dead Man Found," headlined the *Las Vegas Review*. "May Be Hyde." M.J. Barone, an Italian naturalist traveling up the Colorado River near Las Vegas, had found a small stone monument near the mouth of a small wash. A note stuffed into the monument read: "Slim, I am taking this road. It looks good to me." Barone, curious, followed the trail into a small dead-end canyon. At the end he found the body of a young man. Authorities were quick to assume the body was that of Glen Hyde.

It was not long before papers in the dead man's pockets gave them the name of Frederick Cutler of Salt Lake City. Cutler rushed to the scene and identified the man as his son Cecil, twenty-six, who had last been heard of in Zion Canyon on December 2, heading for Las Vegas. Death was from starvation and exposure.

ELLSWORTH KOLB had spent two weeks visiting with Emery at the South

Rim and was on the train back to Los Angeles when it stopped for a few minutes at Peach Springs. "Getting off the train at Peach Springs I ran into Mr. Hyde, who had gone upstream on a fruitless search," recalled Kolb. "He couldn't get over a sort of obsession that his son was alive, perhaps injured, and needing help.... He came back to Los Angeles with me, then returned home. ...The editor of a Shoshone Falls paper wrote us a letter of thanks for our efforts and stated that the family was highly respected."

It was day forty-one of the search when Hyde finally threw in the sponge. At least for a while.

On January 30, Jeanne Hyde wrote again to Mrs. Haley:

> I too, wish the youngsters bodies might be found, though sometimes I think even yet that they may turn up alive. It is only a fanciful dream, founded on no facts at all, only an irrational hope so don't let me influence you with it, for I know it is only because I do not want even yet to give up hope. They are undoubtedly dead, but if I only could know, one way or the other. At least we know they were remarkably successful as far as they went. What happened we can never know, but it must have been some foolish trick of fate, rather than lack of skill on their parts...
>
> Papa is home, tho I haven't seen him. He got off the train at Hansen, and I have been snowed in at Kimberly for a week. We tried to drive to Hansen to meet him, but could not get through the snow. He walked out to the ranch and now he is snowed in.

ROLLIN C. HYDE sat alone in his old house by the wood stove. He had no electricity, no plumbing, no phone. The snow shrieked across the barren fields, rattling the windows, howling through the cracks. He shoved another stick into the fire to drive off the chill and bleakness. He was beaten again, busted again, but he was not through. He would go back. Somehow, somewhere, he would find them.

"I am going back to the river again," Hyde wrote Mrs. Haley. " I don't know when. I will try to find out when would be the best time. I think after a while I can get Ellsworth Kolb to go with me and Jeanne wants to go. I have very little hope of finding anything, but it will maybe satisfy me. I have notified the Sheriffs on both sides of the river offering a reward."

He wrote to Emery Kolb, asking when the best time to go down the river might be. Should he wait until fall, after high water? Or would it be better to go now? Although he acknowledged he was only looking for their bodies now, he could not stop looking.

> Hansen Idaho
> Feb. 22, 1929
> Dear Mrs. Haley;
>   Your kind letter received a few days ago. There is little I can write in reply...
>   Bessie was a wonderful girl and different from any I have known, and Glen—you know, he and I had been together just we two for a long time. If it ever came home to me that they would not come back, I don't know what I would do.

R.C. and Glen

Upper Granite Gorge, near mile 103, looking upstream, November 21, 1928, Hyde photo

Dreams
Foolishness you say
For many times they are broken.

I wonder
From all your dreams
Have you no tiny token?

— Bessie Haley

20

⌒ November 17–30 1928 ⌒

℞. *C.* HYDE had gained a masterful knowledge of the lower Grand Canyon. He knew exactly where he had, and had not, looked. Now in the frozen winter of southern Idaho, he had little else to ponder and few clues outside of Bessie's cryptic journal on which to base his reasoning.

Ellsworth Kolb, hoping to figure out what had happened to the Hydes, had taken the liberty of copying Bessie's notes before returning the journal to R.C. Hyde. Since their story was well established above Phantom Ranch, Kolb only transcribed their entries following their visit with Emery. Jeanne Hyde later said she destroyed the original journal, although she did write a much-embellished version that survives. Unfortunately, in Jeanne's rendition it is difficult to distinguish Bessie's record from Jeanne's elaborations. Kolb's unadulterated copy of the journal, then, is the only authentic document that can give us some idea of what the last two weeks of the honeymoon voyage were like. A thorough examination of the journal helps to illuminate those ruminations that R.C. Hyde, the Kolb brothers, and others made about Bessie and Glen's fate.

Copy of Mrs. Glen Hydes notes.

KOLB BROTHERS

Fri. at Kolb Studio ART SHOP, LECTURE ROOM STUDIO
Grand Canyon, Arizona

Sat. (Oct.17) Mr. Sutro with us. left about noon. Bad headwind 6 Rapids. Had to use rope at one. Camped without springs.

It is unclear whether the dates in parentheses were in the original diary, or were added by Ellsworth Kolb. They do, however, match the 1928 calendar. Trying to replicate Bessie's count of rapids is difficult, as every person perceives rapids differently.

Emery Kolb assumed the Hydes had tried to line the scow through Horn Creek Rapid. Yet trying to line Horn Creek with a two-ton boat and insufficient manpower would have been disastrous. "Had to use rope at one," more likely refers to their escape from the eddy where John Baer described them: "They hauled the boat from the shore upstream…"

After discussing the trip with Adolph Sutro, Marston concluded the Hydes had spent the night a mile below Horn Creek Rapid on the left bank.

Sun. (18th.) Head wind. 4 Rapids. 2nd Monument Rapid. Met guides and had lunch at Hermit Rapids. 3 Hermit Rapid. 4 Bouchre.

After running Granite Falls (Monument Creek) in the morning, the Hydes bade Sutro farewell at Hermit Camp and continued downstream through Hermit and Boucher Rapids.

Mon. (19ᵗʰ.) 6 Rapids. nos. 2-3-4 ―almost ―one. Crystal Creek Rapid Camped in afternoon

The first rapid below Boucher is Crystal Creek, which at the time was a relatively minor rapid. Glen and Bessie had no trouble there and continued down through Tuna Creek and Agate Rapids. Below Agate they pulled ashore in a small driftwood-clogged eddy on the north shore and camped for two nights.

Tues. (20ᵗʰ.) Camped all day as I didn't feel well.

Some of the after-the-fact reminiscences from the Hydes' visit to Grand Canyon Village give the impression that Bessie was not feeling well even then. If Francy's story is accurate and they had had an altercation at Hermit, that too could contribute to a lack of spunk. Another theory is that Bessie was pregnant. Glen's comment in a letter to his father from Lee's Ferry, "Bessie is feeling fine and eating everything but the boat," could allude to an anticipation of morning sickness. And the photographs of Bessie by Kolb and Sutro show a fullness that one historian guessed was due to pregnancy. Or she could just have been sick. Regardless, a photograph Glen took below Agate shows a bedraggled Bessie in a disheveled camp.

Wed. (21ˢᵗ.) 16 Rapids, Cable after 8ᵗʰ. Rapid. 9 at Bass Creek Rapid. Cable before 12ᵗʰ Rapid.

Layover camp below Agate Rapid, November 20, 1928, Glen Hyde photo

There were cable crossings at both Bass (8th Rapid)—where Francy and Harbin had ejected Patraw and noticed Glen's tracks—and just above Hakatai (12th Rapid). Depending on what Bessie termed rapids, they would have camped that night in the vicinity of Mile 115 to 120. This would have put them below the Upper Granite Gorge, the forty-mile long dark and foreboding stretch of river that holds the lion's share of major rapids in Grand Canyon. They would have had good reason for optimism as the walls opened up.

Thurs. (22nd.) 18 Rapid's. High walls on right between 17 and 18. 18th Rapid bad. Got caught in eddy. Glen stayed up with boat all night.

The Hydes made good progress, running down through Stephen Aisle and Conquistador Aisle and into the Middle Granite Gorge. At

Portage at Bedrock, November 23, 1928, Hyde photo

Bedrock (18th) Rapid, however, they had a particularly nasty run. At Bedrock, the current pinches toward the left side of the river and piles straight into a monolithic island of granite. The safe run here is to go into the shallow water to the right of the island. The force of the current, however, piles to the left of the island and down a corkscrew bedrock maze. Glen and Bessie were hurled down the left.

Halfway down the left side there is a tight and nearly inescapable eddy on the left shore. Many a modern day boatman who has missed the right run has ended up trapped in the left eddy and required many attempts to get out. Glen and Bessie were solidly marooned in the eddy.

Throughout the night, Glen struggled with the boat in the surging eddy, trying to keep it from dashing itself to bits on the granite crags.

Friday. (23ᵈ:) Spent all day getting boat on rocks. Smashed sweep.

Rain-in-the-Face weighed approximately two tons. How the Hydes managed to drag the boat up onto the boulders along the left shore boggles the mind. They may have carried a block and tackle. The photographs they took show merely that they accomplished it. One of the sweeps had been shattered during the struggle.

> Sat. (24ᵗʰ.) Launched "Rain in the Face" (boat) about noon. Minded boat. 2 Rapids. (no.) 2 Mean. Rocks and bad waves.

The boat was damaged during the adventure at Bedrock, but not irreparably. Rapid No. 2 was Dubendorff, and Bessie was understating it as being mean. In low water the current piles down the violent left side, where several fang-like rocks protrude between the crashing waves and holes. It is doubtful they could have avoided all the violence.

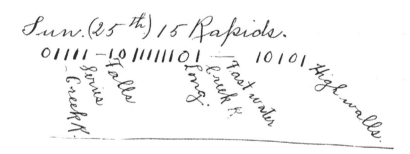

> Sun. (25ᵗʰ) 15 Rapids.
> O I I I I — I O I I I I I I O I — I O I O I
> Serio Creek R. / Falls / Long. / Duck R. / Fast water / High walls.

Here we are introduced to Bessie's code. An 0 is presumed to be a riffle, a 1 is a rapid and a dash is flat water.

Once below Dubendorff the Middle Granite Gorge ends, and there are few serious rapids (Upset Rapid at mile 150, and Lava Falls at mile 179) until the Lower Granite Gorge begins near Diamond Creek. Glen and Bessie were making good time again. They passed Tapeats Creek on the right, a beautiful clear spring-fed stream, then Deer Creek Falls, which plunges over a hundred feet from a cleft in the rocks to a pool at river level. Below Deer Creek the rock strata slowly dive below river level until the river is bordered by sheer Muav Limestone walls on both sides. Their camp appears to have been in the Muav Gorge somewhere below Kanab Creek.

Mon. (26ᵗʰ) *Rapids.* *Rocks in middle river.*
(?) *Creeks.*

That morning they likely passed a small creek at Matkatamiba Canyon and ran Upset Rapid. Five miles below is a large pile of lime-stone boulders in mid-river, and two miles past that is Havasu Creek. From Havasu it is another nine miles to a small beach on the right below Tuckup Canyon. This may well have been their campsite, as they paused here to take five photographs. Looking upstream at the boat, Bessie took two of Glen, posing at the sweeps. Then, switching places, Glen took three of Bessie. These were the last photographs they took.

There is little in the journal or the pictures that gives insight into how Glen and Bessie were getting along. Yet there is, in these last pictures, at least, an implicit understanding, a cooperation to pose for portraits. Glen, hair neatly combed and pipe in mouth; Bessie, hair combed, hat on, hat off, challenging the camera. It seems likely things were going well.

Tues. (27ᵗʰ) 101001 000+ 01 0000+1+
Long Brook(?)p *Spread* *Long Rock in River* *Hot Springs*
Rain *at end of 2ⁿᵈ+* ." *P.*
Did wash.

Bessie has now added a + to her code. Perhaps a landing made? They worked their way on down through several riffles to Vulcan's Anvil, a large lava boulder resting prominently in the middle of the river. One mile below is Lava Falls, one of the most notorious rapids on the river. They appear to have run it without ceremony and landed at the springs

Glen below Tuckup Canyon, Bessie Hyde photo

below on the left. In the midsummer heat, most present-day river runners fail to notice how warm the water is. On a freezing sunless afternoon in late November, it must have felt positively hot. It appears they
camped there, and perhaps did the wash as well.

> Wed. (28th) // 00000000000 /
> Fast water in between.
> Could only travel a little on account of
> bad wind.

Below Lava Falls the current speeds up noticeably, and the river
winds through gravel bars and riffles for several miles. Even with good
current, however, the winds forced them to call it quits after a few
miles. Their final rapid of the day may well have been at 185-Mile Rapid,
just five miles below Lava Falls, or could have been three miles farther
at Whitmore Wash. It was the night of the full moon, and their camp
was lit as if with a searchlight.

Bessie below Tuckup Canyon, Glen Hyde photo

Thurs. (29ᵗʰ.) Thanksgiving Day.
1001 – 12 Riffles 1 – 6 Riffles (꘏꘏꘏)
– 1 0 0 0 0 0 0 1 0 0
Fairly bad   *Series*   *long & long*

Saw a deer.

On the move again, Glen and Bessie snaked their way down through the broken walls of the Hurricane fault zone and through 205-Mile Rapid, which is, indeed, fairly rough. From there they drifted through a series of riffles and a small rapid at Mile 209, and pulled into camp a short distance below. John Nelson later found their camp, their tracks, their lima beans, and their fruit, lard, and Prince Albert tobacco cans.

The river, which had been steadily falling for ten days, began a slow rise while they were at this camp. With the haphazard tie-up arrangements Sutro complained of, their boat could easily have escaped. But it didn't.

Friday (30th.)

0 0 0 0 1000 11101 10001 1111 11101

Series.   *Long.*   *Creek.*   *Small Creek.*

This ends the notes.

Leaving their final camp at Mile 210, they entered the Lower Granite Gorge, ran 217-Mile Rapid, a long S-curved affair. Francy and Harbin had made note of Glen's final tracks at the head of this rapid. The Hydes continued on through a series of small rapids and riffles above Diamond Creek. The creek with a series of rapids almost has to be Diamond Creek. A few more rapids follow, then Travertine Creek pours in from the left, mid-rapid. Bessie notes one more riffle and a rapid, and the journal ends.

THE KOLB BROTHERS tried to piece together what might have happened, based on what the journal said, what they themselves found in the lower gorge, and what they knew of the Hydes' history. "Someone told me Mrs. Hyde said she would hold the painter of the scow while her husband looked the rapids over," wrote Ellsworth Kolb. "Once she was nearly pulled in when a sudden gust of wind blew against the boat. This gave me the idea that such an incident could have been the cause of their trouble. That she was dragged in, and her husband went to rescue her and was unsuccessful."

Just days after he returned from the search, Emery Kolb wrote to Julius Stone, the river runner who had helped Emery and Ellsworth get started on the river years earlier.

The last definite place they mention is Lava Falls, then three days more, long stretches of quiet water, then 16 rapids in a day. We all know there is no such run of rapids above Diamond, and we do not think that big boat with both sweeps down could go from Diamond to near Separation without smashing at least the oars, especially when we consider that we turned it loose and in the first little rapid it shipped much water, ran into the wall and smashed one of the oars off.

Yet less than one month later, Emery wrote a puzzling letter to riverman Dave Rust, apparently referring to R.C. Hyde's final trek upstream.

> ...reporting the last eight miles above Diamond, Mr. Hyde found his son's tracks a mile below. Track showed a leisure stride going down to end of the rapid and never returning. So it is with Hyde as my first impression that she was holding the boat and was pulled in, possibly with aid of wind as Lee's Ferry, and he jumped in after and both went down.

Kolb appears to be confusing John Nelson's sighting of Bessie's tracks below their final camp, with Francy and Harbin's (and later, R.C. Hyde's) sightings of tracks at 217-Mile Rapid. Hypothesizing a loss of the scow at 217-Mile Rapid appears to contradict both Kolb's letter to Stone a month earlier, and the diary itself.

In later years Emery dropped the story of the one-way tracks above Diamond Creek and became increasingly certain that Bessie had been pulled in by gusty winds while scouting 232-Mile Rapid, and that Glen dove in to save her. Most river runners who have tried to decipher Bessie's final string of code agree on the location. If indeed they had passed Travertine Creek and another riffle, the final rapid noted would be the long, rough, sinuous, but relatively easy 231-Mile Rapid. The next obstacle would be 232-Mile Rapid, with its strong currents hurling the river, and anything floating in it, into a nasty cluster of rock fangs on the lower right. Pulling in to scout 232, especially with the limited maneuverability of a scow, would be tough. The eddy above is small and beachless, the rocks steep, polished, and slippery.

Yet R.C. Hyde, now back in Idaho, still was not inclined to think Glen and Bessie had made it past Diamond Creek, and was still focusing on their last camp. Nor was he fully aware that 232-Mile Rapid was a serious threat. "Between the place where their tracks were last found and the place the boat was found, is no bad water—only minor rapids to run," he summarized in a full report to the *Twin Falls Daily News*. "What accident occurred in that stretch of comparatively quiet water will never be known."

R.C. Hyde on
Spencer Trail

The first fall frost
In shining silver,
Comes at night.

And soon beguiles
The fluttering trees
With jewels.

At dawn…
The barren ground
Is carpeted with brown,
Dry, crackling leaves;
Who can no longer whisper
Soft, low songs;
For they—
Are dead.

— *Bessie Haley*

21

~ *February 1929 – June 1930* ~

THE MORE R.C. HYDE pored over maps and Bessie's diary, the more
he began to think the accident happened below Diamond Creek
after all. In corresponding with Ellsworth Kolb, Hyde began to
realize the magnitude of the rapids in the lower gorge. The gap in his
search began to grow in his mind. But as Hyde, in snow-swept Idaho,
mulled the fate of his son, history continued to unfold in Arizona. On
February 6, 1929, Dr. Charles Vivian of Phoenix, the man who had told
Emery Kolb he needed an emergency appendectomy a month and a half
earlier, died of double pneumonia. Kolb, meanwhile, continued fine, as
did his appendix.

Two days later, Jeremiah Johnson of Lee's Ferry reported seeing sus-
picious footprints twelve miles downriver at Soap Creek. Johnson had
gone in to Soap Creek to recover the body of Royce Dean, who had

drowned along with Johnson's son Dolph and Lewis Nez Tsinnie in the ferry accident the previous June. Dolph Johnson's and Tsinnie's bodies were never found.

While packing out Dean's body, Jerry Johnson spotted the tracks of a man and a woman who had apparently hiked some three miles up Soap Creek Canyon before returning to the river. It was Johnson's guess that they were the Hydes' footprints. He postulated Glen and Bessie had tried to abandon the river after seeing the ferocity of Soap Creek Rapid, but had not been able to find their way out of the gorge. Unlikely. Although the tracks could have been the Hydes', neither Glen nor Bessie made much note of the rapid, or the hike, in their letters.

ON FEBRUARY 20, 1929 tragedy struck. Park Naturalist Glen Sturdevant, Ranger Fred Johnson, and Chief Ranger Jimmy Brooks were coming back from a ten-day natural history expedition on the north side of the river. They reboarded the small canvas boat they had stashed above Horn Creek Rapid—the same boat Sturdevant, Brooks, and Brown had used in November twenty miles upstream. Halfway across they lost an oar. Johnson lunged for it. The boat went over. Sturdevant and Brooks had life jackets, while Johnson clung to a buoyant roll of blankets.

All three men were swept into Horn Creek Rapid. Although the river had risen somewhat after the extreme lows Kolb and Francy had seen two months earlier, it was still only 5,800 CFS, a level that makes Horn Creek one of the most violent on the river. Brooks washed ashore on the north side, beaten, bruised, and barely conscious. Once he got his breath he looked for Sturdevant and Johnson. Finding no trace, he climbed to the Tonto Platform and began the long hike upriver to Phantom Ranch, across the new bridge, and a vertical mile up to the South Rim. At midnight he woke Superintendent Tillotson, and by five o'clock the next morning Brooks, black and blue from head to foot, was heading back in with one of four search parties.

Down on the canyon floor, somewhere above Hermit Rapid on the south shore, park ranger Carl Lehnert, his wife Edith Kolb Lehnert (Emery's daughter), and Michael Harrison were on an exploration, inventorying resources and shooting feral burros. They were just packing up when they heard a distant holler. It was George Pifer, from

Hermit Camp, shouting for them to call headquarters. Back at Hermit Camp they got the bad news, and were sent down to Hermit Rapid to start an all-night watch fire.

The next morning there was a new plan. Bob Francy hiked in with Dick Mueller and Ray Tankersley, all veterans of up and downriver runs in the old Pathé-Bray movie boats. In fact just one week earlier, Mueller, a blacksmith, had hiked in and repaired the last boat of the fleet. It had been sawed in two for a stunt shot and left on the beach at Hermit two years earlier. Mueller had used a huge strip of copper to fasten the two halves back together. Now Francy and the rest of them planned to row and drag the boat upstream to search for bodies. They had one life jacket for the four men. In an egalitarian move, they stowed the jacket below decks.

At the giant eddy below Granite Falls, Harrison shouted "There's Glen!" All he could see was one stiff finger protruding from the river, but Harrison recalled Sturdevant had always had a stiff pinkie. They hauled him aboard, still in a life jacket, and took him to the Monument Trail to be packed out at Hermit. They headed upriver again. On the third day, after scaling Granite Falls, Horn Creek Rapid and a dozen riffles, they reached the foot of the Bright Angel Trail. Bert Lauzon was there, sitting on a box of dynamite, smoking a pipe. He sent them back to Horn Creek to see if they could dislodge Johnson's body with explosives. All they produced were geysers. Johnson's body was never found.

Back at the Rim, Harrison met Superintendent Tillotson at headquarters. Harrison still remembers his reception:

> As long as I had known Tilly I never heard him say anything profane, not even "damn." He said, "Mike Harrison, you're a damned liar!" "What?" I replied. "You're a damned liar! When we held that conference on who was going on the river to look for the Hydes, you said that you had a trunk full of medals you had won from swimming. I just learned that you can't swim a stroke!"

"I still can't!" says Harrison, more than seventy years later, with a chuckle. "I only take showers."

That weekend was to be the grand celebration of the tenth year of Grand Canyon National Park's existence. Instead it was spent mourning two of the park's prominent men. Michael Harrison, Fats Harbin, and Les Carr sang at the double funeral.

The *Daily Arizona Silver Belt*, of Miami, Arizona, praised Sturdevant as a great naturalist who knew more about Grand Canyon than anyone, but went on to say:

> ...The water of the Colorado is so heavily burdened with silt, that it quickly enters the clothing and weighs down to death the strongest swimmers.
>
> Only naked swimmers have a chance.... Had they taken the precaution to remove all clothing before attempting the descent of the rapids, they probably would have escaped from the maw of the stream. As it was, doubtless their silt burdened clothing dragged them down before they could reach land.

Although it is hard to imagine that boating nude in near-freezing water would have saved Sturdevant, Johnson, or the Hydes, it is remarkable how many drowning victims were never found. Of those without life jackets in 1928 and 1929, only Royce Dean's body had been recovered, washed up at Soap Creek some twelve miles below the drowning. "You have to remember," asserts Michael Harrison. "In those days, the river never gave up its dead. Never!"

DOWNRIVER, still another unrelated search was taking place. Dr. Arthur L. Inglesby, a dentist, geologist, tourist guide and, in later years, boatman, launched a small expedition from his friend Warren Cox's home in Saint George, Utah. Having followed the saga of the Hydes in the newspapers, the two men, together with Dr. J.K.W. Bracken of Pasadena, drove across the Arizona Strip in an old Model-A, down Grand Wash to Tassi, and upriver to Pierce's Ferry. There they met Alger, the ferryman, who had an ancient fourteen-foot boat. "A heavy wooden affair," recalled Inglesby. "We used outboard motors... We managed to sneak up and tow the boat over several rapids but were finally stalled, mostly because of mud and quicksand along the shore." After struggling some twelve miles upriver, still thirty miles shy of where the Hyde scow lay wedged, they retreated downriver and returned to Saint George. Although they took some rare pre-lake movie footage of the lower canyon, they contributed little toward solving the Hyde mystery.

On June 13, 1929, the Ætna Life Insurance Company, which carried a life insurance policy for Glen Hyde, wrote to Emery Kolb, asking for "such facts as you can supply in determining whether our insured is dead or alive."

Kolb wrote back describing the search, stating: "There is no doubt in our minds that the pair are dead." He went on to point out:

> They did not have many more miles to navigate and had they succeeded in getting through, their success would have been of far greater value than that of obtaining insurance by purposefully disappearing. Our short acquaintance leads us to believe that the Hydes, including the father, are of high type honorable people. We personally would trust them to the limit.

Back in West Virginia, William and Lottie Haley began to wonder if Glen and Bessie could have been captured by Indians. Mrs. Haley wrote to the Hydes. Jeanne Hyde responded in April, assuring her that the Hualapai were a good and docile people, that the Indian Agent was in touch with virtually everything they did, and that they rarely, if ever, went down to the river:

> I don't want to dishearten you, Mrs. Haley, but we know that would be an impossibility. We don't know exactly where the accident might of occurred. It may have happened below where Papa thought it did, and in that case in rougher water than we first thought...If Glen and Bessie had been marooned ashore I feel certain they would have made their way to some settlement. I can't see any slight hope of their being alive....
>
> Lovingly, Jeanne Hyde

William Haley responded, wondering if not the Indians, what about outlaws? Could it have been murder? R.C. Hyde replied on July 13, describing the remoteness of the region and the infrequency of visitation. "There have been outlaws known to be hiding from arrest in some of the almost inaccessible canyons along the river, but rarely, and it seems to me that they could have but two purposes in attacking Glen and Bessie—money and food," wrote Hyde. He reminded Haley that all food, supplies and money had been found on the scow. "It is all a mystery to me. I hope to go back next winter but I fear there is little I can learn."

True, there was little left to learn, but it was enough to draw him back. By autumn Hyde had convinced himself that Glen and Bessie had definitely passed Diamond Creek, and that the twelve miles between there and where the scow had been found had not been adequately examined. He continued corresponding with Haley, and together the men planned another search in late December. Because it would have been relatively easy for Glen and Bessie to escape on the south side of the river via Diamond Creek, Hyde focused on the extremely remote northern shore.

On October 24, 1929, Black Thursday, the stock market collapsed, signaling America's formal entry into the Great Depression. This time Hyde, who had lost everything in the Panic of 1893, had nothing to lose. He was already destitute. Haley, still crawling out of his own bankruptcy of two years prior, was also unaffected. Hyde and Haley's expedition went forward as planned. Ætna paid off Glen's life insurance, which covered William Haley's way from West Virginia and Jeanne Hyde's passage from Honolulu where she had been teaching. Hyde drove south to meet them in Saint George, Utah. After a full year of shared sorrow and angst, it was the first time the two fathers had met.

Hyde secured the services of George Weston, another Arizona Strip cowboy with a reputation for questionable cattle dealings. When they gathered in Saint George, Weston realized he knew Hyde. They had met near the turn of the century when Weston was a boy of fourteen and the Hyde family was working land up near Tiger, Washington. He recalled young Glen Hyde as a solitary sort of boy, and thought R.C. Hyde "as fine a man as I'd ever seen."

They drove the seventy miles south toward the Shivwits Plateau and made camp. Weston supplied five mules and a dog. Weston rode one saddle mule, packed gear and food on three mules, and gave the remaining saddle mule to the Hydes and Haley to share. They began their trip at John Stutzneggar's ranch on December 20, once again on one of the shortest, coldest days of the winter.

Weston had consulted with Jimmy Pymm, a cowboy who claimed to have run animals along the route Hyde proposed. Pymm had said it could be done but that it would be tough—really tough in a couple of places. "Take plenty of food," he recommended. He felt the hardest part would be getting the mules to water. It was.

They descended into Separation Canyon and worked their way down toward the river. Upon reaching the main canyon they found they were still hundreds of feet above the river on the Tonto Platform. They had to go four miles upriver before they could find a way down through the jagged Precambrian granites and schists to water the stock.

"From there we made our way upstream to where Glen's camp was, 31 miles by river," R.C. Hyde wrote to Emery Kolb. "I estimate that we walked 200 miles to make it. It was very hard and dangerous, especially for the mules."

"Old man Hyde and daughter was fine," Weston told Dock Marston twenty years later. However:

> Haley was a problem. A good judge of bad whiskey. He was a character. Haley would get into camp before Hyde. Wood was scarce. I'd get into camp around four, hobble or tie mules, rustle wood or ocotillo. Roots would burn fine. Old Haley would burn last stick of wood before he'd go to bed. Haley used up all my tobacco.

Weston had an equally disagreeable recollection of Jeanne Hyde. People who got along well with Jeanne adored her, but to those she did not particularly like, she could be extremely standoffish. "She was just as coldblooded as any fish I'd ever seen," recalled Weston:

> Very uncommunicative in camp—came into camp—the soles were gone off her shoes. I had some horseshoe nails and some leather off saddles. She took off her shoes and threw them to me. I used mule shoe as last and nailed on soles. When I finished she said "Thank you." Nothing else.

They investigated huge caves in the lower end but found nothing more recent than thousand-year-old Indian ruins. They could look down on the river itself and the small beaches at some of the sidecanyon mouths, but they could rarely descend to the river. All the while

George Weston, William Haley, R.C. Hyde.

they scoured the shale slopes for any sign of Glen and Bessie's passing—a pile of rocks, a trail, an article of clothing. They had Christmas
dinner by the river. Jeanne celebrated with a Tarrytown cigarette.

R.C. Hyde was so quiet, so austere, that Weston assumed he was a
minister. "The Lord must have had a Hell of a time building this country in six days!" Weston kidded Hyde. Hyde agreed and quietly kept
searching.

"We got just above Diamond Creek on opposite side," said Weston.
"Followed burro trail, passed poison spring. Came back and here was
Haley filling up on spring. One mule also filled up—we had no trouble
following mule or Haley back to camp."

They spent more than three weeks making their way upriver to the
Snyder Trail. Hyde went as far as what he believed to be Glen and
Bessie's last camp. Finally they ran out of food and patience. After
emptying his revolver at a wild burro he hoped to slaughter and eat—
and missing—Weston hurled the gun into the river in disgust. It was
another two days before they made it to the top of the Snyder Trail, and

food. Weston had lost seventeen pounds.

"Hyde paid me so much a day," said Weston, "and paid me a hundred-dollar tip." But they had found not a single clue. "We took lots of pictures," said Weston. "I wrote regarding pictures. She claimed she lost them all. I figured she threw them away on purpose. At the end she said, 'Well, I want to forget this trip, forget the Canyon and everything pertaining to it.'"

Jeanne didn't forget it, however. Years later she described the scene in a romantic short story set atop the Snyder Trail:

> Jack gazed down on the most beautiful and awe inspiring scene he had ever witnessed. Ever since he had come to the West he had noted Nature's extravagance, but never before that day had this tendency of Nature's been so apparent. Already they had descended several thousand feet. Below them stretched several thousand more of what seemed almost a perpendicular wall to the river channel below. Nature had paintbrush as well as her pick and shovel when she built this canyon. Gold and red and brown vied with green along this stupendous pile of rocks called the Grand Canyon of the Colorado.

Weston drove the party back to Saint George and Haley returned to West Virginia, visiting his brother on the way. Hyde had now searched nearly everywhere his son's body could be. But *nearly* did not satisfy him. He wanted to scour every square foot of some of the roughest terrain on Earth, every possible spot where Glen and Bessie could have perished. Instead of returning to Idaho, the Hydes drove south and returned to Peach Springs, headquarters of his original search, and home of the tireless Deputy Sheriff John Nelson.

Hyde explained his wish to Nelson. At the end of his search a year earlier, Hyde had covered the south shore from Glen and Bessie's last camp to Diamond Creek. From the north shore he had seen enough to be certain Bessie's diary took them below Diamond Creek. He had even picked out the spot the diary ended, a few miles downstream of Diamond Creek's mouth. Now he wished to go there. Nelson, who had had a year to recover from Hyde's last search, agreed to guide him. Jeanne, exhausted and exasperated from the fruitless twenty-six day trek on the north side, checked into the Harvey House and waited.

George
Weston's mule
train on the
Haley/Hyde
search, 1930

Mr. Haley, dear friend;

Got your letter at Peaches Springs as I came out from the river.
Jeanne and I drove to Peaches Springs. She staid there while I and
John Nelson went down the river on the South side.

Starting at Diamond Creek we went down to below where the
record in Bessie's book ended. We followed right along the river bank
by the water. It was very tough traveling. We had frequently to climb
over points of rock. Not very high, not more than 100 feet high but
very difficult in places. Nelson had been along there before and knew
where to go. I doubt if I would have tried it alone. There were so
many places it looked as though we could not go. It really was amazing what we succeeded in climbing over. We packed our grub and
blankets on our backs as horses and mules could not be used.

I saw every Rapid and checked them and the Creeks with the
notebook and know absolutely where the record ended. It was at
Leonetine Rapids some six miles below Diamond Creek. Leonetine
is a heavy rapid, makes big waves, but is, I would say, safe. It is long
but straight from start to finish and not a rock in it. Leonetine Creek
comes in a little below the head of the rapids. It is the largest creek on
that part of the river except Diamond. It is not on the record. It could
not be seen from the head of the rapid nor from the right at this head,
as it came out some twenty [yards] below the head. It would surely
be seen as they went down the rapids as it is plainly to be seen and is
quite a stream and makes a real wide cut where it comes through a

sand bar. It is possible that they might not look that way if they were busy with the boat. But that is not likely. From what Jeanne tells me there would be nothing to do in the boat—just keep it hard on. There was nothing to dodge.

I went on to the next rapids which are not on the record. This one like Leonetine is straight and no rocks. It is the smaller rapid of the two. There was a good landing place on the north bank above Leonetine and could walk along that bank to below that rapids. When I get home I will have a copy of what I wrote down on both sides banks and send you.

…We had a tough time getting over the mountains to California. Stayed three days at Las Vegas waiting for the storm to be over. Over the mountains the snow was four and five feet deep. The road had been opened for one way traffic which made it a job passing cars. Give my regards to Mrs. Haley and Bill,

Yours very truly,

R.C. Hyde

Hyde had deduced that Bessie's journal ended at Travertine Canyon, which he had inexplicably come to call Leonetine. (It may be that the transcriptionist simply misread Hyde's scrawl—Jeanne had noted that Hyde's hand was nearly illegible.) Most subsequent researchers felt the record went a mile or two farther. Regardless, Hyde, once again, had found no trace.

Jeanne and R.C. Hyde returned to Idaho in time for the spring planting. On June 17 in Twin Falls, Glen's estate was probated, his land and two thousand dollars going to R.C. Hyde. But still Hyde could not let go. He had now walked everywhere he could, searching for Glen and Bessie. Everywhere, that is, that could be reached from land. But as they had worked their way along the north side with Weston, they had peered down into numerous dead-end gulches, inaccessible from above. This had troubled Hyde. Two days before the probate, the Sunday magazine section of the *Denver Post* ran a full-page story on the mysterious disappearance of the Hydes. It closed with this:

And now the two fathers, R.C. Hyde and William L. Haley, are laying plans for a last search. With the assistance of a guide, they will make a trip down the river from the last point at which the young couple was seen. They will explore all of the river banks and the little ravines which extend at right angles to the main gorge. They will leave no stone unturned in their endeavor to learn something of the disappearance of the vanished bride and her young husband.… Almost two years later, the fathers of the two ill-fated youngsters are going to penetrate the wild gorge again, hopeful only of solving the riddle.

Looking upstream near river mile 235; James Ervin's escape route in center

The old tavern,
Grey and deserted for years
By all but the ocean's roar.

Now, sometimes,
A dead seaman comes back,
And taps softly at the door.

— *Bessie Haley*

22

~ *1931* ~

HE GREAT DEPRESSION engulfed the nation. In Chicago Al
Capone was king. Glen and Bessie Hyde continued to fade into
the background of American consciousness. Even so, 1931 brought
several events that, although their bearing on Glen and Bessie's fate is
tangential, draw increasing shades of definition around what can and
does happen to desperate river parties in lower Grand Canyon.

In the Arizona Strip country just downstream of Lava Falls lies
the tiny settlement of Bundyville. For many miles from the Colorado
River northward, the area has long been ranched by the Bundys, the
Iversons, the Heatons, and other Mormon families. On April 19, 1931,
Iven Bundy, twenty-three, and his cousin Floyd Iverson were tending
sheep in the lower end of Whitmore Valley, a short and easy hike from
the Colorado River. In the midday heat, the two young men attempted
to swim across the river. The river was running at around 11,000 CFS,
which, although a little low and sluggish, was undoubtedly still quite
cool in April. Floyd made it across easily. But even when the river is low,
it is unpredictable. A whirlpool swirled up from nowhere and caught
Iven. After a brief struggle he was sucked beneath the surface. He did
not reappear.

Within the week Floyd and his uncles, Chet and Pat Bundy formed
a search party. They had a small metal boat, weighing 180 pounds. This
they loaded with provisions—jerky, beans, and cookies—then went on

to overload the tiny boat with their own three bodies, and cast off.

The river is quite benign for the first fifteen miles below Whitmore Wash. Even so, the small boat upset near Parashant Riffle. The men lost not only much of their food but, said Chet, "a box of dynamite we brought to blow up fish."

Five days out they reached Diamond Creek and pulled in to scout the area. High on the beach they saw the *Bright Angel*, the large boat that Bob Francy and Jack Harbin had abandoned after their fruitless search for the Hydes. They explored what remained of the old shacks left by the Girand drillers in the teens and early twenties. Chet Bundy stepped into what he thought was an old blacksmith's shop. In his journal, Bundy noted the *Bright Angel* and its use in the Hyde search, and went on to say, "We also see where they carved their names on the blacksmith shop for the last time." He later elaborated, "A big two-foot wide plank had served as a place to put tools. I lay down to rest on an old bedsprings, which lay partly under this bench. Of course I looked up, and there I saw written the name of the young couple!"

According to Bundy, it read: "GLEN & BESSIE HYDE, NOVEMBER 31, 1928"—likely misprinted or misread, as November has but thirty days, and Bessie's diary indicates they passed Diamond Creek on November 30. Apparently the Hydes had lain on the same springs as Bundy, and signed in. Other than the cryptic notes in Bessie's diary, this was the first, and last, indication that the Hydes were alive this far down the river. Their final campsite had been discovered fifteen miles above here, their abandoned scow found some twelve miles below.

Deputy Sheriff John Nelson's original search party recorded no tracks at Diamond Creek. But the Hydes could easily have landed on boulders rather than mud, leaving no trace on shore. Any tracks at the drillers' camp might well have been obscured by blowing sand in the two weeks since the Hydes had passed.

Was the signature genuine? We will never know. Bundy's sighting was not common knowledge until he contacted Dock Marston with the tale in the late 1940s. By then the shacks, and the board, and the signature, were long gone. In 1940, river runner Norm Nevills had camped there with his passenger and fellow pyromaniac, Barry Goldwater. They had torched the camp for the thrill of watching it burn. "The result was spectacular," wrote Goldwater. "Long after we retired, the fire threw its red glow on the canyon walls, adding fitful firelight to the soft beams of the moon."

It is likely the name was genuine, however, for there is no motive for Bundy to have made the story up, nor for an impostor to forge the name. Besides, Floyd Iverson attested to seeing the signature as well. Yet even if the signature was genuine, it throws little light on the mystery. Although it narrows the question of where the Hydes vanished, it does nothing to clarify how or why.

CHET BUNDY and his companions, half-starved, could find no fish to speak of in Diamond Creek. Recalled Chet of his brother, "all that he caught I could swallow whole." They pushed on. Below Diamond Creek the rapids worsened. They rowed off to the side of some of the waves, and lined and carried the boat around the obstacles they could not miss. Two days later they passed the point where the Hyde scow was found and arrived at the next major rapid, Separation, where three of Major Powell's men had abandoned the river back in 1869. The Bundys and Iverson began lining the boat along the shore, only to have the current snatch it, pin it against the rocks, and sink it, bursting one of the airtight chambers. After a risky and protracted struggle the men pried the boat loose, bailed it out, and weighed their options. They were down to their last rations, and the rapids appeared to go on without end. Presented with the same predicament that Powell's three men had, they made a similar choice. They had this advantage, however: if the Bundys and Iverson could just get to the rim, they were almost home, instead of far, far from it.

The next morning they filled their one-quart canteen and began the trek out. At a point where the canyon broke into three forks the men took turns reconnoitering. Pat Bundy went first, returning an hour later saying that "a bird would have to fly straight up to get out of there." Iverson's reconnaissance took a little longer, but he came back saying, "Not even a bird could get out of it." With no other options, the three men headed up the final canyon and found the going difficult, but possible. "We found a bird's nest," said Chet Bundy, "and sucked those eggs right now!"

They made it out that day and, foodless and waterless, began walking home. A jackrabbit fell to Chet Bundy's six-shooter and a stock tank supplied water. They spent the night in Penn's Valley with George Weston, the cowboy who had guided Hyde and Haley in their 1929 search of the North Rim country. Two days later, on May 6, 1931, they were back on the ranch.

ONE HUNDRED AND FIFTY miles downriver from the Bundy ranch, the world's largest construction project was in full swing. The Boulder Dam Act had passed while the initial search for the Hydes was in progress in December of 1928. Excavators were now ripping into the canyon walls and gouging the canyon floor, while the biggest cement factory ever known blossomed on the rim. Men from all over the country swarmed to the site, eager for any sort of job in the difficult Depression era. But once they went to work, many wished they had stayed home. Temperatures soared on the canyon floor, heat radiating from the black canyon walls throughout the night. Sand, pebbles, rocks, and occasional boulders cascaded down on them. But it was a job, and the fact that board and room were included was a tremendous lure.

James Ervin, thirty, and a twenty-seven-year-old friend who called himself Bill Paine had been working for several months in the dam site mess hall for Anderson Brothers Boarding and Supply. As spring simmered into early summer, the heat and ever present risk grew intolerable. Paine said he had relatives in Denver that might give them jobs. Leaving instructions to send their final pay checks to Denver, the men climbed into Ervin's stripped down Model-T and drove north, east, and four thousand feet up to Denver. It was cooler to be sure, but they found no work. Worse, their paychecks never arrived. Hungry and irritated, they fired up Ervin's flivver and headed back to the dam project to collect their wages and perhaps go back to work. They drove south through Albuquerque, then west. In Cubero, New Mexico, Ervin's car choked and died. They left it with an Indian at a gas station, telling him if they didn't come back for it in a few months, he could have it. They hitchhiked with little success. They hopped freights but were tossed off at every station. They had made it to Peach Springs, Arizona, when Ervin looked at a road map.

Although they were not terribly far from Boulder Dam, the only way to get there by road was to go west, well into California, then double back northeast to Las Vegas, Nevada, then back south to the dam site—a journey of over 150 miles. At this point neither Ervin nor Paine, scruffy and desperate, were likely to be offered a ride. Staring at the map, Ervin noticed the Colorado River flowed just twenty miles north of Peach Springs. From what he knew of the river above the dam site, it was gentle water. Grand Canyon National Park, famous for its rapids, was well upstream of Peach Springs. Ervin had served in the Coast Guard and was comfortable in a boat. Or a raft. Or whatever they could put together. They were out of time now. They were beginning to starve. They had not eaten in two or three days, since Ervin had snitched a wiener in a Fred Harvey restaurant in Albuquerque. It was June 21, the longest and one of the hottest days of the year. They decided to try the river. Ervin, who claimed to be an adventurous sort, figured they could float down to the dam site overnight, or at least within a day or two.

They asked Old Tom, a Hualapai Indian sitting outside the butcher shop, the way to the river. Perhaps Ervin and Paine did not state their full intentions or perhaps Old Tom just chose not to warn the foolhardy white men. He pointed them down Peach Springs Wash, and told them to stop at Charlie McGee's for water.

They began the long tramp to the river. By midday the heat was excruciating. They missed McGee's place and ran out of water. Paine did not come from the same hard-working background as Ervin, and lacked his stamina. At length he laid down beside the road to rest. Ervin marched on, finally coming to Diamond Creek where he found cool, clear, running water. Nearby was an old coffeepot. He filled it and headed back up the wash. He found Paine, stumbling down the road sobbing, afraid Ervin had deserted him. They walked back down to Diamond Creek and followed the stream another mile to the Colorado River. There they found the same shack Chet Bundy had rested in two months earlier. It was late evening and they spent the night on the old bedsprings, apparently without noticing Glen and Bessie's signature above their heads.

In the morning they explored the beach and were amazed to find a large boat dragged up on the shore. It was the old *Bright Angel*, that had been in the Pathé-Bray movie in 1927, that Francy and Harbin rowed down from Phantom Ranch in December, 1928. When Bob Francy arrived there with the boat on New Year's Day, he gave the boat to deputy sheriff John Nelson, who dragged it up to where Ervin and Paine found it. The *Bright Angel* was about to launch on its third, and final, expedition.

The boat seemed to be in good shape although the sideboards were dried out and appeared leaky. It had a watertight chamber at the front end, which Ervin figured would keep the boat afloat in spite of the leaky hull. It had two good oars with it. In the hatch they found a cork life jacket. Ervin, fresh from the Coast Guard, felt comfortable swimming in rough water, so he gave the preserver to Paine, who was afraid of the water. They pried the boat into the river and prepared to launch.

There was no gear to load, nor food. All Ervin could think of to do was tie some line around the oars in case he lost his grip on them. Paine remained deathly quiet. Ervin, nervous as well, asked: "Why don't you say something?" Paine replied: "I don't know anything to talk about." Ervin looked the boat over once more, the name *Bright Angel* painted across the bow, and said: "It might be *Dark Angel* before we get out of here."

"Yes," said Bill, "it will be a great story to tell your grandchildren, if you live to tell it." They cast off.

Within a hundred yards they were in Diamond Creek Rapid—long but not overly difficult—and things went relatively smoothly. But it was downhill from there. The leaks were so bad that the cockpit was soon awash. In assuming that the bad rapids were all upstream, Ervin had been badly mistaken. They had some thirty miles of rapids downstream of them, including Separation and Lava Cliff, two of the most notorious on the river.

They had considerably more water than the Hydes, Kolbs, Francy, or Bundy had had—just over 23,000 CFS and rising. This had the advantage of covering most of the rocks, but increased the speed, power, and turbulence of the river. The lower gorge is notorious for the boils and swirls that develop at higher flows.

Of the next five or so rapids Ervin remembered running, they swamped or capsized in every one. "I went thru that first rapid bow first," Ervin wrote to Marston. "However that was the only one. Well, there was one other. However the boat was bottom side up that time." Ervin climbed back aboard, threw the rope to Paine, pulled him aboard and continued. In their last flip, the rope securing one of the oars broke, and the oar was swept downstream. They floundered to the south shore with the boat near Mile 233. They tied the *Bright Angel* to a boulder. They could not control the craft with just one oar. Paine was not about to get back in the boat anyway. Ervin felt there was no choice but to abandon the river, yet Paine, in a cursing, whimpering heap by the boat, was in no condition to scale the walls. Ervin told him to stay with the boat and he would go for help. When Paine, weak from hunger, pointed out that Ervin hadn't eaten in several days either, Ervin replied, "Maybe not, but I can make a lot of tracks before I cash in."

Ervin first scaled the steep craggy Precambrian schist cliffs that border the river, topping out on the Tonto Platform some eight hundred feet above the river—a hair-raising task in itself. It was now midday, June 22, and scorching hot. Ervin had the blind luck to reach the Tonto near a good spring. He drank as much as he could and looked for the best way out.

Given this predicament, most veteran Grand Canyon hikers would likely have walked upstream on the Tonto Platform, which provides relatively easy, level traversing throughout much of the Canyon, to Diamond Creek, then back up the road to Peach Springs. Perhaps that did not occur to Ervin, or perhaps the prolonged terrors of the morning had made it seem like they were much too far downstream to return to Diamond Creek. The other factor was hunger. Ervin had not eaten in four days. He was at the end of his tether and looking for his best shot at getting out fast. He eyed the massive Redwall Limestone cliffs above him. Throughout Grand Canyon, many of the trails are chosen for their rare access to a route through the Redwall. Ervin was about to forge a new one.

His first attempt was a dead end. He returned to the spring, watered up, and walked to the edge of the Tonto to see what Paine was doing. He spotted Paine halfway up the schist cliff, blubbering and shouting, "Wait for me!"

"Go back to the boat and wait!" shouted Ervin, and returned to the Redwall. This time he found a crack and was able to squirm to the back of it and work his way up. When he had reached a considerable height a large overhanging chock-stone blocked his way. By bracing his feet on one wall and his back on the other he was able to chimney out and around the boulder and continue climbing. By late afternoon he had worked his way most of the way up the cliff, when he found what he felt was a gift from god—the first and only barrel cactus he saw on his climb. He hacked it to bits with a sharp stone and began chewing and sucking on the bitter pulp. Although the taste was repulsive, there was enough moisture to sustain him. Just before sundown he reached the top.

In most of Grand Canyon there would still be another fifteen hundred feet of cliffs to scale above the Redwall. Fortunately for Ervin, the upper cliffs have eroded away in the far southwestern corner of Grand Canyon, and he gazed south over a rolling flatland. On his way up the cliff he had decided that if he got to the top and found himself on an isolated spire, he would end his life there and then. But from what he could see, he was out of the Canyon. He took his bearings on some distant hills and plodded until the last moonlight faded in the early morning hours on June 23.

Midmorning, Charlie McGee heard his artesian tap running and came outdoors to find Ervin beneath it, trying to drink it dry. McGee—the same McGee they had missed on their hike into the river two days earlier—dragged Ervin away from the tap and made him take just a little water at a time. Once Ervin was rested and watered, McGee took him into town to none other than Deputy Sheriff John Nelson, whose boat Ervin had unknowingly stolen.

Nelson listened to his story and began gathering a search party. He dispatched a team of packhorses that night, and Ervin, Nelson, and a few others drove out to the rim the next morning. Nelson was able to verify Ervin's tracks coming straight up off the Redwall. They then met up with the packhorses and went west to the Bridge Canyon Trail—which Ervin could easily have used had he known of it—dropped down to the Tonto and headed back upstream. There they found Ervin's tracks crossing to the base of the Redwall from the rim of the inner

James
Ervin

Ervin's
escape
crack
through
the Redwall
Limestone,
John Evans
photo

gorge. But upon looking over the lip of the Tonto, all they saw was river. No boat. No Bill Paine.

Normal surges of the river could have snapped the weathered hemp bowline of the *Bright Angel* and swept her away. Moreover, the river had risen several inches the day Ervin and Paine struggled ashore there and could easily have washed the old tub loose. Or Paine, feeling abandoned, could have pushed the hulk into the river. Whether he was aboard, dove after the boat, or died of starvation and heat stroke in the vast, trackless convolutions of the Lower Granite Gorge, is a matter of conjecture.

Nelson's party scanned the area for tracks or traces of Paine but found nothing. Meanwhile, Ervin left the group and walked the edge of the Tonto downstream for a mile or so, then cut across toward the Bridge Canyon Trail. Something about Ervin's behavior caused Nelson to suspect he was not getting the whole story from Ervin—that perhaps Ervin was lying about Paine ever getting to shore at all. Yet it is hard to see why Ervin would have altered or fabricated his tale. Old Tom had seen the two men head down Diamond Creek, Sheriff Nelson's boat was missing, and Nelson himself had seen Ervin's tracks leading to the base of the Redwall and coming off the top. If Paine never made it to shore, what reason could Ervin have had to claim he did? Ervin attested to the veracity of his tale until his dying day.

Some have speculated that an untrained climber could not have made the climb. In 1967, armed with Ervin's notes and interviews, river runner and historian Bill Belknap brought his future son-in-law, climber John Evans, into the area to attempt to retrace the route. They found most of Ervin's landmarks, and Evans made the climb. Rejecting what he thought were far too technical moves for Ervin—tricky maneuvers like laybacks and jam cracks—Evans worked his way back and forth along the ledges until he found his way to the top. It was exposed, scary, and not something a non-climber would do for fun. But Evans believes an untrained person, if persistent, could have made it. It helped that Ervin was a strong man; small, wiry, and 130 pounds. Thirty-five years later, at the age of sixty-six, Ervin could still do six one-arm push-ups on either side. Moreover, his sense of direction was uncanny—a raven could not have flown a more direct route back to Peach Springs.

The *Bright Angel* was never seen again. Nor was Paine. In fact, Paine never existed in the first place. Bill Paine was a name assumed by Jack Talmadge, a man about whom little is known. Ervin knew this, and said Jack [Bill] claimed to be a brother of the famous Talmadge sisters of Hollywood. Norma and Constance, the two elder sisters, still in their early thirties, had already retired from spectacular careers as silent movie stars. The third sister, Natalie, had married Buster Keaton. If Jack Talmadge was really their brother, it seems likely he was an illegitimate son of their deadbeat father, Fred. Absent for most of the early years of the Talmadge girls' life, the father was finally brought back into the family fold a few years before he died in 1924. No mention of Jack was made in Fred's obituary, nor would one be expected.

Ervin traveled to Hollywood to try and deliver word to Talmadge's relatives. He went to a cafeteria where Talmadge had worked. There he was told that Jack Talmadge had left quite some time ago with a day's receipts—some seven hundred dollars—and was a wanted man. Hence the assumed name.

IN LATE JUNE, 1931, Vernon "Happy" Castle and Tex Harvey, prospectors, were fishing in a huge eddy upstream from Pierce's Ferry at the foot of Grand Canyon. "Hey!" hollered Harvey, "I've caught a man!"

"Pull him in!" said Castle, thinking his partner was kidding. He wasn't. Harvey dragged up the decaying body of a husky man in a tattered undershirt. They rolled it in canvas and buried it in the sand, later notifying the county sheriff. "Kind of spoiled our fishing trip," recalled Castle.

A year later one of the prospectors met Chet Bundy's brother Omer in Kingman, Arizona. When Omer heard the description of the body, he felt sure it was Iven Bundy. A few years later, when Boulder Dam was about to flood the area, the federal government offered to move the grave. When no one else claimed him, the Bundys had him exhumed and moved to Mount Trumbull, near Bundyville. Iven's sister Barbara examined the skull and teeth and felt quite certain it was Iven.

THE EVENTS OF 1931 throw a few glimmers of light on the Hydes. Chet Bundy's find in the drillers' shack helps confirm the common interpretation of Bessie's diary—that the Hydes did indeed pass Diamond Creek. The Bundys and Iverson's escape on the north side of the river, and Ervin's astonishing climb on the south, imply that a strong-willed person can make it out to either rim from the lower river, whether they know the way out or not. Castle and Harvey found that the occasional lifejacket-less body does reappear, although only by the rarest coincidence. Or, as in Paine/Talmadge's case, a person can disappear forever.

Talmadge sisters
playing card, 1920s

R.C. Hyde

The tide
Glides out;
And the smooth,
Cool sands
Are strewn with
Many broken things.

— Bessie Haley

23

~ *1938 – 1970* ~

R. C. HYDE and William Haley gave up the hunt. Their final search by river died on the drawing board. Money was undoubtedly a factor as the Depression deepened, further aggravated by the Dust Bowl drought. Perhaps, too, with the passage of two years, Hyde and Haley began to accept the unacceptable. Hyde continued to work both the Home Place and Glen's old farm near Murtaugh. Haley went back to wallpapering. But although their search had ended, the saga of Glen and Bessie was just beginning.

Occasional rumors surfaced that Glen and Bessie had reappeared. Some came from the Grand Canyon area, where searchers fed the fires of speculation. George Weston had gotten it in his mind that both Hyde and Nelson knew exactly what had become of Glen and Bessie, but were covering it up. He hinted there had been foul play of some sort. Jack Harbin let it be known that, based on the tracks he saw, Glen Hyde may have known a lot more about the lay of Grand Canyon than he had let on. Francy said he thought Kolb had paid them to hike out Diamond Creek so that Kolb could get publicity for the search. And he thought R.C. Hyde knew about it.

In June of 1938, O.J. Pusey, Acting Chief of the Salt Lake Bureau of the Associated Press, wrote to William Haley in West Virginia:

> I am loathe to revive memories deadened by time but am writing to you in the hope that rumors floating in the west can be squelched.

> We have received reports recently that your daughter and her husband, Mr. and Mrs. Glen R. Hyde, who disappeared while boating down the Colorado River nearly 10 years ago, survived a capsized boat and are now living in Utah or Idaho.
>
> If this seemingly impossible thing happened, I am sure you would be among the first to hear of it. Would you be gracious enough to write me a denial of these rumors?

Haley wrote back, stating that Glen and Bessie were, to his knowledge, quite dead, but put forth his theory that there had been foul play—murder perhaps. He asked Pusey where the rumor came from. Pusey responded only that the story had come from "the vast wilderness along the Utah-Arizona border." He asked Haley for details on his murder theories. Correspondence trailed off.

By 1950, when Dock Marston was collecting interviews, stories, and artifacts of anyone who had ever run the Colorado, both R.C. Hyde and William Haley were dead. Marston picked up bits and pieces of the rumors of Glen and Bessie's survival from Francy, Weston, and others, and followed whatever leads he could. Marston, a river runner himself, had become obsessed with the history of the Colorado River and those who had floated down it. His initial plan, in the late 1940s, had been to write a short history of river running, but as he continued to dig for material, the hunt took over and the book, always due out within the coming year, took a back seat. When he could find no more facts on a particular story, he sought opinions.

River runner Norm Nevills wrote Marston: "I remember a long story in a Sunday *Los Angeles Times* to the effect that both the bride and groom were believed to have disappeared permanently, on purpose, to seek some kind of Utopia or Shangri-la."

Marston responded:

> The hideout theory on the bride and groom was bunk, but Hyde Senior believed it and went back to the river three times in the hope he would find them. The escape theory is possible and I want to run down the clues. It is probable they drowned between Diamond and Mile 237. Generally it is true that the simple theory proves correct, but it is not true often enuf to warrant questioning the simple solution."

"About the Hyde escape rumor," wrote Ellsworth Kolb. "No, I never heard it, and can't think it possible. There are always 'witch hunters' who dig up scandal whenever possible."

"...Personally," wrote Nevills, "I have always felt that they just plain and simple drowned." Marston finally agreed, finding no basis whatsoever to believe they were alive.

Marston found Glen Hyde's sisters, Edna and Jeanne, both married and living near Twin Falls. Unfortunately, as often happened with Marston's forthright—sometimes even gruff— approach, both Jeanne and Edna clammed up and refused to give Marston any details of the family history, or even let him view the family papers. Bessie's original journal, Jeanne told him, had been destroyed.

Eventually Marston found Lottie Haley's address and wrote her for details of her daughter. "Your letter of the 6 kinda opened a soar we try to heal," wrote Mrs. Haley. "We broke up 5 years ago last May. Mr. Haley passed on 4 years ago. I am living with my cousin's niece & they are lovely to me but get very lonely." She sent Marston her collection

River runner and historian
Otis "Dock" Marston

of letters from the Hydes to copy. "I have mailed you what I think will help with my Bessie," she wrote. "She was a bright girl but passed on too soon to do much."

Marston investigated William Haley's murder theories, sorting through suspects and sniffing for conspiracy. No one was immune from suspicion. Bessie's brother Bill told Marston that there were rumors around Parkersburg that Earl Helmick had played a role in the Hydes' disappearance, that Earl had a violent temper and was very angry when Bessie divorced him. Yet every murder theory proved too far fetched for Marston to swallow.

When Marston died in 1979, after more than thirty years of compiling his river history, his manuscript was little closer to publication than it was in 1950. In the end, Marston had concluded the couple had crashed in 232-Mile Rapid, been tossed overboard, and drowned. Emery Kolb, too, suspected 232, but felt they were ashore when the accident happened. In the tape recording that accompanied his South Rim movie for decades, Kolb stated:

> 'Twas our opinion they had been lining this scow, that is, dropping it from the walls with the rope attached to it through rapids—rapids they didn't have the courage to attempt to run—dragged in by the force of water against the boat and drowned. Whatever happened we think happened from on shore.
>
> And of course it's possible a sudden rise took the boat away from them while on shore inspecting channels, and they have starved on the walls as have many others.

With the river running community generally agreeing that the Hydes met their fate at 232, boatmen began to suggest renaming the rapid in their memory. Bride and Groom Rapid and Honeymoon Rapid both made it into guidebooks, and riverman Frank "Fisheye" Masland went so far as to formally apply to the United States Board on Geographic Names to have the name changed to Requiem Rapids. To date, however, the official name remains Two Hundred and Thirtytwo Mile Rapids.

Historian Edwin Corle wrote to Emery Kolb in 1942, asking for the full story on the Hyde couple. "Their tragic case should be treated with dignity and compassion," Corle wrote. "After all, the Hydes went in where angels may well fear to tread, and their sacrifice has acted as a warning to the impetuous or the ill-advised." Four years later, in *Listen, Bright Angel*, his history of Grand Canyon, Corle gave his version of the Hyde's fate:

> The Hydes were well equipped and the scow was a capable craft. They had almost made it and by all odds they should have come through successfully. The Hydes are not to be blamed. It was the river. Nobody thought in advance that the beast had never seen a girl before, that he would study her for a long time, and finally he would take a wife.

By 1970, virtually all rumors of Glen or Bessie's survival had withered. Most historians agreed that the Hydes had perished in the river, at or near 232-Mile Rapid.

Glen Hyde's bungalow in Murtaugh

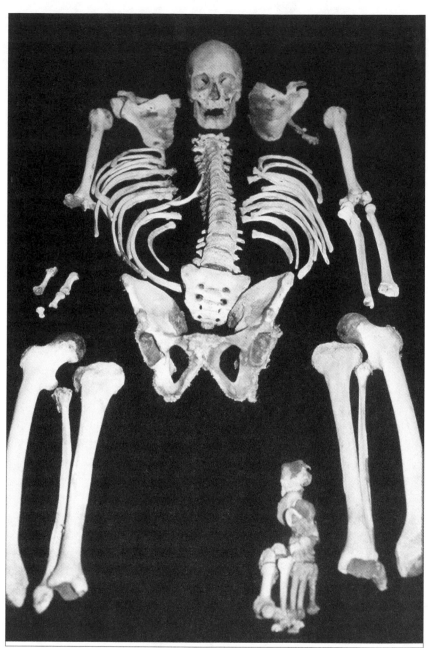

The bones from Kolb's boathouse, Dr. Walter Birkby photo

Part Three

Glens and Bessies

Front
sweep
retracted,
steering
with rear
sweep

Like passing friends—
Is the moving ship;
With shadowy outline
And paling lights,
That slowly fade
In the harbor fog.

— Bessie Haley

24

~ 1996 ~

*J*ERI'S EYES WERE WIDE, her countenance grim. She crouched cat-like in the stern of the scow, calculating her pounce. I stood on the dance floor, fists gripping the sweeps, eyes fixed on the crisp line where the entire river dropped from sight. It is difficult enough to enter a major rapid in a boat you feel comfortable with. But this horrid, uncontrollable contraption had filled us with a unique dread. I was cottonmouthed, tingling with adrenaline, soberly awaiting our fate. That peculiar calm had finally descended, when a boatman sets aside indecision and the urge to flee, casts off from shore, and commits to the will of the river. From that point it becomes a matter of actions and reactions, of total awareness and constant reassessment, of seamless transfer to plan B, plan C, plan D.

Although it was a blistering August day in the desert, I wore heavy jeans and a long-sleeve denim shirt to ward off the worst abrasions. My dual life jackets were cinched so tight I could scarcely inhale, and my helmet snug. The roar of unseen whitewater grew louder, and the occasional flash of an exploding wave leapt above the horizon. I glanced back at Jeri but her eyes were fixed downstream.

Valiant? Heroic? More like quixotic. Closer to downright goofy. Yet it is hard to fully savor the absurd when you are about to be violently beaten yet again. Harder yet when it's your own damned, stupid, stubborn fault; when you have been begging for it for weeks. Our two-ton, roughhewn anachronism of a boat drifted peacefully and inexorably into Crystal Creek Rapid, one of the nastiest on the modern Colorado.

"I could not believe what I was seeing," boatman Mike Yard told me afterward. "This—this—horse-trough, floating into Crystal with people standing on it! I was paralyzed! I couldn't react! I couldn't believe anyone was really *doing* that!"

Yard had arrived at the head of Crystal in a motorized raft with several passengers just as we were about to launch. He had asked if there were any way he could help. We had told him to go down to the slow water midway through the rapid and coordinate with Brian. We felt we could survive the first half of Crystal, but fully expected to be out of control by part two, the Rock Island—an acre of boulders, most of them barely covered, several jutting above the water—a nightmare for any boat. The first half of the rapid is extremely violent, and routinely throws boats toward the left side of the river, into the Island. Only a thin thread of current goes completely to the left of the Island. Of the remaining current, roughly half goes to the right of the Island. The rest of the river crashes through the boulders. The survivor of the first half of Crystal, then, is faced with a predicament: whether to try and get into the right half of the current and miss the island, or to fight through the left half of the current to get to the far left chute. General wisdom says, "when in doubt, go right." Yet time and again boatmen ignore general wisdom and pay the price.

We had agreed with Brian that as we neared the bottom of the first part of Crystal we would make our call, left or right. At that point, he would assist us with a T-Bone push if needed. Now Yard waited as well.

I made an extremely tight entry on the right side, pulling hard right as I dropped in, in an effort to miss the main violence that throws boats to the left. We were doing well for about fifteen yards before the scow began to plunge left, into the heart of the New Wave, a fifteen-foot crashing breaker. Jeri was already sprawled on the rear floor; I dove to the front. We blasted through the wave and I jumped back up to regain the sweeps. We were heading left fast. A quick eye-to-eye conference with Yard and Brian and we agreed to attempt the left run. Together they pushed against our right side, giving a combined thrust of a hundred horsepower toward the left chute.

From where they stood at their motors, looking slightly upstream at

Crossed sweeps
in Crystal Rapid,
heading for
trouble

us, things appeared to be working. But Jeri and I could see that we were losing ground. All three boats were heading straight into the gut of the Rock Island. I started gesturing frantically for them to abort and leave us to our fate. "We're going right, pal!" I screamed at Brian. I never say "Pal." "Save yourselves!" I shouted. Brian was gone instantly, a blur vanishing upstream. Yard, overloaded and underpowered, made a miraculous slalom run of the right side of the Island. We dead-centered the rock pile. We were backward by then, so Jeri had an intimate view of the onrushing calamity. I dropped the rear sweep into the river and began plunging it between rocks and prying. Astonishingly, the scow once again began to perform, threading cleanly between the boulders. Well, all but one. We collided abruptly, stopping dead from a good fifteen miles an hour. The boat shuddered, buoyed up as the water piled beneath us, then floated across the obstacle and out the bottom of the rapid.

For years Jeri and I had been rowing fragile, thin-shelled plywood dories. After a crash like that, we assumed we would only be afloat for a matter of a few more seconds. We beached at a small spit of sand just above the next rapid and examined the boat for damage. We could find none. Nothing. Even after the trip, with the boat out of water, we could not locate the point of impact. Two tons of spongy, waterlogged pine have a remarkable squish factor.

We launched again and entered Tuna Creek Rapid, a long two-part rapid with a right-angle bend, which then shoots straight into a midstream rock. Brian was hovering above the rock ready to push, but we were sailing on down the left. We knew each bend, each errant current, each obstacle, long before we got to it, and could prepare well in advance. It was in prolonged stretches of tricky water like this that we really began to appreciate Glen Hyde's genius. That he could think that fast, react so decisively in unknown water in a four-thousand-pound scow, is uncanny.

It was late afternoon by now and I was an utter mess. I was beaten, bloody, and exhausted. I had a swollen bruise on my thigh the size of a cucumber. Jeri was hammered. We wanted to camp. Yard asked us if we would join them for dinner at their camp eight miles farther downriver. I started to whimper, and said I'd be glad to if he would switch boats with us. To our astonishment, he did.

For the next five rapids Jeri and I motored Yard's raft and laughed as we watched first Yard, then Brian take turns getting pummeled in the scow. Brian, at six-foot-five, is massive enough to maintain more control of the sweeps than I. Yard, an athletic five-ten with few self-preservation instincts, resorted to flying tackles of the wayward sweeps. Watching the twenty-foot wooden tub bound through the waves with these hapless victims dashing about on the center platform was almost more than we could bear, especially knowing that we had been looking even goofier for a full week. All I recall about camp that night were the margaritas and a short crawl to bed.

Two days later we were feeling ill again. Glen Canyon Dam, which controls the water flow in Grand Canyon, had throttled down to a paltry 8,000 CFS, and we were headed for Bedrock Rapid. Bedrock, with the giant monolith in the center and the tough choice: the difficult shallow run to the right, or the violent corkscrew consequences of the left. Going left is almost always accidental, and rarely enjoyable. We had hoped to have high enough water to go right and slide over the shallows, but it was not to be. We had almost exactly the flow Glen and Bessie had, and were doomed to their fate: a left run.

Although we could imagine the scow, if everything went perfectly, negotiating the left side without disaster, the odds were against it. We talked it over at length as we approached. The cost-benefit ratio of attempting Bedrock was decidedly unfavorable. What, after all, were we trying to prove? "I-Beam," snapped Brian. We strapped onto the front of the powerboat for a quick sneak down the narrow right run.

It was only much later, after a full analysis of Bessie's journal and reconstruction of their photographs, that we learned just how bad Glen and Bessie's run of Bedrock had been—a resounding crash on the left side, followed by a two-day portage. At that water level, given the choice, I would motor it again.

Dubendorff Rapid, a mile downstream, is equally ugly at low water in its own way. "Mean," wrote Bessie Hyde. We scouted briefly and prepared to run. Up until now we had been fortunate not to encounter crowds of onlookers. But all of a sudden at Dubendorff we caught up to three commercial river trips, their passengers and crew lining the banks in ghoulish anticipation, cameras glinting in the afternoon sun.

We put on a good show. We missed the hoped-for right run, of course, and snaked down through the boulders on the left, diving to the floor of the scow two or three times, and bounding out the bottom of the rapid to the cheers of the crowd. We cheered too. We had survived the Upper and Middle Granite Gorges, and we had already run the Lower Gorge on our test cruise. Only two major rapids remained: Upset Rapid and Lava Falls.

For the next half hour we drifted downriver with one of the commercial river tours, chatting. "I saw on TV where Bessie is supposed to have murdered Glen and hiked out," said one woman. "And then come back on a river trip a few years ago."

"What about that skeleton that was found up at the South Rim?" asked another. "Wasn't that thought to have been Glen?"

We grinned. Until now we had been so concerned about our own survival we had not really thought much about the tales of the Hydes surviving their trip. Yet it seemed that nearly everyone who had heard of Glen and Bessie knew at least some variant of them leaving the river and reappearing somewhere else. "You haven't heard the half of it," I said. We popped open a few beers, and began to tell them what we knew of the wild twists, gyrations, and tangents the Hyde legend had taken in the last twenty-five years.

George Billingsley
and Elizabeth Cutler,
October, 1971,
Richard Rogers photo

Eucalyptus trees
With mystic whispers
Sing leaf songs,
Of softer music
Than we can make—
Or understand.

— Bessie Haley

Tall pine trees
In sombre silhouette,
Seem made for
Martial music;
And pageantry
Of stately grandeur.

— Bessie Haley

25

~ *1971* ~

"ONIGHT I'M GOING TO TELL YOU the story of Glen and Bessie Hyde," said Rick Petrillo, shifting his weight from one foot to the other, dodging the campfire smoke. It was a cold night, his audience was small and close. Of the seven passengers who had started the river trip two weeks earlier, two had left due to injury; five remained. After that the rains began.

"It was back in 1928, just a few miles downstream from here, that the Hydes disappeared." The group had now seen the worst the Canyon had to offer. They were survivors; they were a close group; they knew each other. It was late October, 1971. The days were short, the nights too long to sleep through. Predawn temperatures were dropping into the thirties. Silently, they listened. Petrillo went on to tell them what was now the most famous of Grand Canyon legends, the tragedy of the honeymoon couple.

By 1971, river trips through Grand Canyon had become common-place. What was considered a daredevil stunt in the 'twenties had become a commercially available commodity by the late 1930s when Norm Nevills began offering rowing trips in wooden Cataract boats. In the 1940s war surplus inflatable rafts became available and boatmen soon adapted them to whitewater use. During the 'fifties whitewater tourism surged when the Sierra Club began taking hundreds of people a summer down the Green and Yampa Rivers during their fight against a dam in Dinosaur National Monument.

In 1963 Glen Canyon Dam was completed, flooding most of Glen Canyon and over half of Cataract Canyon. Once the reservoir rose high enough that water could be released through Grand Canyon, commercial river tourism exploded. By 1971 some fifteen thousand people a year were floating through Grand Canyon, most of them on large motorized pontoon rafts. Running boats down the river became a small industry. Hundreds of young men and a few dozen young women joined in the evolution of a new career, whitewater guiding. Running the boats was only part of the trade. A boatman—the term preferred by most guides, male and female—had to learn the river, the rapids, the canyon; cook for a crowd over an open fire, cope with weather, keep people safe and happy, handle emergencies; and of course, tell stories around the fire. It was challenging and rewarding; there were few role models and fewer rules. And in 1971 there were still quite a few rough edges.

PETRILLO took another sip of cheap, strong whiskey from his tin cup, sidestepped a waft of smoke, and began telling the saga of the Hydes. All boatmen knew the basics of the tale—Glen Hyde, the Idaho farm boy, and Bessie, his petite new bride, were lost on their honeymoon through Grand Canyon; Emery Kolb had met them at the rim and offered them life jackets in vain, and Bessie had uttered her poignant question, "I wonder if I'll ever wear pretty shoes again?" They returned to the river and, perhaps less than amicably, resumed their trip, never to be seen again. The Kolbs found the scow upright and loaded, but the Hydes were never found.

Some guides knew more, some knew less. Some added their own details. Rick Petrillo doesn't recall just how he told the story that night, but another boatman who was there, O'Connor "O.C." Dale, said Petrillo was a great story teller. He imagines it was a fairly elaborate rendition, with a deliciously mysterious ending.

Tired from the day's run, Petrillo went to bed, as did most others. Dale remained around the fire. So did boatman George Billingsley, and Liz Cutler, the eldest passenger of the group. A small woman in her sixties, Liz had enjoyed the trip so far, never complaining about the hardships. "A real trooper," recalled the boatmen. It had been quiet around the fire for some time when Liz made a startling announcement:

"I'm Bessie Hyde."

Liz Cutler had signed up for the end-of-year, extra-long rowing trip with Grand Canyon Expeditions. Petrillo, a boatman with several years experience, was the trip leader. Dale and Billingsley, newer to the job, were the other two boatmen. Dale's father, Eben, and cousin Regan rounded out the crew. Between them they were operating two boats: a thirty-seven-foot motorized pontoon raft, and a smaller oar-powered contraption called a triple-rig, composed of three eighteen-foot rafts tied side-by-side with one oarsman on either end. Petrillo had limited experience in the triple-rig; Dale and Billingsley had none. Triple rigs are not operated like a motorboat or a rowboat, but similar to the Hyde sweep scow, with one oar upstream, one oar downstream. They are not for the faint of heart. "The little rowing triple rigs," recalls Petrillo, shaking his head. "The dangerous ones. Those are just a deadly rig. Basically it was a sweepboat, and they're very difficult anyhow. You know, you just couldn't move 'em. And you'd run into the same trouble with sweepboats—I'm amazed that Hyde ever got that far down the Canyon. I'm absolutely amazed."

The trip was fraught with calamities. The days were short, the water was low, rocky, violent. By the time they got eight miles to Badger Creek, they had already wrecked their only spare motor. That night at House Rock Rapid, they almost sank the triple-rig as they crashed through the rapid in near twilight. Liz Cutler was unfazed.

"She was quite a character," recalls George Billingsley:

> She was very thin and wiry. She was very, very—what's the word?—hearty. And didn't worry about all the troubles we were having every rapid. It didn't seem to bother her at all, she just went along with the flow. She was really comfortable down there, and the rougher the better. Liz was a lot of fun. She was pretty gung ho. Never complained, never complained, no matter what happened on the trip. If the boat sandwiched on 'em, she'd just hang on. I liked her a lot.

Rick Petrillo's memories are more general. "I remember more about how she impressed me than I do about details about her—that she was

Bessie Haley, 1928, Kolb photo

Liz Cutler, 1971, Richard Rogers photo

calm and confident. I remember that quality. So she'd be a great candidate for that story, that mystery. I thought she was a pretty neat old gal."

On day six they had a bad wreck. Dropping into Horn Creek Rapid, they slammed into a series of waves and holes. The triple-rig buckled and whipped, and Priscilla Dannies' forearm shattered. They continued downriver to the next camp with trail access. That night Billingsley hiked out. With little moonlight and a littler flashlight, he wandered lost for much of the night in a rockfall that blocked the trail. At 3:30 A.M. he reached the rim at Hermit's Rest and, finding no one there, began walking the six miles to Grand Canyon Village. Just before dawn he fell asleep on his feet and slammed into a juniper. He was back at the river by eight in a helicopter, and left again with Priscilla and Bob Dannies to attend his grandmother's funeral.

The next day the triple-rig nearly foundered in Crystal Rapid, but wallowed on through with all aboard. Four days later Billingsley hiked back in at Havasu Creek and they floated on down to camp. Cold rains plagued them for the next few days. They bounced through Lava Falls and that night were hit with over an inch of hail. The weather began to let up the next day and they made camp at Spring Canyon. "We were feeling good so we celebrated with what little beer we had left and sat around the fire warming," recalls Billingsley. "Well, Rick was telling about all these river stories, and the Bessie Hyde story came up and he told that, that's when she piped up." In an addendum to his journal, Billingsley later wrote down what happened next.

> At that time Liz spoke up and said "I know." O.C. then asked "Well, what happened?" She answered while staring into the fire, "I'm Bessie Hyde." No one said anything for a while and we looked at each other with a grin. Then O.C. asked "What did you do with Glen?" Without looking up she replied "I killed him." O.C. said "Oh," then laughed, then asked "How did you do it?" Still looking into the fire she said "Somewhere along here we had a real bad fight and he beat me up. So late that night I got a knife and stabbed him." Nothing was said for a short while and we just looked at each other and Liz never looked up. Then O.C. asked "How did you get out?" She replied "After I drug him into the river and turned the boat loose, I started walking downstream because we knew Diamond Creek was not too far. I finally reached the road and no one was there so I walked up to Peach Springs and caught a Greyhound bus and went back east."

> We just stood around the fire still looking at each other and still grinning and someone said "Well, now we know." And nothing was said about it again and Liz never smiled or looked up from the fire all that time. We went on with other stories. We all figured she was making up the story and let it go at that.

> But after that we began to wonder.

Liz and O.C.
Jim Bonney photo

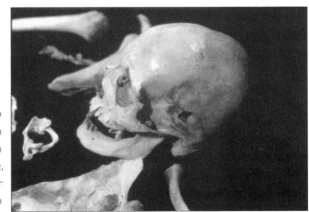

Skull from Kolb
boathouse with
bullet hole in
temple,
Dr. Walter
Birkby photo

Most people have the notion,
Cowboys are something grand,
With guns, silk shirts and lassos,
Quite rulers of the land.

'Tis stories make you think they're such,
But what a fake they are,
For I have never found them so,
And I have traveled far.

Patched overall, and minus guns,
Just ordinary men you'll find,
And all the glorious romances,
Are from some fertile writer's mind.

— *Bessie Haley*

26

~ *1986 – 1985* ~

EMERY KOLB died on December 11, 1976, after spending much of his life bickering with the National Park Service. He and his brother had been well established at Grand Canyon long before the Park was founded, and the question of whether Kolb had the right to maintain and operate his studio perched on the rim was a continuing source of contention. The Park finally agreed that Emery could run the studio as long as he lived, but could not sell it or pass it on to an heir. So in one of the world's greatest acts of living vengeance, Kolb refused to die. He lived to the age of ninety-six, showing his movie four times a day. At the time of his death, it had become the longest-running film in history. The Park Service closed the studio the day after he died, but could not easily tear it down as they had originally planned. The building had been there so long that even the newest additions were now deemed historic, protected by law.

Two months later Kolb's grandson, Emery Lehnert, was packing up his grandfather's possessions and made a telephone call to Superintendent Merle Stitt. Stitt was recovering from a heart attack and was a little jittery, as there had been a double murder at the Powell Memorial on the rim just one week earlier. "Hey Merle," said Lehnert. "I've got another body over here for you." Stitt nearly dropped. Lehnert chuckled, then explained that this was nothing sensational—just an old skeleton in Emery's garage.

Stitt sent Park Anthropologist Robert Euler to the Kolb Studio. Lehnert showed him to the garage. Suspended in the rafters was an old canvas canoe that boatman and guide Dave Rust had given Kolb decades earlier. Climbing up to the boat, Lehnert reached in and began handing down bones—human bones. In fact, a nearly complete skeleton. He then passed down a small bundle of clothing fragments that had once clothed the skeleton. Finally, in a Chase and Sanborn coffee can, he handed Euler the skull.

Lehnert told Euler his grandfather had found the skeleton below the rim many years earlier. Lehnert recalled when he was a boy in the 1930s, helping Kolb assemble the bones on the dining room table. Euler examined the remains and noted that the teeth had fillings, ruling out any prehistoric date. He packed up the bones and turned them over to Ranger Gordon Noreau. Noreau investigated further. In his report, both Emery Lehnert and his mother, Edith Kolb Lehnert, stated that they believed the skeleton had been found below Yavapai Point, Edith adding that she believed Kolb had retrieved it before Grand Canyon became a national park in 1919. Stitt asked that the skeleton be turned over to the County Sheriff.

An inexplicable three years passed before Lloyd Hoener, of the National Park Service, called the Coconino County Sheriff's Department. Sergeant Jack Judd arrived that afternoon, May 5, 1980, to retrieve the remains. Three days later the County Medical Examiner sent the bones to Dr. Walter Birkby at the Human Identification Laboratory in Tucson, and the clothing and other artifacts to the FBI. The *Arizona Daily Sun*, in Flagstaff, began covering the case on May 7, describing the finding of the bones and adding this:

> A honeymoon couple disappeared downstream from Phantom Ranch, but the bodies, if any, were never recovered. Judd says he

plans to check even the possibility the remains are those of one of the honeymooners, identified as Glen and Bessie Hyde. However, Judd emphasized he isn't drawing any conclusions about the case at this point.

Three weeks later, Dr. Birkby called. He had identified the bones as those of a male, approximately six feet tall and around twenty years old. More interesting, he had found a bullet in the skull.

Art Gallenson, a river runner and an old friend of Emery Kolb's, wrote to Judd in May, explaining what he knew of the bones. Kolb had told him that the skeleton was indeed found just below the rim, and was thought to be an indigent with no known relatives. Kolb had loaned the skeleton to a school teacher at the South Rim, who had used it in classes for many years, but returned it to Kolb when she left the school. "Art," Kolb had told Gallenson, "when I die and somebody finds that skeleton, it's gonna cause a lot of commotion." He asked Gallenson to take it to a school in Kanab, but at the time of Kolb's death, the bones remained in the boathouse.

In spite of repeated testimony that the bones predated 1920, the sheriff's department pursued the Hyde angle because, Jack Judd later told the *South Idaho Press*, "That's the only missing person case that we know of during that time, in which the remains have never been found." In June the Los Angeles Police Department Vice Squad sent Judd information on all the living relatives of Glen Hyde. Meanwhile the FBI identified the bullet as a .30 to .32 caliber, but could not identify the weapon, nor could they draw any conclusions from the clothing.

Birkby sent Judd his analysis. The bones were of a Caucasian male, eighteen to twenty years old, six feet tall, plus or minus two inches, with blonde to light brown hair. The body, he said, had lain exposed for one to three years before being brought indoors. Birkby planned to have his class reconstruct the facial features of the skull. Early in 1981, Judd sent the bullet to the Tucson office of the Arizona Department of Public Safety, and sent a series of photographs of Glen Hyde to Dr. Birkby.

"Bones May Be Missing Man's" read an August 24, 1981 Associated Press dispatch from Flagstaff. Dr. Birkby released a picture of his reconstruction of the skull's face and, according to the news report, "Some observers say it resembles Glen Hyde." Sergeant Jack Judd was quoted as saying there was a "fair chance" the bones were Hyde's. Moreover, a silver belt buckle that was found with the bones, "resembles a buckle Hyde was wearing in a picture taken of the newlyweds."

Birkby questioned the facial resemblance, and said there was an eighty percent chance that the bones were those of a man between the ages of nineteen and twenty-one and "fairly robust." Based on the angle of the bullet entry, and the fact that all bone fragments had not been blasted free from the point of entry, Birkby ruled out suicide or point-blank shot. That left homicide. But by now the news writers were hearing only what they wanted to hear. Lowering Glen Hyde's true age from twenty-nine to twenty-four, they said all the evidence matched. "So far," the *South Idaho Press* quoted Birkby, "It's looking rather strongly like this could be the missing Glen Hyde."

Bob Emerson read the story in Twin Falls and called his mother in Honolulu, Glen Hyde's sister Edna. Edna was the last of the honeymooners' immediate family—Glen and Bessie's parents were gone by the mid-'60s, Edna's little sister Jeanne had died childless in 1970, and Bessie's only brother Bill had died just five months earlier, also childless. "That was the first I had heard anything about it," Edna Emerson said. "It just left me horrified." Her daughter Barbara Hall, in Seattle, immediately wrote to Judd and Birkby asking for details.

Although Judd saw no indication that Emery Kolb was involved in the shooting, nor did he see any motive, rumors soon began to circulate that Kolb must have shot Glen to save Bessie from certain death in the scow. This tied in nicely, if not precisely, with the growing myth of Liz Cutler, who had stabbed Glen and hiked out at Diamond Creek. Both myths amplified Bob Francy's second-hand rumor of Glen and Bessie having a fight just before they vanished, and Glen forcing her aboard the scow. Glen, in either myth, now became a brute, who could only be dealt with in one way.

Perhaps, hinted some, Liz only *claimed* she stabbed Glen to cover Kolb's involvement. Ellsworth Kolb was not immune to the rumors either. He was, after all, a bachelor, had vanished from South Rim life in the 1920s, and was living out of the limelight in California. Probably with Bessie. Another variant had Emery Kolb fabricating his visit to Dr.

Vivian in Phoenix prior to the search for the Hydes. Instead, the story went, he had driven to Diamond Creek, gotten Bessie, dispatched Glen, tossed him in the trunk, and stuffed him in the boat in the garage. And then killed Vivian a month later to keep him quiet.

A bizarre but true twist to the Kolb myths stems from Emery's plan to make another river trip. Shortly before his wife Blanche's and brother Ellsworth's deaths in 1960, Emery decided to build a new boat. Scrawling his design on pieces of paper and cardboard, he contracted with Seth Smith of Phoenix to build it. Although neither of the Kolb brothers knew how to run any other type of boat than a simple rowboat, Emery had designed a scow—an enormous scow. His only experience with scows had been during the rescue attempt of the Hydes, when Ellsworth ran the Hydes' waterlogged scow through a small riffle before abandoning it to the rapids. Although Ellsworth later said he was impressed with the ease of handling the craft, it is hard to figure what possessed Emery to build one. Painted as white as Moby Dick, the huge scow eventually arrived at the South Rim.

In early 1962 Kolb, then a frail, diminutive eighty-one years old, began asking old river running colleagues if they would care to join him for a trip through Grand Canyon. Bert Lauzon, from the 1911-12 trip, declined, as did Leigh Lint from the 1923 trip. "You spoke one time as though you would be interested if I tried out my new scow on the river," Kolb wrote to river runner Harry Aleson. "Well, I may try it some time in May. If I do I would like to have you along."

Emery Kolb and his great white scow, 1960

"I have always appreciated your kindness and consideration in wanting me to accompany you," replied Aleson gently, "and I had hoped it would work out. I must forgo it this year." Dock Marston wrote to an acquaintance, "What [Emery] needs is to get someone who will see that he does not do things, and one of these things is any running of that goofy boat of his."

With no one to accompany him, Emery let the boat languish in the garage, eventually giving it to friends in Utah. But years later, as the Hyde rumors and myths swirled around Kolb, the question resurfaced: "What strange connection did Kolb have with the Hydes that would cause him to build, of all things, a scow?"

The story of Liz Cutler grew, although neither Billingsley nor Petrillo nor Dale remember actively spreading the rumor. They told a few other boatmen around the warehouse, and maybe a few passengers on subsequent trips. Petrillo soon left Grand Canyon and went to Idaho for ten years. In 1982, he returned to Grand Canyon.

> I no sooner got back than I was runnin' every trip. And many of the stories had become little legends. Grand Canyon seems to have produced a couple of generations of river boatmen who've almost made a cult out of being on the river, and boy, they repeat those stories, and repeat 'em and they just, they change. I know those older boatmen, and I remember some of those young boatmen just hanging on to every word, and I remember how we hung onto the words of the group who learned just before we did. We just accepted it, and some of those were not true.
>
> I was surprised when I went back in '82, after being away from the story for a long time, to find out that it was a big story. I just thought it was something that we heard about that we didn't put much credence in. But I know in '82 they were really solid on that story. And it got reinforced when they found the skull with the bullet hole in it. And all of a sudden everybody was pretty sure that it had to be Glen's skull. Maybe Kolb was involved, maybe Kolb lusted after her, or maybe he just hid the body after she shot him because he beat her up...but there never was any foundation for that. But it sure got to be

a widespread story being told every day in the Canyon.

You can grab hold of a rumor and remember it for fifty years, exactly the way that rumor happened. Never miss a lick. But still it's based on nothing.

Liz Cutler's story continued to evolve. Her campfire story became a confession, her knowledge of Grand Canyon became vast and inexplicable, her every move or act on the trip seemed somehow to support the fact she was really Bessie Hyde. It was too good a story to ignore, and too wild not to pass on.

A mutant strain of the Liz myth had evolved by the early 1980s. *Another* woman, it went, on a *different* trip, told a *similar* story. Of the trip with Glen, she said, "I realized I had made a mistake." She, too, had stabbed Glen, with a butcher knife. She, too, had hiked out, but had gone out the *north* side. She, too, had started a new life, but as a waitress in Circleville, Utah. Even Rick Petrillo recalls a hybrid strain nearly thirty years later:

> Hyde got swept off and never showed up again and she eventually got into shore and just had to leave the boat, 'cause she was afraid to run the river. I think she said he drowned. And then she got out of there. I believe she had settled for a while in a little quiet Mormon community in northern Nevada or Southern Utah. But, you know, I'm not very clear about that.

Several boatmen recall hearing this version, but none can agree on details. Cheryl Whitaker, who has lived her entire life in tiny Circleville, says such a waitress never existed. Most likely the story arose from repeated retellings, time, and strong drink.

AUTHOR SCOTT THYBONY of Flagstaff, Arizona, began looking into the Liz Cutler story in 1985. He telephoned Cutler, then seventy-eight, at home in Pomeroy, Ohio. She denied any knowledge of the tale or the Hyde name. But who, Thybony wondered, would admit to a capital crime, over the phone, to a complete stranger? Murder, after all, has no statute of limitations. Thybony talked to law enforcement officials who stated that many missing persons, after a period of roaming, are finally found not far from their old stomping grounds. Pomeroy was just forty miles from Parkersburg, West Virginia, Bessie's home town. One detective doubted Liz's story, telling Thybony he had never heard of a case where a bride had killed her husband on their honeymoon. Thybony pointed out they had been married over seven months by the time of the disappearance. The detective mulled that over, paused, then nodded. "I guess that's long enough," he said.

Thybony wrote a short piece, entitled, "What Happened to Bessie Hyde?" that appeared in the back of the October, 1985, *Outside Magazine*. He gave a short synopsis of Glen and Bessie's story, followed by the tale of Liz Cutler. He finished it with a teaser, "When she finishes her story, the others don't know what to think. Liz tells them she isn't worried about getting caught. Nobody would believe her anyway."

Martin J. Anderson, an amateur river historian who learned the trade from Dock Marston, had also been studying the Hyde story. Believing Liz might be Bessie, he called her. "Sir," she said, "I think somebody's mistaken. I don't know a thing about it and never did." Anderson explained the story in a bit more detail, but Cutler replied, "I never heard of Bess. I never heard of such a person."

Anderson pressed the issue. Cutler, irritated, said, "I happen to have a fabulous memory and never heard of Bessie Hyde in my life. I'm purportedly known for this fabulous memory at seventy-six. No, I never heard of it in my life."

Glen Hyde

One of the Human Identification Laboratory's reconstructions of the Kolb skeleton

Anderson was undaunted, writing to historian Norm Tessman, at the Sharlot Hall Museum in Prescott, Arizona, "The story was told on the river trip, she made the claim that she was Bessie, O.C. joked with her about Bessie, and now she claims she never heard of Bessie? For a person who has a fabulous memory, somebody is kidding somebody."

RESEARCH ON THE SKELETON case continued. Norm Tessman began working with the skeleton's clothing. Upon careful examination he found the belt buckle, reputed to be identical to the one in Glen Hyde's last photograph, to be markedly different. The skeleton had a standard heel-bar buckle, with the belt and tongue attached to one side; Glen Hyde's was a center-bar buckle. The skeleton's buckle was hammered metal; Hyde's was smooth.

Based on stories from the Kolb family, Tessman located a small mining adit on a precipitous hidden ledge below Yavapai Point where Kolb could have found the skeleton. He did an archeological screening of the diggings in hopes he would find some evidence linking the skeleton to the site. He found none.

Meanwhile, the Department of Public Safety found that the bullet came from an H & R Topbreak hammerless .32 caliber revolver, an obscure type of handgun first manufactured in 1903. And in Tucson, Birkby was having serious doubts about the morphology of the skull compared to Hyde's face.

 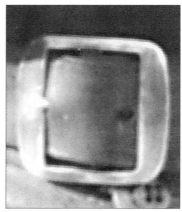

Buckle from the skeleton, Tessman photo

Glen Hyde's buckle, Kolb photo

Although the rumors continued to evolve, there were few factual developments until August, 1985, when Glen Hyde's niece, Barbara Hall, frustrated that she had gotten no replies from her earlier queries, wrote again, this time to Arizona Governor Bruce Babbitt. She wanted copies of all the reports and investigations, and any information on the disposition of the remains. Furthermore, her mother, Edna Emerson, now eighty-nine, wanted the belt buckle returned.

Babbitt, known for his fondness of Grand Canyon and its history, took a personal interest in the story. He urged the sheriff's office to summarize their findings. Birkby submitted a final report, stating that in addition to the age being wrong for Glen Hyde, six different facial reconstructions all failed to resemble him. "It is my professional opinion," he wrote, "that the submitted skeletal material in the above cited case are not the remains of Mr. Glen R. Hyde…"

On November 13, 1985, Judd sent final reports to the governor and Barbara Hall. "The…investigation proceeded through several resources; the FBI Laboratory, DPS State Laboratory, Northern Arizona University, University of Arizona Human Identification Laboratory, and Sharlot Hall Historical Society. They concluded that the skeletal remains are not those of Glen Hyde."

Liz Cutler,
Grand Canyon,
1971

Just a tiny thought,
And commonplace you'd say,
But for me it made a dream
Of loveliness, one lonely day.

— Bessie Haley

27

T TEN O'CLOCK in the evening on December 3, 1987, an estimated 20,330,000 Americans tuned their televisions to NBC. In his most dramatic Elliott Ness voice, Robert Stack began: "In 1928 Glen and Bessie Hyde disappeared on a perilous rafting trip on the Colorado River. Both were assumed lost until a woman claiming to be Bessie Hyde said she murdered her husband." Glen and Bessie had finally made prime time, headlining on *Unsolved Mysteries*. After a quick telling of the Hyde's voyage and the finding of the skeleton at Emery Kolb's, Stack went on, "Tonight, we'll examine these mysteries of the Grand Canyon. What happened to Glen Hyde, and his bride Bessie? Is their disappearance connected to the secrets of the bones in the boathouse?"

After lowering Glen's age to twenty-seven and Bessie's to a delicate eighteen, Stack built a suspenseful case for the Kolb bones being those of Glen Hyde. Then, on cue, Dr. Walter Birkby dealt a *coup de grâce*. After superimposing a portrait of Hyde over the actual skull, Birkby stated:

> The skull is of a different shape than the face of Glen Hyde. The eye orbits themselves are angled in a different direction than Glen Hyde's. The cheeks are wider. Even the shape of the chin is wrong. Glen Hyde's chin was somewhat rounded as we can see in the photograph, whereas the chin of the submitted skull tends to be fairly squared off. So, those features alone do not match. These remains— these remains that were submitted for analyses—are *not* the remains of Glen Hyde. Period. End of story.

"But the story, in fact, does go on," continued Stack. "The mystery deepens." He told the story of "an unknown woman" on a 1971 river trip, and introduced George Billingsley, one of the boatmen who was there, to describe her. "She was a very serious person," said Billingsley. "She was always just watching the Canyon. And helping out a little bit around camp, all the time wanting to do something. And, uh, fairly happy, but quiet. Pretty much to herself."

On screen, an actress by a campfire confessed to being Bessie Hyde. "It was right along here we had a bad fight. He beat me up," she said, "I got a knife and I stabbed him."

Billingsley went on, "She told it seriously enough to where we wasn't sure what else to say, but we all figured she was just making up her own story. But later on we got to thinkin', now maybe she really was Bessie because the age was right. And she never smiled when she said what she said. As if she really knew."

Scott Thybony capped the story:

> I got the full name of the woman, and eventually contacted her back in Ohio. But when I asked her about the Hydes and their disappearance, she denied everything. She said she hadn't told the story, she said she didn't know anybody named Hyde, and she said she wasn't Bessie Hyde.
>
> My gut feeling, though, is that she was.

Stack closed the show with haunting questions for the nation, "The mystery surrounding the story still remains unsolved. If the bones in Emery Kolb's boathouse are not Glen Hyde's, whose are they? And why did Kolb keep them hidden in that canoe for so many years? Did Bessie Hyde murder her husband on that turbulent river trip fifty years ago? And is she still alive at the age of seventy-nine?"

The Hyde story had leapt from a regional myth to a nationally-known legend, and the audience was left with the distinct impression that Liz Cutler was, indeed, Bessie Hyde, and that Glen Hyde was little more than a bullheaded brute. Bob Emerson, Glen Hyde's nephew, watched the show. Aghast, he called his uncle, Leonard Emerson, in Twin Falls. "I asked Len—because Len saw it too—if he thought Glen was really like that. And he said 'No. Not at all.'"

LIZ CUTLER's story finally began to crumble. Others who had been on the trip with her never bought it in the first place. Few were even aware of the story. Passenger Jim Bonney recalls, "Yes, I remember Liz. But I don't remember that particular story or Liz's comment about being Bessie Hyde." Richard Rogers remembers Liz fondly as active and cheerful, but says, "I don't remember a campfire gathering where Liz says she was Bessie Hyde. But that doesn't mean she didn't say so. If she did say it, everyone assumed she was kidding."

Recalled Roy Seylor, a fellow passenger: "Liz was a saucy and witty gal who teased everyone, gave as good as she got, mothered us all and made us love her for it." He elaborated in his journal, "Liz Cutler continues to be a character, to everyone's amusement. 'My doctor told me I mustn't do any cooking or dish washing…' We nickname her Queen Mother for her imperious attitude, which is a complete and delightful put-on… Liz…was soon running the boat. She looks like an aging Cleopatra sitting high and dry on that big barge, giving O.C. orders. It is impossible to get mad at her. Really a delightful woman."

But when asked about the Hyde myth, Seylor wrote, "As for the legend that Liz Cutler is Bessie Hyde, I feel you can discount it as just Liz's wild imagination. She was a very lovable gal, but full of 'stories,' so don't take her Bessie Hyde story too seriously. B.S. around the campfire sometimes has a way of being perpetuated too seriously, and this story is a case in point."

O'Connor Dale, who was there at the campfire that night, recalls a more jocular version than Billingsley:

> It was around the campfire, and after the story people sat around and talked for a little bit, but pretty soon everybody wandered off, and George and I were up by the fire. And Elizabeth joined us. And she had a little sparkle in her eye, and she comes up and says, "I have a confession to make."
>
> And I said, "What's that, Elizabeth?"
>
> She said, "I'm Bessie Hyde."
>
> She had kind of a little grin, and everything. And I asked her, I said, "Well, how'd you do old Glen in?"
>
> And she had a little knife, had a blade on it that long. [Dale holds

his thumb and forefinger about an inch and a half apart.] She said, "I did him in with this." You know, and we kind of chuckled a little bit. I think we joked and kidded with her a little bit, and then she went off to bed. And George and I went off to bed. And for the rest of the trip I don't know if George did, but I'd call her Bessie once in a while. And she was havin' fun with it, you know. She got a little attention and stuff like that.

Rick Petrillo, who had spawned the tale with his telling of the Hyde story that night, missed the whole thing:

> It was something that came out of the blue. There hadn't been any lead up to it. And later on George told me that this woman had said she was Bessie Hyde. I know when he told that story we didn't have any reason to buy it. I just couldn't quite believe it.

Norm Tessman, who had studied the Kolb skeleton, looked into Liz Cutler's background. He wrote the Meigs County Museum in Pomeroy, asking if they could tell him about Elizabeth Cutler. Margaret Parker, museum president, wrote back. "We knew the lady and had no problem with proving who she was prior to 1928, or for that matter, since." She mentioned that Marty Anderson had recently obtained Liz's birth records, and sent Tessman newspaper clippings of the Arnold family reunions that Elizabeth attended in 1925 and 1926. At that point both Tessman and Anderson dropped the case.

Anderson, in fact, wrote an essay in 1988 called "A Perfect Place to Hyde," wherein he claimed, unequivocally, that Elizabeth Arnold Cutler was not, is not, and never would be Bessie Hyde. "Tennyson once said that a half truth is the blackest of all lies, because it is harder to prove. This is the case here," Anderson blasted. He did not blame

Pickwick, the first bus line to Peach Springs, had not begun service to Northern Arizona in 1928, when Liz Cutler claimed to have taken a Greyhound back East

Liz Cutler, but rather those who spread the tale. "It would be unfair to accuse Liz of being an impostor. She was cherished by those who were with her. Her antics provided pleasure and enjoyment, and all knew that her statements shouldn't be taken seriously."

Although Anderson died before he was able to publish the story, it was placed in several Western library collections, where future researchers would have access to Liz's defense. Since that time, most historians who mention the story of the Hydes still mention the Liz Cutler variant, but do not endorse it.

THE ENTIRE THIRTY-YEAR CONTROVERSY could easily have been avoided with a trip to the tiny town of Pomeroy, Ohio. A beautiful town perched on the steep northern bank of a bend in the Ohio River, Pomeroy has a population of less than three thousand. The town is small enough, says Cutler's cousin Jean Seidenable, "that everyone knew when you threw the washwater out last." There were no secrets. Although Liz Cutler died in 1998, you can still mention her name and most residents will smile, or even laugh. "Liz! Big hats!" one woman remembers, referring to her huge collection of outlandish hats, one of which she was always modeling. "You never knew what she was going to say," says another old friend. "I used to see her in church every Sunday," says another man. "She would always have on one of those hats and long gloves on and say, 'Good morning, friend.'"

In Pomeroy, nearly everyone over forty remembers Liz; many knew her much or all of her life; several, in fact, are related to her—cousins, nieces, nephews. Mary Elizabeth Arnold was born there on December 2, 1908, the third child of Hoadley Arnold and Ida Duerr Arnold, who had been married at the County Fair five years previous. She was a wild and incorrigible child, but excelled in the public schools, graduating at the age of sixteen. Liz was the short sister in a tall family—her siblings were both six feet, while Liz barely reached five-foot-four. She and her sister Thelma were caring for their mother throughout a fatal bout with cancer at the time young Bessie Haley Hyde's disappearance was making headlines across the nation.

In 1938 she married Donald "Doodle" Ridenauer. "He was a doodle, all right! Merciful Heavens!" recalls Jean Seidenable. "He was as wild as she was. He had a convertible and drove like the wind." The marriage did not last.

Having lost both their parents, the three siblings, James, Thelma, and Liz, were especially close. When James registered for the draft, Liz insisted on registering too. When the draft board balked, she asked them just where it said she could *not* register. They gave in and Liz was soon drafted. She enrolled in the Women's Army Auxiliary Corps and rose to the rank of First Lieutenant. Liz's great-nephew, Tony Bibbee, often visited her in later years and was enthralled by her tales of flying bombers from one base to another under the famous pilot Jackie Cochran. During one flight to London, she told him, she received a distress call from an American ship. Dropping down through the clouds, she spotted a German U-Boat just beneath the ocean's surface and a torpedo trail heading in the direction of the ship. She swooped over the U-Boat and dropped the contents of the bomb bay, one depth charge. The U-boat surfaced, deployed life rafts, evacuated, and promptly sank. Later, in London, as Bibbee recalls the tale, Liz got to meet the imprisoned U-Boat captain. He was outraged that this tiny woman had sunk him. Liz Cutler's other relatives dismiss this as another of her tall tales.

Elizabeth remarried after the war, this time to J.J. Cutler, who was in the oil business in Belpre, Ohio, just across the river from Parkersburg. In 1950 she earned a B.A. from Marietta College, and went on to get her masters at Ohio University in Athens. After J.J. Cutler died in 1958, Liz taught psychology and served as Dean of Women at Rio Grande College, in Rio Grande, Ohio. She later taught at a Methodist college in Missouri. When she retired, she returned to Pomeroy and moved in with her widowed sister, Thelma Dill. The two sisters traveled much of the world together.

After Thelma died, Liz continued to be active in church and the local bridge club, but still took time off for travel and adventure. When Jean Seidenable asked what possessed her to want to go down the Colorado, Liz said simply, "I've never done that. And I always wanted to." So she did.

OF THE MANY people who thought, wondered or wrote about Liz during the last three decades, only one, Eleanor Inskip, a publisher from Moab,

Elizabeth Arnold Cutler: grade school, undergraduate, Dean of Women

Utah, bothered to visit her. She came away convinced that Liz was not Bessie Hyde, but suggested that Liz could have known someone else who really *was* a surviving Bessie. After spending an afternoon with Liz, warming up to the Bessie myth and getting off a few laughs here and there, Inskip told her she was surprised at her height, that she was taller than she looked in the portrait with Glen. With a twinkle, Liz said, "Well, Glen was really quite tall, you know."

Inskip later sent Cutler a manuscript by geologist Donald Baars—a lurid novel based loosely on the "Liz" variation of the Hyde myth. It was laced with sexuality, crudity, and physical abuse, and ended with a grisly murder. Liz was understandably livid. "Why can't they leave me alone?" she said, but followed that with an enigmatic, "Can't a person just make one mistake?"

WHEN ASKED about the Liz Cutler story today, George Billingsley expresses remorse.

> I really feel bad that we even started the story. We shouldn't have said anything at all. The whole story is just nothing more than just talking around the campfire. But at the time, being young boatmen, the way things were, we mentioned it a couple times. You know how boatmen are. You hear a story and it goes on to the next person and pretty soon after a few years, it recirculates. But I am sorry people have bothered her about this. I'm sure she did not want to be bothered. I think that's wrong.

Elizabeth Cutler's relatives back in Pomeroy had never heard Liz's Bessie Hyde story. A few had actually seen the *Unsolved Mysteries* program, but never realized the "unknown woman" was Liz. Her cousin Phil Windon says he can understand Liz saying it. "She was quite a joker," he laughs. Grand-nephew Tony Bibbee says, "She would be likely to tell a story like that if someone was grinding her gears, to shut up a know-it-all." Cousin Jean Seidenable chuckles, "I can just imagine her spinning a yarn like that. And I can just imagine the kick she got out of it. And the bigger the reaction, the more she would have laid it on."

When Elizabeth Arnold Cutler died in 1998, she left a legacy—a scholarship for students from Meigs County, named after her and her two siblings—the Dill Arnold Cutler Scholarship. Yet her fireside jest lives on in the West, primarily because *Unsolved Mysteries* made no attempt whatsoever to solve her mystery. It would have ruined the show. It was quite simple to persuade an entire nation that Bessie Hyde had murdered her husband and escaped. But it would have been far harder for a murderous refugee to convince the entire town of Pomeroy that she was a native, not to mention persuading Thelma and James Arnold to believe she was their sister. Besides: Liz Cutler was four inches too tall.

THE CASES WERE CLOSED, and Glen and Bessie Hyde were once again officially missing. But not for long. Shortly after NBC ran their *Unsolved Mysteries* segment, they received a call from Glenda Buklis. She had heard of the show and was curious if it could have been about her father, Glenn Hyde. He too had disappeared in 1928, not reappearing until the mid-1930s. While gone he had rafted rivers in Idaho and Canada, and had attempted Grand Canyon as well. But about the Colorado River trip he had never elaborated, except to say, "It didn't work out."

Georgie Clark,
Woman of the River

When I am very old,
I hope that I can say,
Life gave me all she could,
And filled each single day.

— Bessie Haley

28

~ *1992* ~

I N 1992 one of the most famous of all river runners, Georgie Clark,
"Woman of the River," died at the age of eighty-one. Bill George of
Salt Lake City was to deliver the eulogy:

> We bought Georgie Clark's company when she died. And I was
> conducting the funeral, down in Las Vegas. And her trusted friend
> and nurse—the person to whom she left her company legally, Lee
> McCurry, who has since passed away—called that morning, two or
> three hours before the funeral, and told me, "Bill, we don't know
> who we're burying today." Those were her words. I said, "What are
> you telling me, Lee?" I went over to Georgie's trailer and sat down
> with Lee.
>
> And I threw my funeral talk out the window. I mean it was not
> even *close*! Georgie's name was never Georgie. It was *Bessie*.

Since the mid-1950s, when she introduced the large inflatable motorized pontoon boats to Grand Canyon, the name of Georgie White—
later Georgie Clark—had been synonymous with river running. For
over thirty-five years Georgie took dozens of groups a year down the
rivers of the West, Mexico, and Alaska. In 1971 she divorced James
White and took back the name Clark, that of her first husband. For the
next twenty years she continued her trips through Grand Canyon at the
helm of her gigantic raft.

She was an extremely private woman. "You know, she was always so
secretive" recalls Bill George:

I knew her probably as well as about anybody, and I was never *ever* at her home until she was extremely sick. She lived in a mobile home in Vegas, but she would always meet you at the Silver Slipper. All of her business was transacted at the Silver Slipper. She never even let her *boatmen* come to her house. Nobody who *worked* for her ever came to her house. No *friends* came to her house.

In 1977 Georgie coauthored her autobiography with Duane Newcomb, and gave a rendition of her early life. She said she was born in Chicago to the destitute DeRoss family, and raised by her laundress mother in the absence of a deadbeat father. "My roots in Chicago go very deep," she wrote. She told of learning to swim in icy Lake Michigan at the Oak Street Beach. On January 22, 1928, when only a sophomore in high school, Georgie married Harold Clark because, she said, "I had strong sex needs." Their daughter, Sommona Rose Clark, was born on March 21, 1929.

Leaving Sommona Rose with Georgie's mother and older siblings Paul and Marie, Georgie and Harold went first to Miami, then New York, looking for work. Then, with a few dollars in their pockets, they bicycled to Los Angeles, where Georgie's family joined her. She soon divorced Clark. "Husbands," she said, "have always come second with me." Georgie and Sommona Rose spent much of their spare time over the next few years hiking, skiing, and bicycling. Georgie remarried, this time to James White, a chronic alcoholic. Working odd jobs, they were able to make ends meet. During World War II Georgie, like Liz Cutler, trained as a pilot to ferry planes in the face of acute pilot shortages.

In 1944 tragedy struck. During a bicycle ride to Santa Barbara, Sommona Rose, then fifteen, was struck and killed by a hit-and-run motorist. Georgie was devastated and went into a severe depression. Months later friends dragged her to a presentation by an eccentric desert enthusiast named Harry Aleson. Georgie found a kindred spirit in Aleson. The two of them soon began hiking the remote country of the Arizona Strip north of Grand Canyon. Their first hike was from the lower Grand Canyon, up, out, over the cliffs, and across the desert to Saint George, Utah—a route very similar to what Glen and Bessie Hyde might have attempted had they been stranded on the north shore.

Aleson and White soon progressed to river travel, swimming down the lower seventy miles of Grand Canyon in their life jackets. They soon began to experiment with inflatable rafts and in 1952, Georgie and another friend rowed Grand Canyon in a small ten-man raft. Georgie had found her calling.

In 1953 Georgie began taking passengers on "Share-the-Expense" trips. Finding the ten-man rafts too small, she began strapping them together in various configurations to make a larger, more stable craft. In this manner she invented the triple-rig—the same sweep-boat type of craft later used on Liz Cutler's trip—a rig run in the same manner as the Hyde scow. Eventually she began buying huge thirty-three-foot bridge pontoons and running them with an outboard motor. By strapping three pontoons together, she came up with her *pièce de résistance*, the unflippable floating island called the G-rig. With her crash helmet strapped around her chin and a Coors beer in one hand, she motored her G-rig for the next thirty years.

She attracted a devout following, some passengers returning year after year. In 1984 Georgie hired Marty Hunsaker as a truck driver. He soon advanced to one of Georgie's boatmen. Hunsaker's sister, Lee McCurry, hired on the same year as a caretaker for Georgie's ailing sister Marie, who had long run Georgie's business. After Marie died, McCurry took over the role of office manager. Roz Jirge, a long-time passenger and later crew for Georgie, knew Hunsaker and McCurry well. "For a long time there," Jirge wrote to river historian John Weisheit, "Marty Hunsaker and Lee McCurry thought that perhaps Georgie was actually Bessie Hyde." Perhaps, Jirge speculated, their theory may have had some roots in Georgie's "joking statement to the effect that she wished she could become a black widow spider after her death so that she could come back, mate with a man, and then kill him!" This fit in nicely with the common myth that Glen Hyde was a hard-edged brute.

In 1989, Hunsaker's raft flipped in Crystal Rapid. In his attempts to make sure all his passengers were out from under the boat, Hunsaker drowned. Two years later, after the 1991 river season, Georgie began to lose weight. By December she was in such bad shape she finally had McCurry take her to a doctor. It was cancer, terminal. She sold her company to Bill George, a long-time friend and owner of Western River

Expeditions. She then had her pets put to sleep and peacefully awaited her fate. On May 12, 1992, she died in her sleep.

Four days later Bill George sat agog in Georgie's trailer with Lee McCurry:

> Lee said, "You won't believe the stuff I've come up with in the last three or four days" She said, "Number one, here's her birth certificate. She was born Bessie DeRoss. And they lived in Denver."
>
> They never lived in Chicago like she says in her book. She never *saw* Chicago. But you never know, from any of her books, what's real and what isn't. You can't take her word for *anything*. So we got to doing some other things and then Lee hauls out a marriage certificate. A certified copy, stamped with the original notary stamp in the corner of it, of one Glen R. Hyde and Bessie Haley.
>
> Well, so Lee gives me that copy. It's in Georgie's lingerie drawer. She said in that same lingerie drawer was a pistol. And so my mind starts going round and round and round. Then all these things start to come down. One of 'em I knew—I was aware of it, cause Georgie had mentioned it. She *hated*, with a *passion*, Emery Kolb. For what reason, she never said. She would go into a meeting—if he were there—and walk away. She would not be around him *whatever*. And then, these other things...
>
> But this marriage certificate that was in her drawer just blew me away. How would she *get* it? Why would she *want* it? It's just been an intriguing enough story. There are just so many parallels. I'm not saying it's one and the same, but it has crossed my mind more than once.

Georgie and Harry Aleson's hikes in and out of Grand Canyon in the same area the Hydes vanished are certainly curious. Her invention of the sweep-style triple-rig even more curious. And when Georgie first met Harry Aleson, she was living in Los Angeles—the very city Bessie was moving to when Glen Hyde came into her life. And at that time Bessie was traveling with Greta Granstedt, the role model who had shot her own boyfriend in the stomach some years earlier.

But Sommona Rose's birth in March of 1929 would mean Bessie— that is, Georgie—would have been at least four months pregnant—and

Bessie Haley, High School, 1924   Georgie Clark, wedding, 1938

some have hypothesized she *was* pregnant—when they were last seen at Grand Canyon Village. Tight timing. "That's not tight," laughs Bill George. "That's fine. Knowin' Georgie, that's not a problem."

"Well you know, going with visual memories of Georgie and pictures of Bessie," says Gaylord Staveley, another river outfitter and long-time acquaintance of Georgie, "yeah, you can see some bone structure maybe and some stuff facially that…who knows? But if so, what a secret to keep all your life. That's deep dark."

Deep. Dark. But highly unlikely. In researching *Woman of the River*, his biography of Georgie, Richard Westwood found that Georgie was indeed born Bessie DeRoss in Guymon, Oklahoma, on November 13, 1910. Her parents, George and Tamor DeRoss were listed in Denver's 1920 census with children Marie, 16, Paul, 12, and the youngest, whose name was then listed as Georgia, 9. They remained there for another ten years, by which time Georgie had married Harold Clark. Although there are gaps in her life that are unexplained, and her autobiographical notes are often pure fiction, Paul and Marie certainly seemed to think Georgie was their sister. Could that have been faked? With no other living relatives, perhaps they could have been a trio of refugees, adopting the name of a deceased family. That's really stretching.

But the marriage record in the lingerie drawer? Inexplicable. On close inspection, however, it turns out to be a certified copy of the record in the Twin Falls County Recorder's book of marriage records, available to anyone with two dollars and knowledge of where to look. And it most certainly was obtained after the invention of the photocopy machine. Why Georgie had it, no one knows.

But Bessie Hyde and Georgie Clark were not the same woman. Georgie's eyes were a piercing pale blue-gray. No one recalls the precise color of Bessie's, but in every portrait, her irises are dark, rich, and apparently a deep chocolate brown. Bessie had a delicate nose; Georgie, a definite schnoz. And there is this problem: Georgie was five inches taller than Bessie Hyde.

Gravestone two miles from Hyde home in Hansen, Idaho

Just a song
That couldn't be famous,
That no one would ever hear.

To its creator
It was sweet music,
And helped to dry broken tears.

— Bessie Haley

29

~ *1985 – 2000* ~

T HAT LEAVES GLENDA. Glenda Hyde Buklis's tale may be the strangest one yet. Her father really was Glenn Hyde. He died in California in 1951, only two months after Glenda was born. What she knows of her father comes from her mother, older siblings, and her uncle, Glenn's brother Roy. Roy was several years older than Glenn, but lived to a ripe old age, going parachuting when he was in his nineties. Whereas Glenn had been extremely reticent throughout his life, Roy enjoyed telling the stories that Glenn had confided in him. Pieced together, Glenn Hyde's story goes something like this.

Glenn William Hyde was born near Bolivar, Missouri, on February 15, 1905, the seventh of nine children of Luther Hyde. When Glenn was five the Hydes moved to Piru, California, an agricultural valley north of Los Angeles, then south to Brea, a small oilfield town in Orange County. Luther worked the oil rigs and eventually became Superintendent of the Water Department. Glenn's first car was a wreck that he was paid to take custody of. He soon became a rum-runner, and later a truck driver. In 1927, Glenn's girlfriend Nora got pregnant. Luther announced that Glenn *would* marry her whether he wanted to or not. Glenn reportedly said "You can make me marry her but you can't make me stay." Edna Hyde was born on January 28, 1928. Six weeks later, Glenn Hyde vanished.

The next seven years of his life are undocumented. What little is known comes from Roy, and from things Glenn mentioned in his later years. Glenn divorced Nora in Nevada, and began what he called "river rafting." From Glenda's description of the boats, they were flat-bottomed wooden boats that had an oar off either end. Scows, very probably. "He liked rafting," says Glenda. "He built all his own boats. Didn't like how other people built them. Besides, he couldn't afford them." He ran rivers in Idaho, Oregon, and Canada. Roy said Glenn had also tried boating in Alaska, Glenn's only comment being, "It's not a good idea." At some point he made an attempt on the Colorado River, through Grand Canyon. When pressed for details, he invariably said, "It didn't work out." Pressed further he might add, "It was a failure. Nobody wants to hear about failures." The only other details Roy had were that Glenn "pretty nearly didn't make it," and he "was staying with some Indians in the desert afterward."

Glenda gives an approximate date of late 1928 for the trip, because Roy and his wife Jeanne, who had just returned from prospecting in Alaska, heard the story in 1929 when Glenn met up with them in Idaho.

GLENN REAPPEARED in Brea around 1936 and resumed truck driving. Asked why he never told anyone where he was he simply said, "Well, if I were dead you'd have heard." His truck was hit by a train in the late 1930s, and Glenn had one stiff leg from then on.

In 1942, Glenn picked up a young girl hitchhiking from California to New York. Bea Fahnestalk was a descendant of the Van Buren clan and wanted to visit the Van Buren homestead in New York. She was on spring break from the University of California at Berkeley. Concerned for her safety, Glenn drove her clear to New York, then picked her up on his return trip, driving her to her parent's house in Potters Valley, California. When he dropped her off he said to Bea's mother, "Take care of my future bride." They were married three weeks later.

Glenn served in the Merchant Marine during World War Two, nearly drowning after his boat was sunk. The Hydes had been married several years when Bea found out that Glenn had a former wife and child. Outraged, she demanded to know why he had never told her. "It was easier that way," he said. End of story.

Glenda was the last of five children. Her father died of a variant of

Glen Rollin Hyde, 1927

Glenn William Hyde, 1948

black lung, brought on by the toxic dust from the iron ore he trucked most of his life. He was buried on his forty-sixth birthday.

Throughout her childhood, Glenda and the other children heard stories of their father, often just bits and snatches heard between the grown-ups. One tale in particular was never fully explained, as the conversation always stopped as soon as children appeared. But there had been a woman in Glenn's life during his long absence. Her name was Bessie. Just when they met and what went on is unknown. But once, when Glenda was playing under the dining room table unnoticed, she overheard a conversation which explained the scar on her father's back: Bessie had stabbed him. Glenda crawled out from under the table and asked why Bessie had stabbed her father in the back. She was sent away.

The parallels are so uncanny that it seems parallel universes are colliding. Glen Hyde had two sisters, Edna and Jeanne. Glenn Hyde named his first daughter Edna; Jeanne was his brother's wife. Glen and Glenn disappeared in 1928. Both ran rivers in Idaho and Canada. Neither of their trips on the Colorado worked out. Both were about six feet tall. A search for birth records for Glenn William Hyde comes up blank.

During one ten-year period the state of Missouri kept no birth records whatsoever. Glenn falls conveniently in the middle. A 1948 photograph of Glenn Hyde bears a disturbing resemblance to Glen, in both posture and facial appearance. And the story of Bessie stabbing him in the back fits right in with Liz Cutler's tale of murder. The myth could expand to where Bessie stabbed him, left him for dead, but he didn't die. Glen vanished and recovered with the help of local Indians, and assumed the identity of Glenn seven years later.

It is an intriguing story, but there are serious problems, not the least of which are that Liz was not Bessie—and Glenn had a preexisting family in Brea that recognized him when he returned. It's hard to fool relatives. Could it have been a conspiracy? Glen and Glenn could have actually met as children between 1908 and 1912, when both families lived in Southern California, or in 1928, when both Glen[n]s were in Idaho. Could they have made a deal?

Only if Glenn's parents and eight siblings were in on it. And it would beg the larger question of what did they do with the real Glenn, who appears with the family in both the 1910 and 1920 United States Censuses. As to the physical resemblance, Dr. Walter Birkby, the forensic anthropologist who debunked the Kolb skeleton points out, "Glen Hyde had more protuberant ears than Glenn; Glen has a more pointed chin (which is without a cleft) than does Glenn, who appears to have a cleft; Glenn also appears to have more pronounced nasal alae (i.e. more nasal "flare") than does Glen."

Glenda Buklis and her siblings are relieved to know that the two Glen[n] Hydes were not the same person. Their family history is exciting enough without another abandoned wife. Glenda writes:

> It is an amazing coincidence, to find two men with the same name (although slightly different spelling on the first name) who had such similar adventures, during approximately the same time period. Makes me wonder: why didn't anybody record both boat trips? Did my father's fail so early on that nobody cared? Or was it just that he didn't (as this other Glen & Bessie did) call on the media to witness?
>
> That was the one thing that really seemed out of character, for my father, from all I'd been told about him: he did not seem to be the

Glen Rollin Hyde's signature, 1925

Glenn William Hyde's markedly
different signature, 1938

Santa Ana Register
Wednesday, February 14, 1951
Too large a family to fool

kind of guy to care about fame. He did what he wanted to do, for his own personal satisfaction, & didn't apparently care about other people's opinions, or that others would know of his accomplishments.

My father, according to my uncles, wasn't interested in that. He just wanted to know what he could do, for himself. He never tended to brag about what he did, just offhand remarks. Such as his laconic "it just didn't work out," when pressed for results of his trip down the Grand Canyon. He tried it. He failed. End of story. That's pretty much how he tended to explain things, according to my mom & my uncles. If successful, he would say more, but not much more. He just didn't tend to find it important, to tell others of his exploits. They had to ask questions, & if they didn't ask the right questions, they didn't get the answers. Uncle Roy told me that Glenn never volunteered much.

In the end, we must place Glenn with Liz, Georgie, and the bones in the boathouse, as merely another set of admittedly astonishing coincidences, leavened with seven decades of evolving mythology.

THERE ARE STILL MORE TWISTS, of course. Going chronologically through the Polk's City Directories for Parkersburg, West Virginia, a Bessie Haley shows up in 1924 on Myrtle Street on the South Side. Not until 1926, two years later, do William and Charlotte Haley appear on Oak Street, in central Parkersburg, with Bessie L. Haley, a student, living with them. The South Side Bessie disappears. In 1928 there are no Bessies listed. Then, in 1930, Bessie L. Haley reappears on the South Side, on Broadway. In 1932 she is Bessie M. Haley, then from 1937 through 1944 she reverts to Bessie L. Haley. Then she disappears for good. The dates are interesting, bizarre, curious. And in all probability, entirely coincidental.

Two miles southeast of the old Hyde place in Hansen, Idaho, lies the tiny Rock Creek Cemetery. Nestled in the grass is a small undated marker with the name LIZZIE HYDE. Like Bessie, Lizzie is a diminutive form of Elizabeth. There are no other Hydes in the cemetery. A local cemetery record, also without dates, claims Lizzie to have been a daughter of John Weighall, buried nearby, who died in 1932 at the age of eighty-three—not too old to have claimed someone Bessie's age as his daughter. He would have been about fifty-six when Bessie Haley was born. Another small town secret?

A dozen miles east of Peach Springs, Arizona, lies a tiny, dilapidated settlement named Hyde Park. Could a surviving Glen or Bessie have been so bold? "No," says Bob Goldenstein of Peach Springs. "That was founded by Faye Hyde. He ran the only liquor store in the area."

In 1973, Ray Johnson and a few of his friends were on a river trip in lower Grand Canyon. During lunch at Mile 234, recalls Johnson, "A fellow in our small group climbed over the rocky embankment behind us and came back with a porcelain doll face that he had found wedged between some rocks approximately fifty feet above the water." Bessie was known to have written a poem about a doll. The Hydes are thought to have wrecked at 232, just two miles above where the ancient doll's face was found, and the scow was found just a few miles below. Could Bessie, wondered Johnson's group, have floundered ashore with her dolly and lost or jettisoned it as she climbed out 234-Mile Canyon?

The United States Social Security Death Index lists some two dozen Bessie Haleys born within ten years of Bessie Haley Hyde, and a dozen Bessie Hydes. Add to that eight Glen or Glenn Hydes born within ten years of Glen Rollin Hyde. All lived to ripe old ages. Any of them could have switched identities. The imagination runs wild. The fewer the facts, the better the story.

Yet every spicy myth about the reappearance of Glen or Bessie Hyde withers in the glare of rigorous examination. None hold any more credence than Bessie's high school *Prophecy,* which stated "Bessie Haley, who was disappointed in love, is at the southpole collecting polar bear's teeth." As tempting and intriguing as it is to imagine one or both of the Hydes escaping to a new life, there is not a shred of evidence to support it. No, it is back in the Lower Granite Gorge of Grand Canyon, on the last bitter cold day of November, 1928, where our scrutiny must fall.

An unknown friend with
Bessie and Glen, 1928

232-Mile Rapid, looking upstream

Part Four

Pieces of the Puzzle

A calm
moment in
the Lower
Granite
Gorge

Sometimes:
Impatient waves
Break too far out.
And come to shore—
Unnoticed.

—— Bessie Haley

30

"MY GOD!" I shouted. "Did you see what happened to Brian?" After getting the nod from us that we were lined up satisfactorily, Brian had turned, motored his sportboat into Lava Falls, and vanished. Moments later we saw his arms, then the propeller, then spare oars flying. He and Cooper were getting pummeled. I stared, aghast.

"*Forget Brian!*" screamed Jeri. "Look what's happening to *us!*"

I refocused. In my rapt horror I had let our tight left position slip toward the center of the river—the single most common mistake on a left entry to Lava Falls. I lurched at the sweeps, straining left as hard as I could, but with no visible results. By now we both knew that you just *cannot* row a sweepboat sideways. But there was nothing else to do. "*We're going over the Ledge!*" I shouted to Jeri. The Ledge—a steep plunge into a frothing, rocky maw that rarely lets a boat escape undamaged. Or right side up. I once watched a dory flip six times in a row in there. In our case, at a far lower water level, it would be disastrous.

"*No we're not!*" screamed Jeri, in an effort to will us to the left. "Don't give up! Just…"

I couldn't understand her. I was pulling for all I was worth, watching the Ledge draw us in. "What?" I bellowed. My lungs were burning, my limbs were rubbery. She was still hollering at me. "*What?*" I shouted again, panicked and cross, and still pulling for what little I was worth.

I took one last stroke as we dropped over the left side of the Ledge. We missed the rocks in the bottom by inches, and somehow escaped the heart of the pit. I dove to the floor and heard a horrific crash as the rear sweep hit the dance floor. The handle of the sweep snapped off, zinging over my head. We hit another wave, spun sideways, but I knew the worst was over. I jumped up and began struggling with the forward sweep, hoping Brian would be able to catch us before we flushed into Lower Lava Rapid with a broken sweep.

Brian and Cooper motored up, drenched and bedraggled, eyes wide. They nudged us to shore, all four of us shouting our stories at once amid the spirited popping of beers. We had survived. We were *going* to survive. From here to Diamond Creek was little that should harm us. We could let down our guard. For the first time, we could enjoy the trip.

THE NEXT FORTY-FIVE MILES to Diamond Creek are scow country. There are dozens of small riffles, shallow gravel bars, swooping S-turns—the kind of things in which scows excel. We were exuberant, trading from one boat to the other, everyone getting a chance at the sweeps. The horrors of Lava, Hance, and the Gorges dimmed and slipped away. We actually began to like the damnable tub.

Somewhere around Mile 192 we were sucked suddenly off to the right into a vigorously recirculating eddy. Brian was long gone downstream. Jeri made a half dozen attempts to break out, sliding up the eddy parallel to the shore, with the forward sweep reaching out to catch the current. Each time the current spun us back into the eddy. I finally relieved her and tried the same thing—two times, three times, four times—to no avail. At one point I ended up sideways in the eddy and began pushing hard up the eddy, broadside. It couldn't work but we had tried everything else. The whole boat hit the eddy line at once, and seconds later we were in the current, peeling out downstream. A light went on. Ah-hah. The trip was almost over, but we were finally learning a few tricks.

That afternoon we passed the Hydes' last camp at Mile 210. Somewhere along here Rick Petrillo had told the Hyde story to Liz Cutler, launching the most popular variation on the Hyde myth. For many guides, this is still the stretch of river where the Hyde story surfaces. Some tell a short version, just hitting the highlights. Others draw it out, including as many permutations as they know. Some sink so low as to include a dreadful variant I first heard from a dory boatman named Tim Cooper. It is the tale of the slippery Cuban trader, Enrico Haravem.

Haravem had been working his way across northern Arizona in the late 1920s, making shady deals with Anglos and Indians, then moving on when things got too cramped. By late 1928, he was holed up in upper Travertine Canyon on the Hualapai Reservation, having already earned the enmity of many of the tribe. Although only conjecture, it is thought that Haravem may have encountered Glen and Bessie somewhere around Diamond Creek or below. Known as quite the ladies man, Enrico may have gotten an eyeful of wee Bessie and seen the desperation in her eyes. Seizing the unique opportunity, he killed Glen and headed south with Bessie. It stands to reason. Ever since that time no one has seen Hyde. Nor Haravem.

OUR LAST FULL DAY on the river was by far the best. Without the weight of imminent disaster, and with, finally, a feel for the craft, we enjoyed every riffle and rapid. That evening, five miles short of Diamond Creek, two boatmen on a commercial raft trip hailed us in to their camp, asking if we might want a steak dinner. We floated a ways past them, pried our way into the eddy and drifted back up along the shore to their camp. "So tell us:" one of their passengers asked as we docked, "What do you think happened to Glen and Bessie?"

The maddening fact was, as much as we had learned about Glen and Bessie's trip through sheer violent experience, we could still not say what happened. Plain and simple, we did not know. On the other hand, we felt we knew quite a bit more about who they were.

During our weeks aboard the scow, Jeri and I often discussed the relationship between Glen and Bessie. For us, time on the boat had not brought about discord, but rather closeness in the shared sense of adventure. The obvious exceptions were the moments leading up to major rapids. Yet tension is not only natural at the head of a serious rapid, it is an essential tool for survival. It is a readying for extreme danger; it is the basic human instinct of fight or flight. By the time we sailed through the tailwaves of that same rapid, all friction was gone.

We guessed the same was true for the Hydes. To be frank, neither of us ever accepted the "brutal Glen" theory. Loving, devoted fathers such as R.C. Hyde rarely raise wife beaters. Throughout his life, Glen Hyde repeatedly showed signs of a greater than normal respect for women and their abilities. Glen had quietly let Bessie take the limelight at the South Rim. "They were a very nice couple," Kolb had said, of "a very modest, decent type." When Kolb offered them life jackets, "all they did was to look at each other and smile." "Decent," Sutro called Hyde. "Not domineering."

We both felt that whatever incident took place at Hermit was simply a result of extreme tension at a difficult spot, blurred by decades of speculation and elaboration. It was an aberration without lead-up or follow-through. Things had been fine at the South Rim, yet tense at Hermit. And within a few days afterward they were taking pictures of each other. Their signature at Diamond Creek had been written from a supine position on the bedsprings. The tension had eased. They were working together again as a team. And most likely, they died as a team.

So was it the boat's fault after all? We had hoped to learn enough about running the scow on our trip to feel comfortable with it, to redeem its sullied reputation as a killer craft. In this aspect, too, we failed. Although we felt we understood the *theory* of running a sweep-boat in whitewater, that theory simply had not borne out in practice. We had gotten violently pummeled on a regular basis. From what we had experienced, it could well have been the boat that killed them. But perhaps we had missed some basic point of technique. Perhaps a real sweepboater could have slicked through the rapids that knocked us silly. I would have to go to Idaho to find out.

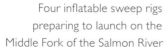

Four inflatable sweep rigs
preparing to launch on the
Middle Fork of the Salmon River

Some ships sail
From port to port,
And never are
So far from home;
While others head
For the open sea,
And go to shores
And bays unknown.

The first feel
Quite content and safe,
So different
From the roving brother;
But they can never know
The wondrous sights,
Of lands or stormy waves,
As do the other.

— Bessie Haley

31

~ July 2000 ~

O N JUNE 30, 2000, I untied the bowline of a twenty-two-foot inflatable sweepboat, pushed the boat from shore, and climbed aboard. Dan Hawley, veteran sweepboat driver, stood on the dance floor with two heavy steel-shafted sweeps in hand. We were running support for a six-day commercial tour of the Middle Fork of the Salmon River. Our job was to carry the lion's share of camp gear from camp to camp, and have it set up by the time the passengers arrived in rowboats. I was the camp flunky and sweepboat helper.

Hawley and I would be alone on the boat most of each day and I could pick his brains about the finer points of sweepcraft. I was particularly lucky to be with Dan Hawley, as he is one of the more senior of the dwindling circle of living sweepboat drivers. He had run his first sweepboat nearly thirty years earlier, and had made well over two hundred trips down the Middle Fork. "Hey Dano," said one of the younger sweepboat drivers at the launch ramp. "Where's the run at Sulfur Slide on this flow?"

"Far left," said Hawley, grinning. The younger man winced. Although it was not late in the year, there had been precious little snow the previous winter, and the river level had already dropped to barely runnable. "Got any advice?" asked another sweepboat driver, looking a little nervous. Hawley told him what little he thought might help—places to be left or right, certain things to avoid—and we went on our way.

The modern sweep rig differs from the old scows in several ways. The inflatable hull can bounce off, squish around, and straddle rocks that bashed and blockaded the old wood scows. The new inflatables are also, by and large, smaller than many of the great scows that ran the Salmon. Most sweep rigs today are between twenty and twenty-four feet. Although old Cap Guleke used to seat a few passengers in the far corners of his scows, out of the way of the swinging sweeps, the newer craft have rounded off those corners, leaving no room for tourists to ride. The sweepboat is now exclusively for cargo.

The sweep-oars are different too. The huge wooden shafts have been replaced with square tubular steel, and a zig-zag kink has been welded into them to bring the blade closer to the hull of the boat and a foot or two lower, giving a distinct mechanical advantage.

The Middle Fork is the last river where sweepboats are run on a regular basis. A few—very few—occasionally run the Main or Lower Salmon, or even more rarely, the Snake River through Hells Canyon, but rowboats are now the craft of choice for most outfits on those bigger streams. The Middle Fork alone provides superior sweepboating. I asked why.

"Gradient," said Hawley. The Middle Fork drops twenty-seven feet per mile. The other rivers have too much flat water and too much wind. And the rapids are too big on the Snake. They would beat you to death."

Within moments of our departure we were barreling downstream, weaving between rocks and waves, walls and pour-overs, Hawley busy prying the boat from one side of the small, steep river to the other. Some of the moves he made seemed impossible. After all, we had no means of propulsion. Yet when I looked over the side of the craft I noticed, to my utter amazement, that we were moving faster than the river itself. I could not recall this happening to us on our scow in Grand Canyon. I asked Hawley just what was going on. It was only then, nearly four years after our scow trip, that I began to understand what was *supposed* to have been happening.

"Sweepage," said Hawley. He explained that a sweepboat, given the opportunity, will quickly accelerate beyond the speed of the current. This speed is called sweepage, and only when you have sweepage can you effectively sweep. Without sweepage, you have little or no control of the boat. "You're just wrestling it," said Hawley. But when I asked how the boat could go faster than the water, I got the same answer from him as I got from every sweep man I asked: "If you figure it out, be sure to let me know."

I later floated the concept of sweepage among a group of physicists. I described the theory, and asked if they thought it physically possible. They all agreed that, in physics talk, the effect is called supervelocity, but failed to agree on whether it was possible for such a ponderous craft to attain it on such a marginally sloped surface. The fastest flow of a stream, they explained to me, is near the center of the current, near the top of the water. This is where the water has the greatest distance from the drag of the river channel. This is where the alert sweepboatman attempts to keep his craft. But could the sweepboat actually exceed that speed? Some thought that since the water is sliding downhill in response to gravity, there was no reason a sweepboat could not slide downhill on the surface of the water like a child on a waterslide. Others felt it impossible, that there had to be another explanation. But like the bumblebee who physicists have said cannot fly, we swept on in blissful ignorance.

Hawley went on to explain that there are several enemies of sweepage. Wind is one of the worst. Consequently, we launched early each morning and ran nonstop to camp to beat the afternoon winds. Another foe is dragging on rocks or the gravel river bottom. It can ruin a perfectly good run, as Hawley demonstrated three days later in Haystack Rapid. We had entered with good sweepage and were prying our way to the left when we dragged across a shallow boulder bar, stalling our forward

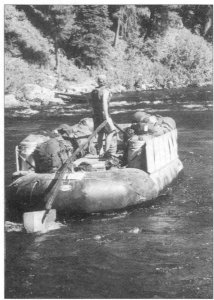

Dan Hawley on the dance floor,
a second sweep rig close behind

Sweepboat departing Boundary
Creek on the Middle Fork

speed. It was momentary, but devastating. "Plan B!" shouted Hawley. He pointed the boat straight downstream into a nest of boulders and waited for his sweepage to rebuild. At the last moment, as I was preparing to swim for it, he pried quickly to the left, then the right, snaking through a slot I would have sworn was too narrow for a kayak.

A third enemy, Hawley explained, was a rapid configuration called pool-and-drop, where the water slows to nothingness at the head of a rapid before cascading over the next drop. This causes the sweepboat to enter each rapid with little or no sweepage. I nodded, realizing in the queasy pit of my stomach that every rapid in Grand Canyon is pool-and-drop. There was one more enemy—big waves. Once the waves get more than a couple feet high they begin to slap the bow of the boat in the rapids, slowing the boat and killing whatever sweepage you have gained. The ill feeling crawled from my stomach right up the back of my neck, standing the hair on end. In the minor rapids in Grand Canyon the boat could gain some sweepage and maneuverability, which struck a familiar chord. The minor rapids had been fun. But in the major rapids, there would be no chance. Just as the sweepage began to build it would be slapped silly, leaving the boatman in a losing wrestling match with the sweeps, dead in the current, out of control.

Back at the Middle Fork launch ramp, I had told Hawley and two other sweepboat drivers that my wife and I had run Grand Canyon in an old wooden sweep scow. There was no look of awe or respect on their faces. "Why?" asked one. They squinted at me as if I were some sort of large, green, nine-legged bug. I later asked Hawley how he would like, with his decades of experience and his modern inflatable sweepboat, to sweep Grand Canyon. He was aghast. "That would be horrible!" he said. "I wouldn't want to be anywhere near it."

He went on to tell me how sane folks stop running sweeps when the Middle Fork gets too high, and described several horrendous sweep wrecks of those who pushed the limit. "Big boat, big wreck." Sweepboats, he reassured me, are for medium-high to low flows on a constant-gradient river. Period.

So Jeri's and my beatings had not been our fault. Our mistake was not that we failed to learn the art of sweeping. No, our mistake was far bigger. Our mistake was thinking that a scow was a viable vessel for Grand Canyon at all. That we would not fare well in the big rapids was a foregone conclusion. For us—and for Glen and Bessie. Little wonder that the Hydes were spooked at Hermit, in the heart of the biggest rapids of the Upper Granite Gorge. It wasn't working.

Glen Hyde knew scows, and was a master sweepman to have made it as far as they did. He had trained under Guleke, the number one guide of the Salmon. He had studied the literature of the Colorado and went into the adventure with open eyes. But what he didn't know—what there was no way to have known in 1928 because no one had tried— was that scows don't work in that sort of water. Even Guleke himself had plans to sweep Grand Canyon. One can only imagine Glen Hyde's struggle between his innate confidence and optimism, and the bafflement, frustration, and fear that the major rapids brought him.

FOR THE LAST TWO DAYS on the Middle Fork I ran the scow most of the time, while Hawley coached, kibitzed, and occasionally praised. We gained and held sweepage and swept swiftly downriver. Paradoxically, sweeps, with no visible means of propulsion, are the fastest boat on the Middle Fork. Rowboats pulled out of the way as Hawley hollered "Sweep!" or "No brakes!" We passed groups of rowboats shortly after spotting them ahead of us, and before long they disappeared from sight upstream. Even though some physicists claimed it impossible, we were on a runaway freight train, weaving our way down the river. It was absolutely exhilarating. No wonder Hyde was sold on the sweepboat. If only he could have known that this beauty of a craft would become, in Grand Canyon, a beast.

The fang rocks at 232-Mile Rapid at the water level the Hydes saw; right-hand rock is about four feet out of water

Oh! mamma dear, please come!
My dolly must be drowned,
When I put her on the creek,
She sunk without a sound.

Wee Betty's eyes filled with tears,
Where could poor dolly be?
Perhaps she'd turned to a mermaid,
And drifted out to sea.

— Bessie Haley

32

August 2000

SHORTLY AFTER DAWN I packed a light sleeping bag, a leaky air mattress, a small bag of victuals, and my camera into my kayak, and paddled into Diamond Creek Rapid. Somewhere in the twelve miles below here, Glen and Bessie Hyde had, in all probability, met their untimely demise. Although my wife and I had run this stretch on our test run of the scow four years earlier, that had been our first day in the boat and the river level had been quite high. We had floated willy-nilly over the obstacles that might well have overcome the Hydes. Scared witless, we had learned nothing.

But during the parched summer of 2000, the Bureau of Reclamation turned down the spigot at Glen Canyon Dam to a steady 8,000 CFS—almost exactly the flow on which Glen and Bessie vanished. On August 22, armed with a far better knowledge of the strengths and weaknesses of sweepcraft, I dropped into the Lower Granite Gorge of Grand Canyon hoping for some last clue as to the Hydes' fate.

It is hard to maintain supreme confidence in a kayak in whitewater when you are all alone. Although the rapids of the Lower Gorge were well within my ability, there was something unsettling in knowing that this was the stage of water that claimed the Hydes, and that whatever got them might be lurking down there. Uncertainty in a kayak breeds instability, and I teetered through the rapids stabbing at the water with my paddle, wondering just how good an idea this really was.

A copy of Bessie's journal in hand, I tallied off the rapids, riffles, and streams starting with the long series of small rapids at Diamond Creek. After a few more small rapids I came to Travertine Canyon, where Bessie had marked another small stream and a rapid. Below that came two more riffles and 231-Mile Rapid. Bessie marked one riffle and a rapid. My best guess concurred with most other river historians—231 was likely the last mark in her book. From my kayak at the head of the rapid I could look down the long winding fall and see no serious obstacle. I could see smooth water below. From the dance floor, the Hydes would have had a far better view, and likely ran it without scouting. "I looked everything over that showed a big drop," Glen had written to Jeanne after Marble Canyon. This rapid showed no big drop, nor had the Kolbs reported finding tracks in the sand patches on either shore.

I pulled ashore, climbed the cliffs on each side of the river to scout the rapid and visualize the Hydes' run. Although there were obstacles, the rapid looked quite easy for a scow. From top to bottom, diagonal breaking waves pushed into the deep-water route, making it simple to remain out of harm's way. I doubted seriously that the Hydes would have come to grief there. I paddled through.

A mile later the river jogs slightly to the left and enters 232-Mile Rapid. Again, I gazed downstream from my boat, trying to imagine the thought patterns of the Hydes. The river swept back to the right, hiding much of the lower half of the rapid behind the shoreline. But the calm eddy on the left, below the rapid, was plainly visible. From what I could see from my kayak, the rapid was short and did not drop more than five feet—much less than many of the major rapids. Although Glen Hyde doubtlessly knew he was only ten miles from a serious drop at Separation Rapid, it is unlikely he had ever heard of 232. It was in none of the literature. Moreover, sweepboats are so slow in getting back into the current from shore that any scouting must be done from several hundred yards upstream—a near impossibility at 232 due to the sheerness of the cliffs. Again, the Kolbs had seen no tracks, and again, my best guess was that they ran the rapid without scouting it.

I paddled ashore on the left and climbed to a ledge fifty feet above the rapid. Although I knew well what I was about to see, my heart still sank. By then I had been working for more than a year on a book about the Hydes, and had developed a great respect and affection for them. It was wrenching to see what confronted them on entry to 232-Mile Rapid.

Entering with little or no momentum—no sweepage—the first giant breaking diagonal wave would have slammed them toward the right. Two more diagonal waves in quick succession would have forced them farther right. A continuous set of waves below would have prevented them from gaining any sweepage, any maneuverability at all. By then they would have seen what was about to happen, but it would be too late. Adrift in the main current, they would have hurtled down the right shore straight into three bedrock fangs that jut five feet above the river. For a sweep scow, it is hard to imagine any other run.

In the seventy years since the Hydes' disappearance, dozens of experienced boatmen have come to grief on the fangs in low water. A book could be written on the calamities and extrications that have taken place there. Rafts and dories have been wrapped, ripped, flipped, and sunk. Whole thirty-seven-foot motor rigs have been brutally violated by the fangs. "If you fail to get fouled in 232 you have probably not had a *wilderness experience* in the Canyon," wrote Dock Marston in 1973. "Study... will probably show that this one has gotten more victims than any three other rapids in the Canyon combined."

On November 17, 1990, on the twenty-first day of his solo raft trip through Grand Canyon, David Whittlesey entered 232 on 11,500 cfs. The fangs flipped his fourteen-foot rowboat. After a failed attempt to right the upside-down boat, he climbed onto the bottom and, with one oar, tried to steer the raft to a sandy beach. 234-Mile Rapid washed him overboard, whereupon the boat ran over him, crushing him against the shallow rocks. At that point impending hypothermia forced him to abandon the boat and drag himself ashore. Shoeless, he tried to work his way downstream along the cliffs of the south shore, but a handhold crumbled. He tumbled into the river, breaking four teeth and knocking himself unconscious. When he recovered enough to proceed, another rock tumbled and broke two toes. He finally reached a small sandy alcove and waited for help. It was another six days before a Park Service helicopter found him there. Meanwhile, Whittlesey subsisted on one stale beer the floods had wedged in a high crevice, one grasshopper, and a lizard.

Most rapids in Grand Canyon are reasonably forgiving. At low water, 232 is not.

I SLIPPED BACK into my kayak and paddled into the current. I entered the rapid, stroked hard to the right shore to avoid the great lateral waves in the center, and pulled into a small pocket in the rocks about one hundred feet upstream of the fangs. I was quite certain the Hydes had made it this far, and felt that their fate very likely rested on what happened in the next hundred yards. Although it was still morning, I climbed ashore and made camp in the rocks, midway through 232-Mile Rapid.

The Lower Granite Gorge is remarkable for the sinuous carving and fluting in the granite and schist along the shore. The tortured rock is at its most magnificent along the right edge of 232. In extreme high flows the river churns wildly here, spinning and whirling its sediment, grinding and polishing a garden of Henry Moore sculptures. At low flows the river exposes its handiwork as it thrashes along the base of the statuary. I camped in a sand-floored pocket amid the spires, sister rocks to the wicked fangs offshore below me.

I scrambled along the shore and climbed a large spire just below the fangs and stared, begging some sort of answer from the inscrutable river. "What did you do to them?" I shouted. "How did you get them *both*?" "Or did they escape from this trap only to enter a worse one on shore?" The river roared and surged against and amongst the fang rocks, but failed to elaborate.

I decided to explore the options the Hydes might have had on shore. Suppose they survived a crash, but lost the boat. Or they somehow lost the boat in an attempt to land before the fangs. Then what? At 232, the Granite Gorge is nearly one thousand feet deep, capped by the Tonto Platform of relatively gently sloping Bright Angel Shale. Above the Tonto, the Redwall cliffs rise another two thousand formidable feet on the south shore and the Kaibab Limestone rises an additional thousand beyond that on the north. But just climbing to the Tonto would have been a challenge. Both Glen's and Bessie's leather boots were still aboard the scow. They were wearing tennis shoes—flimsy canvas affairs that were likely threadbare this late in the trip. One side-

Tough terrain: Looking downstream from 232, &ang rock visible at lower left; looking upstream from near Mile 234, 232-Mile Rapid visible in distance

ways step might have ripped the uppers from the soles. And the terrain was brutal. Steep schist, unscalable in many places, broken and unstable in the rest. In my brand-new ninety-dollar off-trail running shoes I was having trouble getting a foothold in most spots.

Although I fantasized finding two skeletons huddled together at the foot of a particularly steep cliff, the fact was I had no idea which way the Hydes might have gone. Glen's brother-in-law, Carl Emerson, said the Hydes planned to stay along the river in the case of a wreck. Would they have followed the boat, hoping to catch it? Or tried to work back upstream to Diamond Creek, which they knew to be a viable exit from the depths? Or would they, as R.C. Hyde feared, try to scale the cliffs? It was anyone's guess. Within three miles upstream or downstream, the cliffs on both shores become impassable below the Tonto. Any prolonged attempt to escape would have forced them at least up to the Tonto Platform. There are side canyons at the head of 232 on both shores that would provide relatively easy access to the Tonto. But downstream of the rapid, the climb would be far more difficult and chancy. From the Tonto they could have worked downstream until they found their boat, or upstream to Diamond Creek.

But the searchers found no trace. The Kolbs found no tracks, but there is precious little sand along the rocky shore and the Kolbs did not have time to do much exploring. R.C. Hyde found no tracks, no cairns, no cast-off garments, no distress signals. Nothing. But would he have been likely to? In 1931 Deputy Sheriff John Nelson saw James Ervin's tracks both above and below the Redwall—but he had Ervin there to point them out, and the tracks were barely a day old. The Hydes had been gone nearly a month when the first searches began, and it had rained, blown, and snowed in the meantime. "I would be amazed," said Dr. Harvey Butchart, who spent much of his life exploring the trails, routes, and hidden nooks of Grand Canyon, "if their tracks would show." Tracks or no tracks, Butchart, long a student of Grand Canyon history, suspects they died in the river.

Geologist and boatman George Billingsley, who has mapped the entire lower Grand Canyon, much of it by foot, disagrees. "Today it's probably the most remote region in Arizona, other than the river itself," he says. "I tend to think the boat just got away from them. And they couldn't *stay* there. They had to go. And they just simply didn't make it out of the canyon."

Although Ervin and the Bundys proved that strong and determined individuals might climb out to either rim, those folks were wearing decent shoes. From what is known of Glen Hyde's strength and stamina, he might well have made it out if uninjured and sufficiently shod. Of Bessie, less is known.

Was R.C. Hyde's search insufficient? In a sense, yes—one could scour that steep and wrinkled terrain for a lifetime and still miss a human body. It is some of the most uncooperative country in the world for a foot search. Although R.C. Hyde's searches were astonishing in their thoroughness, they were not conclusive and he knew it. He wanted to return again to examine the side canyons he had not been able to descend into from above. Thoughts of unsearched cracks, crevices, and canyons plagued him for years.

But had they been on foot, shouldn't the airplane searches have spotted them? Doubtful as well. When John Evans and Bill Belknap were retracing James Ervin's climb in 1967, Belknap's wife Fran and daughter Loie flew into the canyon to check on them with local pilot Earl Leesburg. Although they knew where to look and had intermittent radio contact, Loie Evans says her father and her fiancée were nearly impossible to find. It took several passes before they spotted Belknap waving a yellow ground sheet. The country is vast and convoluted, humans but tiny specks.

But if we assume the Hydes were fit enough for a serious attempt at hiking out, we must also assume they would have left some sign—a pile of rocks, a rag on a stick, a message stamped in the sand—in the hopes searchers might find them. Had they done so, R.C. Hyde would very likely have spotted it. Like George Mallory, whose body lay in plain sight on the slopes of Mount Everest for seventy-five years before being found, Glen and Bessie may still be out there somewhere. But there was never a clue to indicate they had left the river. Not a trace had been found.

I made several forays to high outcrops looking for likely routes, but found nothing promising. Spooked by the sheer vertical exposure and loose footing and discouraged by the infinite number of wrong places to look, I returned to the rapid.

FROM MY PERCH on the rocky shore, I watched the river boil and rage into the fangs. Seventy-some years of conjecture had been heaped on so few actual clues. When the Kolbs found the scow, everything on the boat was in running order, as if the Hydes had been abducted by aliens midstream. Glen and Bessie had taken no gear with them—their permanent separation from the boat was not intentional. The scow appeared undamaged, although there was substantial water in the boat. And then there was the rope stuck to the floor of the river.

Some feel the boat simply slipped away from them while they were ashore. The records at the Phantom Ranch river gage from a day previous indicate the river was rising on their last day. A slight rise combined with slipshod mooring habits described by Sutro could easily send a boat downstream unattended. They may have stopped to scout 231 or 232, and lost the boat. One or both might have dived in after it; one or both might have died trying to hike along the shore or out to civilization. But no tracks, no sign, no clue.

The Kolb brothers felt one or both of the Hydes were pulled in by the boat, either while scouting 232 or attempting to line the boat along the shore. Emery later stated that the Hydes had told them of Bessie nearly being pulled from shore near Lee's Ferry when the wind shifted the boat. Perhaps, the Kolbs thought, the same thing could have happened here. Landings are small and tricky in the Lower Granite Gorge, and the currents sometimes unpredictable. The boat weighed two tons, and Bessie but ninety pounds.

While there is no record of the Hydes lining at any of the rapids, it is possible they may have tried it. If so, a boat of that size could certainly have ripped loose from their grasp or toppled them from shore. Yet lining seems so dangerous and impractical that it is unlikely they tried it. Kolb, like many other early river runners, may have put forth lining as an option simply because they had often lined themselves—and to admit the rapids could all be run without lining was uncomfortable.

Whether pulled in by a wind gust, or during a lining attempt, the rope would have to actually pull Bessie or Glen or both completely into the river. Wouldn't they have let go before that? Probably so, if they *could* have. But perhaps they were no longer gripping the rope—the rope was gripping *them*. Some critics have said Kolb should never have cut the bowline of the scow, that Bessie might have been affixed to the end of it, snagged in the rocks. Others have poo-pooed the thought. Yet it is a very real possibility.

In the early 1970s a young woman named Cyd Wimberley was working as a helper on a large commercial motorized raft trip through Grand Canyon. At 209-Mile Rapid the engine failed. As the raft washed out of the rapid it slammed the left shore and lodged on a submerged boulder. Wimberley and another crew member climbed gingerly ashore. They began pulling ropes off the front and back of the thirty-seven-foot raft, rocking the boat back and forth in an attempt to free it. Wimberley was pulling on the upstream rope when the boat broke loose and swung into fast current. As her rope played out, she looked down. "It happened so fast," she recalls:

> There really was that moment of ultimate realization of seeing the boat get free, and glancing down and realizing, as coils are going out, my foot was in the middle of them. And it was too late. It was that split instant type of thing where you realize that it's caught but there is nothing you can do about it because it's happening so fast. I could

not possibly have gotten my foot out of that mess in time. The boat was just tearing down in the current and of course the line was just uncoiling until it met my leg at which point it coiled around my leg and picked me up. And I think I screamed.

It dragged me through several of those boulders, as tall as I am, by the side of the river. I mean they were *really big boulders*, because it picked up my left leg and scraped the inside of both of my legs as it dragged me over that first big boulder. And then I hit a couple more. It broke my jaw in three places and the rope cut the muscle right below—you know where your calf muscle bulges out?—it actually, internally, severed that muscle. And then I hit the water.

It didn't knock me out. I remember being towed along with water going over my head. But I had a life jacket on. And so I floated. The boatman had a big knife on his belt, and he reached down and he cut the rope, which freed me. And then somebody came in the water after me and dragged me onto shore.

I think it's really miraculous I wasn't killed.

Had Wimberley been without a life jacket, had she been unconscious, had there been no one aboard the boat to free her, she might well have drowned and sunk to the bottom—or to the end of the rope. Such a scenario could have happened to one of the Hydes—perhaps an escaping boat at a scouting point, perhaps during an attempt to dislodge a boat pinned on the fangs at 232, perhaps during a sudden forced landing below.

Les Bechdel, one of the country's foremost experts on river safety and rescue, admits, "Any time you have a length of loose line, swift current, and a firm anchor point such as a boat or the shore, the potential for disaster exists." The rope the Kolbs cut could have held one of the Hydes by the ankle.

Or not—perhaps the Hydes had merely tied a knot in the end of their frayed rope to keep it from unraveling, and that knot caught in the rocks. The Kolbs felt that the fact the rope was overboard indicated the Hydes were ashore. But the rope, laid in a loose coil across the back of the scow, could easily have washed overboard at 232.

Again, neither Francy, Harbin, nor the Kolbs had seen tracks on

The perfect scow trap: Sweepboating 232 at the water level

Note:
The fang rocks of 232 are under water at medium to high river flows. It is only at low water such as the Hydes saw that 232 becomes an extreme hazard.

Tonto Platform, where upriver and downriver hiking is most feasible. Climbing to Tonto near 232 would best be done up the small sidecanyons near the head of the rapid.

5

Fang rocks. Although a scow might withstand a collision, the violence could injure and/ or eject one or both people. Nearby underwater rocks could complicate the issue.

4

Adrift in the main wave train of 232, a scow would stand little chance of missing the fang rocks which lie directly in the path of the current.

In the Granite Gorge below 232, downstream travel along the shore becomes increasingly difficult and finally impossible. An attempt to reach the Tonto from this area would be extremely hazardous.

Calm water. If uninjured, a swimmer might make shore at this point.

N

encountered by the Hydes

1

The rapid comes into the view of a boatman around Point A. The eddy, Point C, is clearly visible with little appreciable drop. The lateral waves and fang rocks are not yet visible. Note extremely difficult terrain for landing or scouting at this point.

2

By Point B the lateral waves and fang rocks come into view. However, by this time the scow is fully committed to running the rapid. A scow would now enter the rapid with no momentum or maneuverability.

3

A series of three to four strong lateral waves would thrust any unpowered vessel to the right side of the river. The height of the waves would prevent a scow from gaining any momentum or control.

Relatively calm eddy, visible from upstream

Hole

Pourover boulder

Far left entry to rapid

Obstacles prevent an entry on the left side of the lateral waves. Although it is possible to go to the left of these obstacles, it is difficult even for a highly maneuverable rowboat.

shore since the last major rapid at Mile 217, the last rapid too long and steep to be scouted from midstream. Most likely the Hydes were scouting what rapids they could from the boat and had not gone ashore since Diamond Creek. Most likely, they were well into 232 before they saw the fangs at the foot.

ALMOST WITHOUT EXCEPTION, rapids in Grand Canyon are formed at the mouths of side canyons, where flash floods and debris flows obstruct the channel and thrust the river toward the far bank. The river pools, then drops over the obstruction, foaming and fuming along the far side of the channel. A few rapids are formed where two side canyons join the river from opposite sides, their deltas thrusting the river toward the center of the channel. But in nearly all rapids, the deltas are ancient enough that any bedrock obstacles have been ground away eons ago. Although some rapids have relatively recent boulders complicating the main channel, boatmen can run the primary deepwater chute in nearly all rapids.

There are two notable exceptions, where the side canyon delta thrusts the main flow straight into a bedrock projection. One is Bedrock Rapid, where the Hydes crashed and spent two days working themselves free and repairing the boat. The other is 232.

I continued to stare at the fang rocks, mesmerized by the unrelenting violence of the river pummeling the spires. I was overcome with sadness, knowing that these two people in whose lives I had been immersed for so many months now, had died here. I had grown fond of them—too fond—and now, in my mind's eye, I had to watch them die.

I went over and over what I now knew of the strengths and weaknesses of sweepboats. On the Middle Fork of the Salmon I had come to understand how magnificently a sweepboat *can* perform, and why our scow had performed so poorly in Grand Canyon. And 232 fit the definition of everything wrong for a sweepboat. At 8,000 CFS, Glen and Bessie would, in all probability, despite any evasive attempts, have hit the fangs violently. If they ran 232, they likely wrecked. Whether it threw one or both of them overboard is conjecture. There was no apparent damage to their scow—but after our damage-free collision in Crystal Rapid, it seems unlikely that there would have been.

Fluted rocks on shoreline at 232; fang rocks visible in top center

IF WE LEARNED NOTHING else on our scow trip, we learned this: In big rapids, life on the scow is extremely violent. The sheer force of the windmilling sweeps is very possibly the culprit. The side-to-side action of the sweeps can launch a person like a golf ball from a sand trap. Bessie had been ejected once in Cataract Canyon. The vertical swing of a sweep can strike anywhere. Glen had taken a shot to the chin in Sockdolager, knocking him nearly unconscious and clear out of the boat. Anything could have happened during a collision with the fangs. If both Glen and Bessie were sharing the sweeps as they often did, there could have been a dual launch. Environmentalist, boatman, and river historian Kim Crumbo may not have been far off the mark when he joked, "The reason the Hydes' remains were never found was because no one ever looked high enough on the Redwall, where their bodies were flung."

Once in the river, swimming, regardless of Glen's or Bessie's prowess, would have been difficult. In the immediate vicinity of the fangs the water is extremely turbulent, and many sister fangs lie close beneath the river's surface. Within a hundred feet the water slows to a bubbly calm, with a chance to swim ashore. Yet very possibly they were in no condition to swim by then, due to a bludgeoning from the sweeps, entrapment on the fangs, or just plain drowning in their heavy winter clothes in frigid water.

Any number of scenarios can be built around the hazards the Hydes would have faced at or near 232-Mile Rapid, and many of them include one of them diving in to rescue the other. Although we know little of Bessie's heroic nature, we know two things about Glen. He was an excellent swimmer, and he was R.C. Hyde's son. Given his father's relentlessness in searching for the two, it is easy to imagine Glen diving again and again and again for his bride, until the river finally took him. Although it is slim consolation, most near-drowning victims who have been resuscitated report a quick end to panic, replaced by a quizzical sadness, dissolving into a final euphoria. There are worse ways to go.

There are countless possibilities, all entirely plausible, none much more likely than the other. None of them pleasant, none that comforting to think about. But the question then circles back to the same problem we have with death onshore: why was neither body ever found?

Of ten lifejacket-less drownings between Lee's Ferry and the end of Grand Canyon between the years 1880 and 1935, only three bodies were recovered. Peter Hansbrough of the 1889 Brown-Stanton Expedition made it eighteen miles before beaching. Royce Dean, who drowned when the Lee's Ferry boat capsized, went twelve miles. Iven Bundy set a record of nearly ninety miles, running Lava Falls and the entire Lower Granite Gorge. The other seven were never found. By these numbers, the odds are better than two out of three that a body would not have been found. "In those days," Michael Harrison reminds us, "the river never gave up its dead. Never!"

Dr. Tom Myers, former medic at Grand Canyon, and Dr. Larry Stevens, a Flagstaff biologist, analyzed data from some twenty-two lifejacket-less drownings whose victims were recovered during the past century. On the average, they surfaced approximately 41½ days later, 19½ miles below the point of drowning. The colder the water, the longer a body stays under. Statistically, then, Glen and Bessie would not have surfaced until after all the initial searches were over. Even then, they would have been downstream of Spencer Canyon, where the Kolbs ended their search of the river, but still above all subsequent searches of the Lower Gorge.

During the winter of 1928–29, the river dropped to an extreme low of 3,000 CFS. If the Hyde bodies surfaced, they would likely have washed ashore in the sluggish current, somewhere in the remoteness of lower Grand Canyon. The buzzards would have had the remainder of winter and early spring to recycle what they could before the high June flood of 110,000 CFS scattered whatever was left from Grand Canyon to Mexico. So it is not at all amazing that no bodies were found. It would be more amazing if one had.

Perhaps one was. While the Kolbs were building a boat to search for the Hydes, Murl Emery had reported a prospector's story of having seen a leather jacket float by, just above Boulder Canyon, well over a hundred miles below 232. The story died soon after it was printed, yet it begs a grisly question: without a body to buoy it up, would a leather jacket float?

GLEN AND BESSIE HYDE achieved lasting fame for their attempt on the Colorado, although not the sort they had in mind. Had they succeeded—and they nearly did—they would have been celebrities. Instead, their fate remains unknown, their fame macabre. Their story's end probably took the Hydes by complete surprise. They had been doing extremely well for the last week of their trip, and had every reason to believe they would finish their honeymoon voyage on schedule. Until Mile 232. With all evidence weighed, it appears their end came quickly and unexpectedly in the Colorado River. "Like a flash it comes to them that death will reckon with them; as it does with all the world," Glen wrote in 1922. The Hydes "would lie, forever, unseen by any human eye. The thought came of death without end, to the end of time, time without end."

~ *Finis* ~

R.C. Hyde at
home, 1940s

Oft times
Mighty Waves
Come thundering.
To end on the sand—
Forgotten

— Bessie Haley

Epilogue

*A*FTER GRANDDAD CAME BACK from looking for Glen, the Depression hit. At that point my grandfather owned some more property—another farm or two—and he mortgaged everything to go search for Glen. And I know my father gave him all that he could spare. At one time I think that Granddad was worried about losing everything.

I remember he was moving some equipment from the Hansen place to the Murtaugh place. He had a wagon, kind of a buckboard type wagon and a two-horse team. And so I rode with him, because my mother didn't want Granddad to be alone. I couldn't have been more than five or six years old. But it took the whole day. I slept a good part of it in the back of the buckboard. Instead of following the road, which would go into Hansen and follow the highway, he cut across to what we used to call Poverty Flats and he just went across country through the sage brush and old abandoned farms.

Bob Emerson treasures his memories of Rollin C. Hyde. Throughout his childhood, he would visit his grandfather every Sunday out at the Home Place in Hansen, and would often go out there on weekday afternoons. He remembers Hyde as a very soft-spoken, gentle man. He did not socialize. He subscribed to one magazine, the *Literary Journal*, which he read each week, and had a full set of the *Harvard Classics*, most of which he had read. "I never knew my grandfather to take a drink. He may have, I just don't ever remember him doing it. I don't recall him ever going to church. He was just quiet, very quiet. Dignified. And as they say, everyone called him Mr. Hyde."

When Emerson was in high school, he spent several summers working for his grandfather. By then Jeanne Hyde had married Al Brent, and R.C. had given her the Hansen Place. Hyde had moved out to Glen's old farm near Murtaugh.

He had a hired man full time who did the irrigating and he lived in the house that would have been Glen's. Granddad lived in the tarpaper shack across the road. Just a tarpaper shack. There was no electricity there. No plumbing. No nothing. We hauled water from across the road from the other house. It was no more than ten by twelve feet. There were bedsprings on the floor, and a wood stove, and a table.

Granddad did not have a tractor on the place. He always worked

Painting of Glen Hyde's Murtaugh farm by Robert Moore,
Robert and Roberta Emerson Collection

horses. I was usually doing weeding and hoeing and then helping pitch bundles onto the wagons for threshing and haying. And Granddad usually did the cultivating, the plowing with the horses, and often helped with the irrigating.

Granddad would get up and cook breakfast, always pancakes, and wake me up about 5:30. We would be at work by seven. We would have lunch and then work until seven. I would usually go for a swim in the canal, and when I got back he had cooked his own dinner and an extra potato for me. He went to sleep before dark, in a small screened porch on the east side of the shack. I slept under a tree.

My mother said that wherever grandfather went, he always planted trees. Even on the place across the road, there were three or four cottonwood trees that he'd put in. They were only about ten feet tall when I spent summers and worked there. A few years ago we sold off the buildings and took the house down. The farmer that had the property across the road took those trees down. They were huge then.

At seventy-six, Bob Emerson talks about Hyde with palpable homage. It is Rollin Hyde, not Glen the lost river runner, that the family looks up to. The family, in fact, knows little of Glen Hyde's life story. "Glen's loss must have had a very severe impact," says Bob Emerson. "But the Hydes—my grandfather and mother and Aunt Jeanne—were very introspective. They never really talked about the past or about Glen."

"Bob's grandfather was always very accepting of everything that life dealt him," adds Bob's wife, Roberta Emerson. "Except the loss of his son."

BOB EMERSON returned home from World War II after serving as a mule packer in the Tenth Mountain Division. On October 16, 1945, his grandfather was injured at the Savage Produce Company's potato cellar in Murtaugh. Emerson recalls:

It was after the war and I was talking to someone—probably in the pool hall—who had been there, and he was telling me about it. He said that it was kind of starting to rain a little and the ground was a little bit slick. But he said the kid—the truck driver—was a real cowboy. He said he always drove too fast, and that he came in too fast, pulling in to the potato cellar. Granddad was there directing the trucks. He skidded and pinned Grandfather against one of the pillars.

He was eighty-six then. At that time Grandfather was making plans that were at least ten years into the future for developing the farm and trying to add on to it, pick up more land and things like that.

Hyde did not appear seriously injured. Two men helped him up and took him to his daughter Edna's home in Kimberly. As he had throughout life, Hyde was prepared to brush himself off and march on. Indeed, throughout history, the motto of the Hyde coat of arms has consisted of a single word: "Onward." The following morning, Edna took her father into the Twin Falls Hospital for X-rays. At noon Hyde suddenly became ill, and within the hour died of a punctured lung.

His body was shipped to Spokane for burial beside his wife, brother, and two infant sons. Edna, Carl, and Bob Emerson drove up for the funeral with Jeanne and her second husband, Les Allen. Only two people from Spokane came to the funeral. One was a relative from the Rosslow family. The other was an old man who had worked for Hyde in Spokane decades earlier. The *Spokane Spokesman Review* made no mention of Hyde's passing. By 1945, the once-famous Hydes of Spokane were long gone and fully forgotten. Back in Idaho, the Twin Falls paper carried a short article, titled: *Rancher, 86, Hurt at Spud Cellar, Dies.*

"I remember Aunt Jeanne saying something about the obituary in Twin Falls," recalls Bob Emerson. "She said 'Dad would not have liked this. He always considered himself a builder.'"

Glossary of a very few whitewater terms

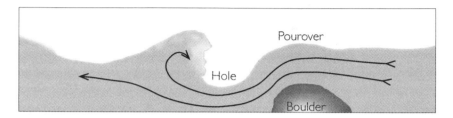

Rapid	A fast-moving, turbulent descent in the river, containing solid obstacles and large waves.
Riffle	A smaller version of a rapid, usually containing few hazards other than running aground.
Falls	On the Colorado River in Grand Canyon: a particularly chaotic or steep rapid; Granite Falls, Lava Falls. Does not contain free-falling water—not a true falls.
Hole	A steep, deep, violent, exploding wave, caused by a shallow obstruction immediately upstream; can stop and/or invert a boat.
Pourover	A shallow boulder over which the river pours, often causing a steep drop and hole immediately downstream.
Lateral Waves	Strong waves breaking diagonally from the shore into the main channel—have a tendency to force watercraft toward the center current.
Tailwaves	The central set of waves, often quite large, at the foot of a rapid, after the main descent is over and the river is slowing to normal speed.
Eddy	A current contrary to the normal downstream current of the river, usually found along shoreline below rapids or other constrictions.
Whirlpool	An ephemeral, three-dimensional eddy.
Boil	The opposite of a whirlpool; an upwelling of water.
CFS	Cubic-feet-per-second. The unit of measure the United States Geological Survey uses to measure streamflow; literally, the number of cubic feet of water that flow by a given point in one second.
Paddle	A shaft with a handle on one end and a blade on the other, used with two hands and no oarlock to power a boat.
Oar	A shaft with a handle on one end and a blade on the other, used to pry against an oar lock to power a boat.

Sweep   A long oar-like device extending from the bow or stern of a sweep-boat, used to guide the boat in the river.

Rowboat   A boat propelled and guided by two or more oars extending from the sides of the boat.

Raft   Originally: a floating assemblage of logs and/or lumber. Nowadays: an inflatable boat, guided by paddles, oars, sweeps, or a motor.

Sportboat   A rigid, inflatable boat powered by an outboard motor.

Motor rig   In Grand Canyon: A large, motorized, twenty- to forty-foot inflatable passenger raft used for whitewater tours.

Sweepboat   A large raft or scow, sixteen to forty feet long, guided by sweeps extending fore and aft. Has no means of propulsion.

Sweepage   Supervelocity: The phenomenon whereby a sweepboat, due to the effects of gravity and the slope of the river's surface, exceeds the speed of the current, thus allowing the craft to be maneuvered.

Scouting a rapid   Going ashore to look over a rapid before running it.

Running a rapid   Navigating the rapid from within the boat without aid from shore.

Portaging   Bypassing a rapid by carrying or dragging the boat along the shore.

Lining   Avoiding a rapid by lowering a floating boat along the shore with ropes. Considered extremely hazardous.

Swamping   Filling a boat with water to the point of impaired navigation.

Bailing   Emptying water from a boat.

Left, right   In river usage, left and right are always as seen looking downriver.

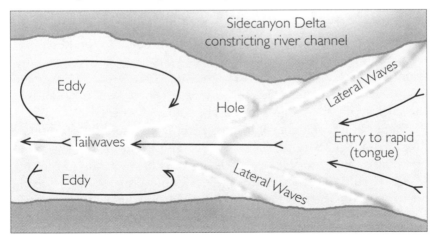

Acknowledgments

*T*HIS BOOK would have been a phantom of what it is without the enthusiasm and generous support of the extended Hyde family. Bob and Bobbie Emerson, Herb and Mary Allen, and Len Emerson took me into their homes and shared not only their memories, but their family photographs and archives. Bob Emerson's tales of his grandfather and Uncle Glen gave more body to this story than any research could have provided. And the more than sixty images from the Emerson and Allen family collections tell volumes that could be conveyed in no other way. Alice Emerson Nelson and Don Olmsted shared family memories and records by phone and mail.

Sadly, Bessie Haley Hyde's family is gone. Both Bessie and her brother Bill died childless. Bessie's father died alone in New York City, her mother died in the Home for Aged Ladies in Easton, Maryland. Neither left papers. Laura Garrett, Bill Haley's widow's niece, shared what she knew of the family, yet Bill left no family materials.

I owe a deep debt to the late Dock Marston for amassing his mountains of material concerning the Hydes and others; in particular, his foresight in transcribing Lottie Haley's entire collection of letters from the Hydes that form the core of Part Two of this book. The original letters no longer exist. For firsthand memories of the search for the Hydes, thanks to the immortal Michael Harrison.

I owe thanks to the entire Flagstaff boating community for their support during the construction of our sweep scow; to our ground support team, Scott Davis, Jim Bowles, and Gregg Wallace; to our river support team, Cooper Carothers, Martha Clark, and Mike Yard, and most especially Brian Dierker, for repeatedly saving our lives. A special thanks to the late Dugald Bremner for the cover photo and others.

Thanks to Jerry Hughes of Hughes River Expeditions for his support on the Middle Fork of the Salmon River, and to Dan Hawley who put up with my interminable questions and was brave enough to let me sweep. Thanks to the Prescott College Alumni Association for getting me to and from the Lower Granite Gorge for my final kayaking sortie.

Thanks to the Utah and Grand Canyon boating communities for

indentifying the Hydes' photographs; especially Dave Lyle, Steve Young, Greg Woodall, Dave Derosiers, Kenton Grua, and Michelle Starr.

For Jess Nebeker stories, thanks to Renae Stastny, and Brenda and Terry McCandless. For help with Greta Granstedt's story: Ted Granstedt III, Annette Granstedt, Alicia Granstedt, and Jason Fabbri.

For help with the Glens and Bessies section, George Billingsley, Scott Thybony, Dr. Walter Birkby, Norm Tessman, Rick Petrillo, O'Connor Dale, Eleanor Inskip, Glenda Buklis, Bill George, Roz Jirge, Gaylord Staveley, Gail Burak, Richard Rogers, Jim Bonney, Art Gallenson, Jean Seidenable, Phil Windon, Tony Bibbee, and James Arnold.

For assistance in analyzing the possibilities of the Lower Granite Gorge, Harvey Butchart, Bob Goldenstein, George Billingsley, John and Loie Evans, Les Bechdel, Cyd Wimberley Martin, David Whittlesey, and Tom Myers.

Librarians and curators throughout North America have aided greatly in obtaining or guiding me to the appropriate materials. I would like to thank: Dr. William Frank, curator of the Marston Collection at the Huntington Library; Karen Underhill, Laine Sutherland, Richard Quartaroli, Kim Kliewer, and Diane Boyer at Cline Library Special Collections, Northern Arizona University; Nancy Compau at the Spokane Public Library; Kim Besom at Grand Canyon National Park Archives; Lisa Bentley of Historic Takoma for help with the history of Takoma Park; Kathleen Larkin of Prince Rupert Public Library; and Roy Webb, Marriott Library, University of Utah.

I would also like to thank the gracious staffs of the following libraries and museums: Utah Historical Society, Idaho Historical Society, Cheney Cowles Museum in Spokane, Pittsburgh Public Libraries, San Francisco Public Libraries, Parkersburg Public Library, Martin Luther King Library, Washington D.C., Easton Public Library, Twin Falls Public Library, Kimberly Public Library, Baltimore Public Library, Marshall College Library, Huntington Public Library, Elko Public Library, Northeastern Nevada Museum, Las Vegas Public Library, and the staff of the Davenport Times in Washington. Thanks also to the following schools for helping the Hyde family retrieve records for this project: University of Oregon, University of Idaho, Parkersburg Public Schools, Spokane Public Schools, Kimberly Public Schools, St. Paul's

School, Marshall University, and San Francisco Art Institute.

Thanks to historians and researchers who shared their knowledge and answered many questions for me: Betty Leavengood, Cort Conley, Dove Menkes, Roy Webb, Jim Knipmeyer, Katie Lee, Ken Sleight, Dave Yeamans, Jerry Hughes, Lew Steiger, John Weisheit, Al Holland, Earl Perry, and Bud Rusho. Special thanks to the great historian David Lavender for encouragement and inspiration.

Inexpressible gratitude to my many manuscript reviewers: Al Holland (a vast effort), Earl Perry, Bob and Bobbie Emerson, Christophe Magny, Achim Gottwald, Dolly Spalding, Logan Hebner, Melissa Niemi, R.J. Johnson, Terri Merz, Richard Quartaroli, John O'Brien, and Jeri, Jaque, and Tom Ledbetter. In many cases I overrode their comments and corrections, and take full responsibility for all mistakes and misstatements.

Thanks also to the dozens whose help has escaped my memory—my deepest apologies for any omissions.

Most of all, my eternal gratitude to my patient wife Jeri Ledbetter, for her support both on and off river during the long and costly process of researching and writing the Hyde saga.

Further reading and research

THERE ARE MYRIAD books on river running, Grand Canyon, and the history of the West, yet none that deal with the Hyde saga in any detail. The Marston Collection at the Huntington Library contains a great wealth of information. However, the majority of material on which this book was based will be housed at Cline Library Special Collections at Northern Arizona University, in Flagstaff, Arizona. Should anyone find more details on the Hyde story, please contact Fretwater Press.

Glen Hyde

Photo Credits

Bob Emerson / Herb Allen Collection (now at Northern Arizona University)
viii, ix, x, xiii, 12, 14, 15, 16, 17, 19, 22B, 23, 24A, 28, 30, 32, 34, 35, 36, 37, 40, 50A, 52, 54, 56, 58, 61, 62, 63, 64, 66, 70, 72, 73, 84, 104, 134, 140, 153, 154, 158, 159, 162, 163, 166, 174, 176, 190, 195, 218A, 237A, 239A, 241, 270, 272, 275, 280

Huntington Library, Otis Marston Collection (listed by source)
Adolph G. Sutro: v, 82, 83, 85, 90, 92 (also back cover)

Woody Claypool, 69	Hyde journal, 156–164
Ancel Taylor: 94, 110, 122, 136	Denver Branden, 56B
Otis Marston, 215	Chet Markley, 112
Haley family, 42B	James Ervin, 187

Northern Arizona University, Cline Library Special Collections
Emery Kolb Collection: p. xiv (detail 208)(NAU.PH.96.568.4035); p. 78 (NAU.PH.96.568.3437); p. 79 (detail 219)(NAU.PH.96.568.656); p. 80 (NAU.PH.96.568.5394); p. 127, (NAU.PH.96.568.5387); p. 130 (NAU.PH.96.568.1186)
Bill Belknap Collection, p. 193 (NAU.PH.96.4.106.67); p. 228 (NAU.PH.96.4.190.214C)
Georgie Clark Collection, p. 233 (NAU.PH.96.91.13.2)

Mojave County Historical Society, Ancel Taylor file, 124, 129, 131, 132, 138
Glen Canyon Natural History Association, Woody Claypool photo, vi
Dugald Bremner, cover, 96, 198, 244
Cooper Carothers & Brian Dierker: 2, 100, 103, 201, 288
Parkersburg High School, *Quill*: 38, 41B, 41A, 233A; *Parischan*: 41A,
University of Utah, J. Willard Marriott Library, Special Collections, Norman D. and Doris Nevills Collection, 66A
Brad Dimock, 6, 7, 46, 48, 50B, 189, 224, 234, 242, 248, 252, 254, 259, 264–265, 267, 277, endsheets

Dr. Walter Birkby, 196, 210, 218B

Jim Bonney, 209, 220	Richard Rogers, 204, 208B
Glenda Buklis, 237B	Rio Grande College Annual, 227C
Raymond Cogswell, 144	Social Security records, 239B
Clyde Eddy, 56A	Ranae Stastny, 24B
John Evans, 178, 187B	Norm Tessman, 219
Jason Fabbri, 44, 46B	Twin Falls Library files, 20, 22A
Marshall College Annual: i, 43	University of Ohio Annual, 227B
Pomeroy High School Annual, 227A	Gregg Wallace, 10

Index

Clark, Owen, xi, 68
Clark, Sommona Rose, 230
Collins, Thomas C., 30
Colorado River, (throughout)
Conley, Cort, iv, 33, 280
Cooper, Tim, 247
Corle, Edwin, 194
Cox, Warren, 170
Crystal Creek Rapid, 103, 157, 200–201,
    208, 231, 266
Cubero, New Mexico, 182
Cummings, Ed, 85
Cutler, Cecil, 151
Cutler, Frederick, 151
Cutler, Elizabeth "Liz" (see Elizabeth
    Arnold)
Cutler, J.J., 226
Dale, Eben, 207
Dale, O'Connor "O.C.," 206, 209, 219,
    223, 279
Dale, Regan, 207
Dannies, Priscilla and Bob, 258
Davenport, Washington, 14, 15, 17, 18,
    279
Davis, Secretary of War Dwight, 107,
    120
Dean, Royce, 67, 167, 168, 170, 268
Dellenbaugh, Frederick, 62
Dellenbaugh Butte, 58
Denver, Colorado, 182, 232, 233
DeRoss, Georgie, 228–234, 239
DeRoss, Marie, 230–233
DeRoss, Paul, 230, 233
Diamond Creek, 91, 94, 107, 108, 111,
    112, 116, 117, 121, 122, 127, 130, 134, 135,
    137–139, 148–151, 160, 164–167, 172, 174–176,
    180–186, 189, 191, 192, 209, 214, 215, 246,
    248, 255, 256, 259, 266
Diamond Creek Rapid, 122, 164, 184
Dickerson, Roy, 147, 148
Dierker, Brian, 9, 98–103, 200–202,
    245–246, 278
Dill, Thelma (see Thelma Arnold)

Dobbin, Old, 18, 22
Dubendorff Rapid, 55, 56, 135, 160, 203
Earhart, Amelia, 57
Easton, Maryland, 39, 278
Eddy, Clyde, 54–56, 58, 61, 66, 71, 155
Elder, Paul, 47
Elko, Nevada, 48–52, 58, 279
El Tovar Hotel, 76, 84, 108
Emerson, Alice, 278
Emerson, Barbara, 214, 220
Emerson, Carl, 27, 119, 149, 259, 274
Emerson, Robert, 19, 28, 53, 149, 214, 222,
    271–274, 278, 280
Emerson, Roberta, 272, 273, 278, 280
Emerson, Edna (see Edna Hyde)
Emerson, Leonard "Len," 23–25, 222, 278
Emery, Murl, 121, 269
Ervin, James, 178, 182–189, 260
Escalante River, 66
Eugene, Oregon, 23
Euler, Robert, 212
Evans, John, 187, 188, 259, 260, 279
Evans, Loie (see Loie Belknap)
Flavell, George, 137
Fernwell Building, 15, 16
Flint, Timothy, 29
Francy, Bob, 82, 91, 108–110, 113–115, 120,
    123–125, 132, 134–139, 148–150, 157, 158, 164,
    165, 168, 169, 180, 184, 191, 192, 214, 263
Fred Harvey Company, 83, 84, 107, 108,
    113, 183
Freeman, Lewis, 62
Gallenson, Art, 213, 279
Galloway, Harold, 46, 47
Galloway, Parley, 55, 59
Galloway, John, 59
Galtsoff, Paul, 91
George, Bill, 229–233
Georgie (see Georgie DeRoss)
Girand, James B., 121, 122, 132, 180
Glen Canyon, 5, 59, 61, 66, 67, 129, 207
Glendale, California, 18
Goldenstein, Bob, 108, 240, 279

The Author

Dimock after a day of abuse aboard the scow, Grand Canyon

BRAD DIMOCK was born in Ithaca, New York, in 1953 and earned a Bachelor of Arts from Prescott College in central Arizona. He proceeded to squander his education for more than thirty-five years as a commercial boatman in Grand Canyon and the rivers of Utah, Alaska, Mexico, Guatemala, Chile, Ethiopia, and Tanzania. He is now a writer, river guide, and aspiring hermit living in Flagstaff, Arizona.

Dimock has written for numerous magazines and has stories in several anthologies. He was one of three authors that collaborated on THE DOING OF THE THING; the Brief, Brilliant Whitewater Career of Buzz Holmstrom, which won the National Outdoor Book Award in 1998. This is his first full length book.

Afterword, 2007

S INCE THE PUBLICATION of *Sunk Without a Sound* in 2001 only one item has surfaced that sheds new light on the story. It is a letter Bessie wrote moments before departing from Greenriver. Significant are her uncertainty about the length and duration of the trip, and the absence of any talk of publicity or breaking records.

To me this casts a shade of doubt on Marston and Sutro's hunch that the trip was primarily about notoriety—a hunch that I may errantly have echoed. Perhaps the Hydes' motives were more similar to Glen and Jeanne's Salmon trip in 1926—running the river just for fun, because it was there.

Brad Dimock, Flagstaff

Green River, Utah Oct. 20, 1928

Dear Aunt Ruth and Uncle Mill,

...This is a funny little town (they claim over six hundred population—but it just isn't possible). We plan on leaving in three or four hours. The boat is practically finished. It's rather large 20 ft. long, 5½ ft. wide and 3 ft. high, and is guided by a large sweep oar at each end. We will go down the Green River and then the Colorado, (how far will depend on how bad the water gets) making about a two or three months trip. From the river we'll go to Los Angeles and spend three or four days there, and then on up to San Francisco. I plan on doing a lot of sketching on the trip, as, of course, the scenery will be wonderful. We had one great scramble getting ready to leave—packing for the river trip—packing the trunk to be sent to Los Angeles—and storing the other things in the attic at the other house. Packing is an awful bother anyway, although I must admit Glen did most of it. I'm terribly excited and awfully anxious to start. Write to me sometime (at Hansen, Idaho), and I'll write you all about the trip when we get out. Love to Sally Lou

Lovingly,

Bessie Hyde

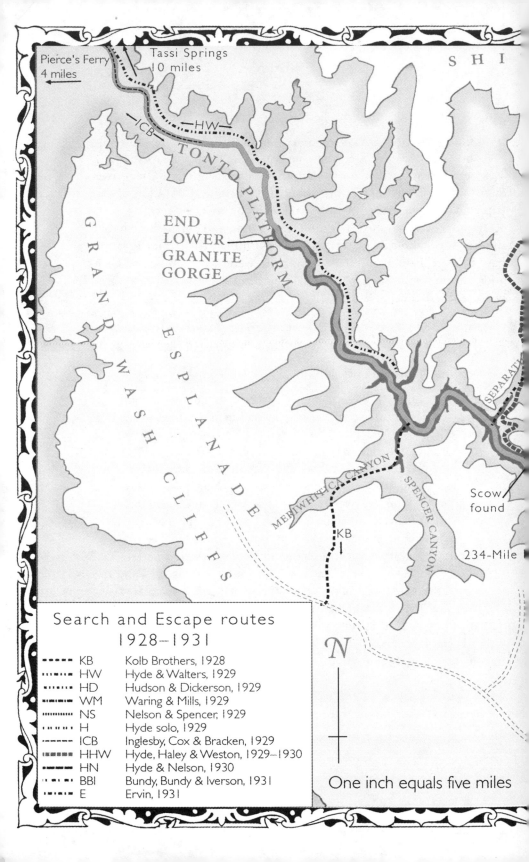

Pierce's Ferry
4 miles

Tassi Springs
10 miles

S H I

—HW—

—ICB—

TONTO PLATFORM

END
LOWER
GRANITE
GORGE

G R A N D

W A S H
C L I F F S

E S P L A N A D E

MEBIWHITICA CANYON

SPENCER CANYON

SEPARATE

Scow
found

234-Mile

KB
↓

Search and Escape routes
1928–1931

▪▪▪▪ KB	Kolb Brothers, 1928	
▪▪▪▪▪ HW	Hyde & Walters, 1929	
▪▪▪▪▪ HD	Hudson & Dickerson, 1929	
▪▪▪▪▪ WM	Waring & Mills, 1929	
▪▪▪▪▪ NS	Nelson & Spencer, 1929	
▪▪▪▪▪ H	Hyde solo, 1929	
▪ ▪ ▪ ICB	Inglesby, Cox & Bracken, 1929	
▪▪▪▪ HHW	Hyde, Haley & Weston, 1929–1930	
▪▪▪▪ HN	Hyde & Nelson, 1930	
▪▪▪▪ BBI	Bundy, Bundy & Iverson, 1931	
▪▪▪▪ E	Ervin, 1931	

N

One inch equals five miles